Managing Marketing Performance
2005–2006

D0192229

DISCARD

The Chartered
Institute of Marketing

Managing Marketing Performance 2005–2006

Helen Meek, Richard Meek, Roger Palmer
and Lynn Parkinson

ELSEVIER
BUTTERWORTH
HEINEMANN

AMSTERDAM BOSTON HEIDELBERG LONDON NEW YORK OXFORD
PARIS SAN DIEGO SAN FRANCISCO SINGAPORE SYDNEY TOKYO

Elsevier Butterworth-Heinemann
Linacre House, Jordan Hill, Oxford OX2 8DP
30 Corporate Drive, Burlington, MA 01803

First published 2005

Copyright © 2005, Helen Meek, Richard Meek, Roger Palmer
and Lynn Parkinson. All rights reserved

The rights of Helen Meek, Richard Meek, Roger Palmer and Lynn Parkinson
to be identified as the authors of this work has been asserted in accordance
with the Copyright, Designs and Patents Act 1988

No part of this publication may be reproduced in any material form (including
photocopying or storing in any medium by electronic means and whether
or not transiently or incidentally to some other use of this publication) without
the written permission of the copyright holder except in accordance with the
provisions of the Copyright, Designs and Patents Act 1988 or under the terms of
a licence issued by the Copyright Licensing Agency Ltd, 90 Tottenham Court Road,
London, England W1T 4LP. Applications for the copyright holder's written
permission to reproduce any part of this publication should be addressed
to the publisher

Permissions may be sought directly from Elsevier's Science and Technology Rights
Department in Oxford, UK: phone: (+44) (0) 1865 843830; fax: (+44) (0) 1865 853333;
e-mail: permissions@elsevier.com. You may also complete your request
on-line via the Elsevier homepage (http://www.elsevier.com), by selecting
'Customer Support' and then 'Obtaining Permissions'

British Library Cataloguing in Publication Data
A catalogue record for this book is available from the British Library

Library of Congress Cataloguing in Publication Data
A catalogue record for this book is available from the Library of Congress

ISBN 0 7506 6653 6

For information on all Elsevier Butterworth-Heinemann publications
visit our website at http://books.elsevier.com

Typeset by Integra Software Services Pvt. Ltd, Pondicherry, India
www.integra-india.com
Printed and bound in Italy

College of
Sutton Campus

Accession
1 2 1 5 4 9

Class
658.802
MEE

Working together to grow
libraries in developing countries

www.elsevier.com | www.bookaid.org | www.sabre.org

ELSEVIER   BOOK AID
            International   Sabre Foundation

Contents

Preface
welcome to the CIM coursebooks

A message from the authors

The redesign of the CIM syllabus and the introduction of the Professional Postgraduate Diploma in Marketing has introduced a number of changes in not only the content of the syllabus, but also the way that it is taught and examined. The CIM is uniquely positioned to bridge the gap between theory and practice and the recent developments in the syllabus are designed to give students real advantages in the world of business, and demonstrate to the employers value that marketing and proficient marketers can contribute to their business. At this level the syllabus is not so much about learning more about marketing, but in demonstrating the ability to apply knowledge in order to produce better business results.

At the Professional Postgraduate Diploma level the examinations integrate in order to allow students to demonstrate how they can apply their knowledge and understanding. This builds on the Certificate and Diploma levels and complements previous learning. Each of the syllabuses at this level may draw on the same knowledge of marketing, but differ in the context in which it is applied. For this reason it is helpful, and indeed desirable, that students have some knowledge and experience of marketing in practice in order that this can give depth and context to their answers.

This unit is entitled 'Managing Marketing Performance', and hence is not concerned so much with learning more about marketing, but is much more involved with how to do the job of marketing and the implementation of marketing strategy. This requires a somewhat wider range of skills to enable you to perform not just as a marketer but as a manager as well. The syllabus will therefore touch on some aspects that are not normally regarded as primarily marketing topics. However the background research that led to the development of the syllabus clearly demonstrated that the knowledge and skills that this unit represents are an essential complement to your marketing knowledge. This is reflected and summarized in the learning outcomes for this module, the full syllabus and a specimen examination paper are available in Appendix 4, which are:

1. Critically evaluate the techniques available for integrating teams and activities across the organization, specifically relating to brands and customer facing processes, and instilling learning within the organization.
2. Identify the barriers to effective implementation of strategies and plans involving change (including communications) in the organization, and develop measures to prevent or overcome them.
3. Demonstrate an ability to manage marketing activities as part of strategy implementation.

4. Assess an organization's need for marketing skills and resources and develop strategies for acquiring, developing and retaining them.
5. Initiate and critically evaluate systems for control of marketing activities undertaken as part of business and marketing plans.

As will be appreciated these learning outcomes do not relate so much to gaining more knowledge on the subject of marketing but in developing the skills to use the knowledge developed from previous modules. These represent the management skills necessary to be an effective marketer, and as can be seen a variety of skills could be needed to address each of these learning outcomes.

The learning outcomes are the result of working through each element of the syllabus, and this is broken down into five elements. You are *strongly advised* to read through the syllabus and be aware of the content. Each of these elements is composed of a number of detailed sub-topics, which are addressed in the units comprising this book. Each unit starts with a description of the learning objectives for that unit and refers to the syllabus elements. In our business lives we draw on a range of interpersonal, financial and other general management skills as well as our own functional skills in marketing. So we draw on and blend these skills appropriate to the context in which we find ourselves. In teaching the syllabus all the contextual variations cannot possibly be addressed and hence the coursebook is arranged in such a way that related material is dealt with in each unit. Other types of learning, such as the use of case studies or your wider reading about business in general provides this important extension into practice and blending of skills. As you work through case studies, consider business examples and review examination questions think more deeply about what the underlying concepts are and how they integrate. Hence the comment earlier that it is desirable for students taking examinations at this level to have experience of marketing in practice.

The following diagram shows how the elements of the syllabus relate to the units and gives a diagrammatic overview of the book.

With the diverse range of subjects that are covered within this unit there is an equally wide reading list. Whilst this study guide is intended to illustrate and inform with respect to the main areas of syllabus, students will benefit considerably by extending their reading into not just textbooks but also business magazines, journal articles, case-studies and so on. You will also benefit by thinking how you can bring your own experience of business to the subject to provide examples and a context in which knowledge can be applied.

The main thing that examiners are looking for is this ability to apply learning. Hence there is an implicit assumption that students approaching the syllabus have already studied the subject quite extensively. This unit takes the student from knowledge to application, and from marketing content to business context. Your ability to demonstrate the application of marketing knowledge to solve business problems and generate shareholder value will ensure your success in this unit.

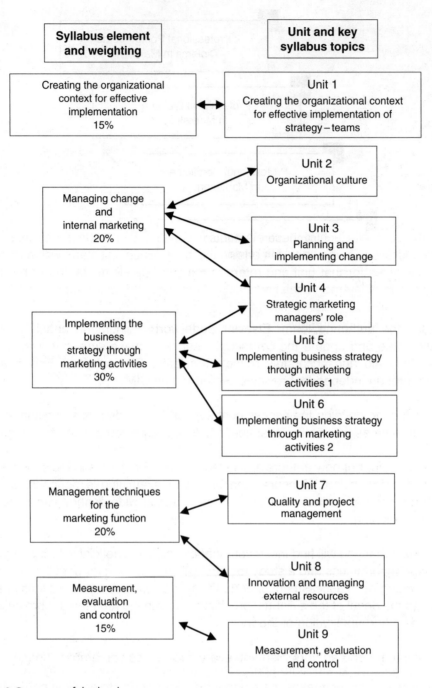

Figure P.1 Overview of the book

An introduction from the academic development advisor

In the last two years we have seen some significant changes to CIM Marketing qualifications. The changes have been introduced on a year-on-year basis, with Certificate changes implemented in 2002, and the Professional Diploma in Marketing being launched in 2003. The Professional Postgraduate Diploma in Marketing was launched in 2004. The new qualifications are based on the CIM Professional Marketing Standards, developed through research with employers.

Study note © CIM 2005

As a result the authoring team, Elsevier Butterworth-Heinemann and I have all aimed to rigorously revise and update the coursebook series to make sure that every title is the best possible study aid and accurately reflects the latest CIM syllabus. This has been further enhanced through independent reviews carried out by CIM.

We have aimed to develop the assessment support to include some additional support for the assignment route as well as the examination, so we hope you will find this helpful.

There are a number of new authors and indeed Senior Examiners in the series who have been commissioned for their CIM course teaching and examining experience, as well as their research into specific curriculum-related areas and their wide general knowledge of the latest thinking in marketing.

We are certain that you will find these coursebooks highly beneficial in terms of the content and assessment opportunities and a study tool that will prepare you for both CIM examinations and continuous/integrative assessment opportunities. They will guide you in a logical and structured way through the detail of the syllabus, providing you with the required underpinning knowledge, understanding and application of theory.

The editorial team and authors wish you every success as you embark upon your studies.

Karen Beamish
Academic Development Advisor

How to use these coursebooks

Everyone who has contributed to this series has been careful to structure the books with the exams in mind. Each unit, therefore, covers an essential part of the syllabus. You need to work through the complete coursebook systematically to ensure that you have covered everything you need to know.

This coursebook is divided into units each containing a selection of the following standard elements:

- *Learning objectives* – tell you what you will be expected to know, having read the unit.
- *Syllabus references* – outline what part of the syllabus is covered in the module.
- *Study guides* – tell you how long the unit is and how long its activities take to do.
- *Questions* – are designed to give you practice – they will be similar to those you get in the exam.
- *Answers* – (at the end of the book) give you a suggested format for answering exam questions. *Remember* there is no such thing as a model answer – you should use these examples only as guidelines.
- *Activities* – give you a chance to put what you have learned into practice.
- *Debriefings* – (at the end of the book) shed light on the methodologies involved in the activities.
- *Hints and tips* – are tips from the senior examiner, examiner or author and are designed to help you avoid common mistakes made by previous candidates and give you guidance on improving your knowledge base.
- *Insights* – encourage you to contextualize your academic knowledge by reference to real-life experience.
- *Key definitions* – highlight and explain the key points relevant to that module.
- *Definitions* – may be used for words you must know to pass the exam.
- *Summaries* – cover what you should have picked up from reading the unit.
- *Further study* – provides details of recommended reading in addition to the coursebook.

While you will find that each section of the syllabus has been covered within this text, you might find that the order of some of the topics has been changed. This is because it sometimes makes more sense to put certain topics together when you are studying, even though they might appear in different sections of the syllabus itself. If you are following the reading and other activities, your coverage of the syllabus will be just fine, but don't forget to follow up with trade press reading!

About MarketingOnline

Elsevier Butterworth-Heinemann offers purchasers of the coursebooks free access to MarketingOnline (www.marketingonline.co.uk), our premier online support engine for the CIM marketing courses. On this site you can benefit from:

- Fully customizable electronic versions of the coursebooks enabling you to annotate, cut and paste sections of text to create your own tailored learning notes.
- The capacity to search the coursebook online for instant access to definitions and key concepts.
- Useful links to e-marketing articles, provided by Dave Chaffey, Director of Marketing Insights Ltd and a leading UK e-marketing consultant, trainer and author.
- A glossary providing a comprehensive dictionary of marketing terms.
- A Frequently Asked Questions (FAQs) section providing guidance and advice on common problems or queries.

Using MarketingOnline

Logging on

Before you can access MarketingOnline you will first need to get a password. Please go to www.marketingonline.co.uk and click on the registration button where you will then find registration instructions for coursebook purchasers. Once you have got your password, you will need to log on using the onscreen instructions. This will give you access to the various functions of the site.

MarketingOnline provides a range of functions, as outlined in the previous section, that can easily be accessed from the site after you have logged on to the system. Please note the following guidelines detailing how to access the main features:

1. *The coursebooks* – buttons corresponding to the three levels of the CIM marketing qualification are situated on the home page. Select your level and you will be presented with the coursebook title for each module of that level. Click on the desired coursebook to access the full online text (divided up by chapter). On each page of text you have the option to add an electronic bookmark or annotation by following the onscreen instructions. You can also freely cut and paste text into a blank word document to create your own learning notes.
2. *e-Marketing articles* – to access the links to relevant e-marketing articles simply click on the link under the text 'E-marketing Essentials: useful links from Marketing Insights'.
3. *Glossary* – a link to the glossary is provided in the top right-hand corner of each page enabling access to this resource at any time.

If you have specific queries about using MarketingOnline then you should consult our fully searchable FAQs section, accessible through the appropriate link in the top right-hand corner of any page of the site. Please also note that a *full user guide* can be downloaded by clicking on the link on the opening page of the website.

unit 1
creating the organizational context for effective implementation of strategy – teams

Objectives

Syllabus links

Learning outcomes

'Critically evaluate the techniques available for integrating teams and activities across the organization, specifically relating to brands and customer-facing processes, and instilling learning within the organization.'

Please see Appendix 4 for full details of the learning outcomes, related statements of practice and knowledge and skills requirements.

Information on the syllabus element (and its weighting) that is supported by this chapter can be found in Figure P.1, in the preface to this book.

Learning objectives

By the end of this unit you will:

  o Have an understanding of the background theories underpinning organizational behaviour

  o Understand the meaning of 'tasks' in the context of implementation planning

  o Have a clear understanding of different types of teams and general team roles

- o Understand at least two perspectives on the evolution of a team

- o Be able to plan how a team should be structured and developed to ensure effective performance

- o To assess teams against their objectives using at least one technique

- o Be able to analyse the causes of sub-optimal performance in teams and provide recommendations to improve motivation, commitment and loyalty

- o Have an understanding of the impact of teams on corporate success.

Key definitions

Strategic choice theory – makes a distinction between formulation of strategy and its implementation. The formulation of strategy includes preparing a plan, the intended actions required to achieve plan objectives and forecasts the consequences of those actions. Implementation is the procedure of designing systems to ensure that plans are carried out (Stacey, 2003, p. 51).

Theory of the learning organization – is the basis of an outstanding organization when it is able to tap the commitment and capacity of its members to learn. Such learning is particularly effective in teams (Senge (1990) cited in Stacey, 2003, p. 51).

A team – is a small number of people with complementary skills who are committed to a common purpose, performance goals, and approach for which they hold themselves mutually accountable (Katzenbach and Smith, 1994).

Work roles – may be defined as, 'The mix of tasks and responsibilities undertaken by individual's or executed within teams' (Belbin, 2004).

Virtual teams – may be considered as 'geographically virtual' where team members are not physically located in relatively close proximity, or 'temporally virtual' separated by time either due to two or three shifts occurring in the working day, or due to shifts in time zones in global organizations.

Gantt charts – a graphical technique for displaying work sequences, usually for a project.

Team roles – characteristic behaviour patterns ascribed to team members. The objective is to ensure a good balance of different team role types depending on the requirements of the project to ensure complementarity and to maximize team performance.

Stages in team development – initially developed by Tuckman, this concept (of which several particular models have been proposed) considers that teams go through various stages once they are formed.

Study Guide

This unit will take you about 4 hours to work through.

We suggest that you take a further 4 hours to do the various activities and questions in this unit.

Introduction

Organizations operate within the external marketing environment. They must align themselves with this environment if they are to maintain long-term competitiveness. The complexity of the marketing environment means increasingly that work is undertaken and implemented by teams rather than by individuals. Teams must work effectively and they too must adapt to the changing requirements of the business environment. This is crucial if marketing strategy is to be implemented fully and effectively. For this to happen it requires positive action within the organization to foster a culture of interdependency and to maximize employee contribution.

In this CIM module we are ultimately concerned with implementing organizational marketing strategy which requires organizational change. People implement programmes that require organizational change. Before we consider a detailed discussion of the syllabus, we must take a step backwards and consider fundamentally how people operate in organizations to bring about such change. Peoples' behaviour is determined in large part according to how they think. Do people working in organizations simply respond to instructions from the CEO, or the senior management team, which is the source of implementation and change programmes? Alternatively, are these programmes constructed based on interactions occurring in groups throughout the organization so that implementation programmes emerge from dialogue and debate within the organization? These represent two extremes of perspective on how implementation and change programmes operate. Many organizations will have a combination of the two perspectives but will tend towards one of these two extremes in their behaviour.

Strategic choice theory suggests that the general strategy and direction of change adopted by an organization is determined by a powerful individual or group and that they design an organizational hierarchy in order to implement it.

> *The structure they design is supposed to be largely a self-regulating one in which people are assigned roles and given objectives to achieve that will realise a given strategy.* (Stacey, 2003, p. 32)

Here change is predictable and implementation is about targets and objectives derived from the strategic plan. In this theoretical approach the role of empowerment and of self-managed teams is unexplained. How the organization copes with unexpected, unplanned change is also not discussed.

In contrast, the theory of the learning organization suggests that the most effective organizations result from high levels of learning by organizational members. Teamwork and team learning are regarded as particularly crucial aspects of the learning organization. Team learning occurs more rapidly than individual learning principally as a result of dialogue and interaction between team members.

The movement towards a knowledge economy creates new problems for the organization. Rather than having traditional assets such as plant and machinery which may be valued and controlled using traditional accounting and human resource management measures, we now have knowledge assets. Knowledge is not generally a traded asset (outside of patent exchanges). Its full importance is not accounted for completely in the balance sheet or by other traditional accounting devices. This creates problems for managing shareholder value. Knowledge workers, it is suggested (Stacey, 2003, Chapter 8), should be managed differently to workers in the traditional economy. Individual knowledge must be shared and become corporate knowledge for such assets to be exploited most effectively in order to create shareholder value.

Extending knowledge

There is some fairly deep, and academic, thinking underpinning these ideas. The text by Stacey (2003) discusses these in detail. The hard-pressed working practitioner is advised to approach this text initially by reading the first chapter, then the part one introduction on pages 15–16, followed by the introduction and summary for all chapters in part one (Chapters 2–9 inclusive). The most relevant sections of this text outside of those already indicated are Chapters 4 and 5, and sections 6.4 to 6.7 and 7.5 and 7.6.

Teams are formed, or exist, to solve organizational problems. They must have clear aims and objectives, comprise an appropriate mix of individuals and be managed to ensure that they make an effective contribution. This does not happen automatically, but requires planning, performance evaluation and strategies to improve the performance of sub-optimal teams when this is diagnosed.

Teams – what are they?

We perhaps assume that we all share a common definition of teams. To clarify our thinking on this subject a definition is helpful:

> *A team is a small number of people with complementary skills who are committed to a common purpose, performance goals, and approach for which they hold themselves mutually accountable.* (Katzenbach and Smith, 1994)

The workplace, or functional, role played by individuals is the basis on which they are recruited, in particular if they are a specialist.

Work roles may be defined as:

> *The mix of tasks and responsibilities undertaken by individuals or executed within teams.* (Belbin, 2004)

Management literature is concerned with teams only in as much as this helps us to understand organizational effectiveness. In other words, how effective were organizations in solving problems and implementing their solutions, i.e. how effective were they in their work? In a text written after reflection on his definitive work on teams, Belbin (2000) concluded that the balance of emphasis was too uneven. It tended to focus too much on teams and hardly at all on work. In *Beyond the Team*, Belbin changes his emphasis to focus on the type of work undertaken and how this affects the social arrangements within the organization for undertaking and completing work. It is useful to remember that the context in which a team operates affects how the team performs and the relationships that develop.

Groups versus teams

A high degree of commitment and loyalty is required for people in organizations to operate effectively as teams rather than simply groups. Katzenbach and Smith (1994, pp. 88–89) make the distinction between groups and teams. They suggest that a working group (common in bureaucratic, hierarchical structures) linked to formal work roles is based primarily on individual contributions. Performance is assessed by measuring each individual's contribution. There may still be a co-operative attitude in which individuals discuss issues and problems to improve individual work.

Group performance is the sum contribution of individual members, however, team performance is synergistic. The team achieves more than that could be achieved with individuals working essentially on their own, even in a co-operative spirit. The main difference is that teams include mutual accountability, in addition to individual accountability. On other dimensions, the differences between teams and groups tends to be of degree; e.g. more information sharing, more joint task and target setting and performance review.

Formal groups, or teams, within an organization may be permanent (e.g. marketing department) or temporary (one off project to set up a CRM system). They must have clear goals and tasks and their purpose within the organization is 'to find solutions to structured problems' (Stacey, 2003, p. 68). They may take various forms and can even be autonomous, and self-managing, democratic and may even be charged with designing their own approach to a given problem. This is in contrast to the traditional command and control perspective of groups within the organization operated more along military lines with edicts from senior management and organizational design focused on reporting and control.

Creating and developing teams

People obviously implement organizational strategy within the context of organizational structures. In the past they operated within highly regimented, hierarchical units. As layers have been stripped out of organizational hierarchies, rigid structures and work groups no longer exist. Flatter organizational structures have resulted in a greater degree of self-management. As structures have become flatter, people are forced to work in fluid, rather than permanent, teams. To understand effective strategy implementation therefore requires the study of management teams and team management.

Marketing team types and contexts

Piercy (2002) argues that if we are going to organize in order to 'go to market' then marketing cannot be a type of ghetto department. His focus of attention is to get better at 'marketing processes' rather than on how to structure particular types of marketing departments.

Summary research indicates the current range of approaches for organizations' marketing to include four main categories of marketing department. These range from low to high in terms of organizational responsibility and from low to high numbers of people employed. The way marketing is organized, and how it links to other parts of the organization, in the organizational structure tends to be determined by strategy. Structure has key attributes, which are a sign of the location of 'power', 'status' and 'organizational culture', and of information flows which in turn support power. New teams increasingly cut across traditional functional structures and can upset organizational balance on all key attributes unless they are well managed. Piercy sees changes required in organizational processes to align the organization 'to market' and these will result in:

- o Changes in organizational hierarchies
- o Increasing dependence on high performing, temporary multi-functional teams organized around market segments
- o Process re-engineering
- o Transnational networks of organizations
- o Learning organizations
- o Increased emphasis on key account management.

Source: Adapted from Piercy (2002, pp. 235–236).

Forming a team, or teams, to complete a major task within the organization may be compared with the external activities of building collaborative networks. Successful internal collaborative networks, just like their external counterparts, are about informal processes based on trust, information sharing, joint decision making and collective responsibility. Ever more frequently, requirements for effective market-led implementation require multi-functional teams that operate across conventional internal boundaries and even external boundaries, as networks including suppliers, distributors and customers are required to solve customer-focused problems.

Extending knowledge

How to transform marketing from its traditional approach to a relatively new approach of organizing marketing in order to 'go to market'. See Chapter 5 'Total integration: processes and teams take over from departments' in Piercy, N.F. (2002) *Market-led Strategic Change: A Guide to Transforming the Process of Going to Market*, 3rd edition, Oxford: Butterworth-Heinemann.

Project teams

The model of 'the project' becomes more relevant as one-off tasks increasingly must be solved. These are solved by teams formed with this sole function but coming from disparate places in one or several organizations. This is a useful perspective to take which traditionally was employed only for major, complex projects common in civil or aeronautical engineering. However, building the next generation customer-focused organization, marketing for example visual information displays as flat screen monitors or a total customer service experience for a hotel group, is just as much a project in every sense of the word.

Brown (2002) suggests that once the project scope and objectives have been defined, the focus of attention is on how the project should be achieved. Three stages are suggested which he terms:

1. *Work breakdown structure* – which decomposes the project into discrete work elements or units. These which are both amenable to control are the basis on which planning, budget setting, financial control and the assigning of responsibilities are based.
2. *Project organization* – in terms of organizing for the project and assigning roles and responsibilities.
3. Setting *milestones or targets* – which acts both as a project route map and facilities control.

The building blocks of the project are to be found in the 'work breakdown structure', in particular within the characteristics of the tasks and information required on each task (Figure 1.1).

Task characteristics

- o Be measurable in terms of cost, effort, resource and time
- o Result in a single (verifiable) end product
- o Have clear start and end dates
- o Be the responsibility of a single person.

Task information

- o Description of task
- o Necessary inputs or preconditions
- o Deliverables
- o Particular resource requirements (with costs)
- o Particular skill requirements
- o Responsibilities
- o Estimated time.

Figure 1.1 Task characteristics and task information
Source: Brown, M. (2002)

Various tools exist to support project requirements including Gantt charts, dependency analysis using PERT (Programme Evaluation and Review Techniques) charts and critical path analysis. Both these help with project planning, task scheduling and control and consequently support implementation.

Extending knowledge

See Brown's (2002) chapters on 'project initiation' (p. 16), 'project organisation' (p. 30) and 'detailed planning' (p. 42) in his pocket-sized, succinct booklet. Brown, M. (2002) *Project Management in a Week*, 3rd edition, London. Hodder & Stoughton.

Adair (2002, p. 34) provides a general guiding approach, also employed by others writing in this area, of a three-circles model (i.e. task, team and individual) for the needs of a group or organization:

1. Achieve the common task
2. Work in harmony as a team
3. Satisfy each individual's needs.

Team skills, characteristics and roles

Belbin (2004), in his research at Henley, concluded that there were only a few ways that people could contribute to teamwork. The essential contributions comprised:

- o Co-ordinating the efforts of the team
- o Creating ideas
- o Motivating and driving the team forward
- o Exploring resources
- o Evaluating options
- o Organizing the work
- o Following up on detail
- o Supporting others
- o Providing expertise.

Belbin as well as other authors have defined important team roles and assign individuals to these roles based on established personality theories as illustrated in Table 1.1.

Table 1.1 Belbin's team roles

Belbin's named roles	Characteristics	Positive qualities	Allowable weaknesses
Company worker (Amended to 'Implementer')	Conservative, dutiful and predictable	Organizing ability, common sense in practical work, hard working and self disciplined.	Lacks flexibility, unresponsive to unproven ideas – tends to stick to the orthodox.
Chairman (Amended to 'the Co-ordinator')	Calm, self confident and controlled	Accomplished in encouraging and obtaining contributions from team members without judgement. A strong sense of objectives.	No more than ordinary in terms of intellect or creative ability. Tends to take credit for the effort of the team.
Shaper	Highly strung, outgoing, dynamic	Has great drive and a readiness to challenge inertia, ineffectiveness, complacency or self-deception.	Prone to provocation, irritation and impatience.
Plant	Individualistic, serious minded, unorthodox.	Possesses 'genius', imagination, intellect and knowledge.	Inclined to disregard practical details. Tends to be preoccupied with ideas and has a strong sense of their ownership.
Resource Investigator	Extroverted, enthusiastic, curious, communicative.	Good at developing contacts and exploring opportunities. Possesses an ability to respond to challenge.	Liable to lose interest once the initial fascination has passed.
Monitor-evaluator	Sober, unemotional and prudent.	Judgement, discretion and hard headedness.	Lacks inspiration or the ability to motivate others.
Team worker	Socially orientated, rather mild mannered and sensitive.	Possesses an ability to respond to people and situations and to promote team spirit.	Indecisive at moments of crisis.
Completer- finisher (Amended to 'Completer')	Painstaking, orderly, conscientious and anxious.	A perfectionist with a capacity to follow through. Delivers on time.	A tendency to worry about small things. A reluctance to 'let go' – perhaps somewhat obsessional.

Source: Adapted from Belbin (2004, p. 72)

Some role names have been amended to fit in more readily with modern approaches to work. Fluid/flexible teams brought together for the life of a task/project result in the term 'Chairman' being replaced by 'Co-ordinator'. Flatter organizational structures rather than rigid hierarchies result in the use of the more appropriate term 'Implementer'. Finally, 'Completer-finisher' has been reduced to 'Completer' to avoid confusion with 'Implementer'. Please note that Belbin (2004) still employs the original, rather than the amended, terminology.

Activity 1.1

Investigate resources available at 'Belbin' (Associates) website

Belbin's work has spawned a website with this as its focus. Visit Belbin Associates website at http://www.belbin.com/index.htm

Activity 1.2

Determine your team role

Online at www.belbin.com (only possible if you have purchased the second edition of Belbin's text (2000))

Team diversity and team success

Discussion of success of teams has developed beyond classical roles considered by Belbin to include the impact of diversity within the team on the success of team functioning. Such diversity issues concern both demographic diversity, i.e. the degree to which team members vary in terms of, for example, age, gender and ethnicity, and diversity in terms of functional specialism. Pelled *et al.* (1999) in reviewing the literature on diversity on group performance found that no conclusive influence was found. Some studies linked diversity to successful performance while others have linked it to unsuccessful performance. Their own conjecture was to suggest an indirect influence on performance though conflict. They suggested that two types of conflict existed:

1. *Task conflict* – is where group members disagree about task issues, including goals, procedures, key areas in which to focus for decision making and appropriate choices for action. Factors that tend to reduce task conflict include repetitive, routine tasks as well as the length of time the group has been together.
2. *Emotional conflict* – describes the outcome rather than the causes of conflict in that it focuses on interpersonal clashes which are characterized by negative attributes such as anger, frustration, etc.

Source: Pelled *et al.* (1999, p. 2).

Pelled *et al.* concluded that 'task conflict' and their resolution leads to enhanced performance, while emotional conflict tends to diminish performance.

Planning teams for effective performance

Belbin (2004, pp. 124–125) concludes that team design should be guided by five interlocking principles.

1. Members of a management team can contribute in two ways to the achievement of team objectives. These are high performance in a functional role in drawing on their professional and technical knowledge and to perform effectively in their team role. Belbin clarifies that this describes a pattern of behavioural characteristics where the manager interacts with others in the team.
2. Each team needs an optimum balance in both functional and team roles. The ideal blend will depend on the goals and tasks the team faces.
3. The effectiveness of a team will be promoted by the extent to which members correctly recognize and adjust themselves to the relative strengths within the team. This includes both in expertise and in ability to engage in specific team roles.
4. Personal qualities fit members for some team roles while limiting the likelihood that they will succeed in others.
5. A team can deploy its technical resources to best advantages only when it has the requisite range of team roles to ensure sufficient teamwork.

Putting a team together

The process of putting a team together must be informed by information on the individual in order to ensure that he/she fits organizational requirements. Principal sources of information for this include:

○ Psychometric tests
○ Self-perception questionnaires
○ Colleague completed assessment of 'perceived team role' capability
○ Information gained from staff attending in-company training courses.

Belbin cautions us also to ensure that recruitment (or internal reshuffling) does not simply recruit more similar people without achieving a balance in team members in terms of the 'team' as well as functional roles that they perform.

With an increase in the number and variety of teams being utilized by organizations, there is an increasing need to understand what in fact makes a team function effectively.

Recruitment

One common mistake in recruitment is to select people to fit in with the organization. The perspective taken is often concerned foremost with organizational culture rather than role. The former approach is focused on the status quo while the latter takes account of the need for evolution and development in team performance. One aspect of effective team performance probably includes further empowering team members. This increases work scope. Recruitment that focuses on the team role that must be filled, taking account of existing skills and roles, is likely to be most successful.

Extending knowledge

See Belbin (2004) for a full discussion on planning an effective team in Chapter 11 'designing a team' and Ahmed and Rafiq (2002, pp. 86–87) on empowerment and recruitment.

Stages in team development

There is broad support for the assertion that teams go through various stages after formation. As long as any dysfunctional behaviour does not develop, team performance grows over time, however, not at a constant rate. This is not simply because people, and therefore teams, vary in their effectiveness over time. It is related to a generalizable pattern of development in which performance initially improves at a relatively slow rate as team members get to know each other socially and in terms of the skill set they possess. As team learning develops about task issues, or the project and how to co-operate in achieving its objectives, a phase occurs in which performance increases rapidly. In contrast, towards the end of the life of a project team, the rate of development slows down as diminishing returns set in.

A significant advance in thinking on effective teams was the realization that this was not a static situation but a dynamic process. Team members interact with one and other over time and similarly over time develop competencies and varying degrees of conflict, both resolved and unresolved. Consequently a perspective of teams is required that takes on board this dynamic process. Various theories of team development have been suggested, the most widely discussed and applied is the theory proposed by Tuckman in which he suggests that team performance goes through four stages of group development over time. These he labelled forming, storming, norming and performing. Later he added a fifth stage which was termed 'adjourning', when a team that had been formed for a project was disbanded upon completion.

Two factors are important in determining, and describing, progression of a team through these stages. These are the resolution of interpersonal relationships and of task activities. In essence, the model by Tuckman describes these two issues, as groups progress through the different stages (Figure 1.2).

Forming

Everyone in the embryonic team is yet to feel emotionally attached to it. Members tend to feel a certain degree of anxiety as roles and relationships within the team are established. Inevitably they will compare the new team with former teams they have been members of.

Group members make an initial assessment of interpersonal relationships and norms within the group. The focus on task is to identify what these are, where task boundaries are and the sort of information required to complete the task(s).

Storming

In this phase people finally understand their function within the team and team relationships settle. It is possible that in this phase, sub-groups start to form and the potential for conflict can foment.

Group members begin to know each other. There may be some conflict not only over leadership but also over how the leader will operate. Members of the group struggle to varying degrees for individual autonomy. Individuals may in fact display a lack of commitment to the demands of particular tasks that they do not favour.

11

Norming

In this stage, group bonding, team spirit and cohesion develop. Their level of commitment to each other, and to the team, increases. People feel sure about their team identity and role. Group 'norms' literally begin to develop to the extent that the clichéd phrase 'that is the way we do things around here' becomes appropriate.

As problems over the demands of particular tasks, and task allocation, have been resolved, conflict diminishes and is more likely manifested in greater cohesiveness in-group functioning. Task co-operation and mutual support develops.

Performing

The team has fully committed to achieving its goals. They are flexible and collaborate freely and willingly. Now that people feel comfortable with each other and their work role, they can devote a substantial amount of emotional, as well as physical, energy to the project. This creates a wonderful environment in which creativity can thrive.

This is the most effective in terms of task activity and interpersonal relationships. The latter are established and almost taken for granted, operating in the background. The focus of activity is on completion of task activity

Figure 1.2 Tuckman's four stages of team development

Tuckman, working with another colleague, added a stage referred to as 'adjourning' in which the group works on finishing off the project. The project is disbanded and some emotional baggage will result. This may be highly positive where group members focus on the success of the team, or it may be negative, due to the loss of friendships and emotional work ties established during the term of the project.

Extending knowledge

If students have access to journal papers they may wish to start with the paper Tuckman wrote with a colleague in which he revisited his original work and added an additional stage (Tuckman and Jensen, 1977).

Another stage?

All organizations wish their teams to remain at the 'performing' stage. However, the management writer John Adair, in his book *Effective Teambuilding* (1986), has identified a further stage (dorming) that can come after performing.

This may be regarded as a stage of relative complacency, where people prefer to live on past successes rather than to devote their energies into further innovations and successes. In a sense team members become institutionalized within their own team and become focused on processes rather than on outcomes.

Each team stage has recognizable characteristics. Sometimes, problems arise during a team stage and other times in the transition from one stage to another.

The Tuckman model is not the only model of team development and it does suffer from some limitations. Perhaps the most important is that not all teams progress through all stages. The model is really an idealized version. With that in mind it still provides a very helpful means of considering team dynamics and progression towards an ideal, highly effective, team.

Activity 1.3

Applying team roles

Consider a team in which you work with all the people in the team. What are your individual roles?

Now answer the following questions. Who:

1. establishes team objectives?
2. co-ordinates most of the work?
3. provides most of the creative ideas?
4. takes most of the decisions?
5. acts as a mediator/peace maker in times of internal dispute?
6. is the main motivator in the team, providing encouragement and support?
7. looks after communication?
8. is able to provide constructive criticism and is able to do this in a way that is accepted without conflict?
9. is good at overcoming difficult issues and situations?
10. takes responsibility for controlling and monitoring work?

Managing teams

Activities that characterize an effective leader, and which can be used as an indicator of an ability to manage the work of teams, is provided by Adair (2002, p. 34). Drawing on inspiration from the writings of Socrates these include an ability to:

o   Select the right people
o   Gain their goodwill and inspire their willing participation (obedience is in fact used)
o   Build good relations with colleagues
o   Set a personal example of industry.

Extending knowledge

The text by Adair (2002) uses examples of leaders from history to inform us about general principles of leadership that may be regarded as universal. Readers may obtain much from this text using a 'short cut' approach by reading the chapter introduction and summaries. These amount to approximately 10 per cent of the text and will provide the essence. However to get the full details and nuances of the ideas, presented by one of the foremost writers on leadership, requires the full text to be read, which many may in addition find to be inspiring. Adair, J. (2002) *Inspiring Leadership: Learning from Great Leaders*, London: Thorogood.

Allocating objectives and establishing role boundaries

A major reason why objectives are not achieved is due to a lack of clarity in who has to achieve each objective and where role boundaries exist. This may even include where the team boundaries with other teams are located. This can affect the very interpersonal relationships on which every high performing team relies. One approach to resolving this problem is to give everyone the opportunity to express their viewpoint.

Activity 1.4

Team responsibilities

Ask every team member, and even some team members in teams with which you are closely associated, to list all the significant tasks in which team members are engaged. Consider all tasks. The three main categories of project responsibilities, meeting responsibilities and education and training responsibilities may be used to assist you. A few suggestions are provided under each heading. These are simply for guidance and in no way reflect the full range of possible tasks.

Project responsibilities, for example

- Creating organizational planning charts
- Gathering data
- Updating team rather than individual files.

Meeting responsibilities, for example

- Organizing meetings
- Ensuring participants are available
- Taking charge of the agenda and of minutes
- Breaking deadlocks during meetings, etc.

Education and training responsibilities, for example

- Teaching project management skills
- Organizing external training, etc.

Normally this activity would be undertaken in a meeting. If you can do this in a team meeting that would be ideal. Otherwise, try and get individual team members to complete this on their own. Perhaps you could arrange a short meeting to discuss everyone's comments?

For each task, list who you think is responsible.

	Individual(s) responsible for the task		
Task	Team Leader	Other team members	Identify one or more other team members who, like the team leader, may require a separate entry.

You must share your views with other team members to assess whether there is any disagreement on roles and role boundaries.

Extending knowledge

See Stacey (2003) on leadership and groups (pp. 67–68) and Chapter 17 on control, leadership and ethics and Section 2.5 on thinking about organizations and their management. Davidson (2002) briefly discusses the linkage between individuals and organizations (pp. 287–290). Ahmed and Rafiq (2002) discuss leadership and internal communications.

Evaluating teams to achieve and maintain team success

We understand then that teams go through stages of development and that this is normal. What can we do to achieve or maintain a successful team?

First we must understand the characteristics of high performing teams. Perhaps ten of the more important include:

1. Members are clear about, and agree with, team goals.
2. Members are clear about the role they are asked to play; have the ability, and skills necessary, to accomplish the assigned or chosen task and agree and accept the role.
3. High degree of interdependence exists, as many team tasks require co-operation.
4. The leader's style changes as necessary to meet group needs as they arise. This may be considered in terms of Tuckman's four stages of group development.
5. A very open communications structure (people as well as systems) facilitates the participation and contribution of all members of the team. In addition, team members provide constructive feedback to each other with the focus on individual performance, productivity and effectiveness and members actually seek this. In addition, they use this to great effect by translating this into improvements on all aspects of their work – i.e. productivity and effectiveness.
6. Time is spent initially on planning how decisions are to be made and problems will be solved. That means that time is spent to ensure that there is consensus as to how decisions are to be made – e.g. majority voting, prior to the occasion when actual decisions must be made.
7. Team solutions and decisions are implemented and they have in place methods by which implementation of decisions is evaluated. This results in rapid detection of poor decisions or indeed poor implementation.
8. Norms of behaviours encourage creative, innovative performance. Unusual behaviour is accepted if this is considered to help individuals to perform at the highest level for the benefit of the team.
9. Suitable structure – as small as is possible to achieve objectives. Sub-groups are encouraged and are not seen as threatening; on the contrary they are considered to be more efficient especially if part of the team can effectively resolve a problem leaving the rest of the team to resolve other problems.
10. Highly cohesive with co-operative members. Conflict still occurs however effective approaches to handling conflict results in their rapid resolution.

Source: Adapted from Wheelan (1999).

Wheelan (1999) states that these conclusions have been taken from many sources, however, these are not detailed apart from a comprehensive set of references at the end of the textbook. Ideas have been pulled together and represented in a highly readable style. A very practical, and clear, text on the subject.

Scholtes (1992), for example, uses the above ideas in a more proactive approach in which he suggests characteristics indicative of problems and provides recommendations for their resolution. Like many writers he favours a list of 10 'ingredients'. Some of these overlap. Consequently these ideas have been adapted and reduced in order to present six clear themes.

Desirable team characteristics	Problem indicators	Possible solution
1. *Clear about purpose and goals* Clear about the larger project and its targets, the steps that must be taken and the purpose of meetings and discussion.	Frequent Change of direction Arguments about the next priority task And substantial questioning of decisions.	Encourage a sense that questioning is okay and that it helps to ensure clarity. It may be because of a lack of goal clarity or too broad a remit is in fact the problem.
2. *Work from an improvement plan* This is an agreed and structured way to proceed. It is not simply about the completion of tasks but also the identification of team member training needs.	Lack of understanding of what to do next when one task has been completed. Frequent realization, in the middle of a task, that it was inappropriate (with regard to timing) to undertake.	Obtain advice from an experienced manager or other similarly knowledgeable colleague in the organization on improvement planning.
3. *Clearly defined team roles* Team members may have been taken from another part of the organization. They must however have a clearly defined job role in the team. This includes the work roles that are to be shared and with whom.	The most junior team member always gets the worst tasks. Frequent confusion about whose role it was to complete a particular task.	The team leader and other managers responsible for the formation of the team must have roles specified clearly from the outset. However consultation within the team, including dialogue between the leader and team members, should be undertaken especially where shared tasks must be allocated.
4. *Complete communication clarity* Clarity, directness, active listening and a sincere desire to understand the perspective of other team members. Information is shared effectively.	Rambling conversations. Over-cautious approach in presenting alternative or counter perspectives, language that does not accept others' viewpoints: 'I think you in fact got that wrong' or 'You really need to get on top of the facts'.	Team members can assess each other on active listening and encouraging open debate in a non-threatening manner. In addition, there is always the opportunity to bring in an impartial external observer to evaluate team communication skills especially at meetings.

5. *Positive team interaction*

Agree procedures for achieving objectives and approaches to encouraging team members to get back on the subject if digressions are excessive. Agree also how decisions are made. Opinions of other team members sought to develop a consensual view of more important decisions. Willingness to be flexible and to adjust your viewpoint on the basis of hard evidence without feeling threatened.

Team members agreeing to arguments that are unsubstantiated by evidence/data. Only a few members of the team actively participating or making decisions. Repetition of particular points. Discussions taking place immediately after the meeting in small groups. Why were these views not expressed in the meeting?

Review by team members as above, or include an external observer to provide feedback on performance.

6. *Balanced participation by team members*

All team members should contribute although it is rare that the participation or contribution is exactly equal.

Team members only talk about their particular area of expertise. Domination of discussion by one or a few.

Review by team members as above, or include an external observer to provide feedback on performance. It may be necessary politically to miss out the internal team review if the problem is serious as the views of an impartial external observer are likely to carry more weight and be taken on board.

Identifying causes of sub-optimal performance and improving team performance

Many studies indicate that teams, and organizations, are successful when people are emotionally engaged and believe in what the team and the organization is doing. In addition, it is important for them to gain some form of psychological satisfaction for the contribution they make to the organization, beyond simple monetary benefits.

Motivation

Understanding motivation and associated attributes of commitment and loyalty is not straightforward when it is recognized that several theories of motivation exist (Stacey, 2003, Section 4.7).

Herzberg (1966)	Suggested that people are motivated to work in co-operation with others by both extrinsic motivators, such as money, and intrinsic motivators, such as recognition for achievement, responsibility, advancement and personal growth.
Maslow (1954)	Maslow in his hierarchy of needs (see CIM Stage 2) suggested that when an organization creates conditions in which people can satisfy their 'self-actualization' needs (the highest level in his hierarchy of needs) then they are powerfully motivated to work for the good of the team and of the organization.
Schein (1988)	One of the several authors to consider three categories of relationships. These are 'coercive', where individuals only do the bare minimum to evade punishment and 'utilitarian' where the individual does enough simply to earn the desired level of reward. The final category is a 'normative' form of relationship where individuals value what they are doing for its own sake, as they believe in it. In this situation the individual's ideology matches that of the organization and this acts as the highest level of individual motivation for the benefit of the organization.

One approach is to consider sub-optimal performance in terms of the three-circles model presented by Adair (2002), and use this perspective to question:

1. Do people know where they are going in terms of their common tasks?
2. Are they held together as a team?
3. Are the individual's needs being satisfied?

Davidson (2002, Chapter 4, especially pp. 286–292) expands on the third element considering the individual in terms of their whole life (employer, family, friends, personal interests and voluntary activities). Ultimately if these are significantly out of balance then the other aspects of life suffer. Too much time working can affect an individual's personal life and ultimately this can have an adverse impact on employed activity.

While teams require people with combinations of attributes discussed so far in this unit, high performance teams are distinguished by their level of commitment and loyalty to one and other. Loyalty and commitment extend beyond simple functionality to complete the job in the highest performing teams, to a strong sense of personal commitment.

A four-category perspective of team problems

Irwin *et al.* (1974) suggest that teams encounter problems whether they are project teams or long-standing operational teams. They highlight four particular categories of problems that are interdependent. These they suggest are problems with:

1. Goals
2. Roles
3. Processes
4. Relationships.

In their discussion of this topic there is a sense that these four factors form a type of hierarchy of potential problems starting with the broadest directional issues to the detailed specific aspects of relationships between team members. This includes team leader–team member relationships and relationships between team members within the team and between teams.

Goal problems

Goals may exist however they may be unclear or misunderstood by team members. In the worst situations goals may be poorly specified suffering and/or may be impossible to measure.

Role problems

Interdependence with the preceding problem is evident on reflection. If there is a lack of clarity about goals, how can there be any clarity about roles for individuals within the team? Once goals, or objectives, have been established, it is possible to clarify individual roles. This, however, is fraught with many difficulties that are frequently overlooked. To what extent:

- o   do individuals understand the boundaries of their roles?
- o   do individuals understand the degree of freedom and authority within their role?
- o   does the individual's perception of their role match others' perception? This may lead to, 'Wasn't I supposed to do that' or that's my job. Alternatively, 'I thought you were to do that'.
- o   inevitably roles interact or even overlap. An inability to cope effectively with this source of potential confusion or conflict will inevitably lead to sub-optimal team performance.

Process problems

There are many potential process issues. One perspective is to consider the more significant as concerned with (a) decision making (b) communications and meetings and (c) leadership style.

(a)   Progress occurs only when decisions are taken. When more than one person is involved this becomes a process issue. Who has responsibility and ultimately authority to make decisions? What rights do team members have, especially in relation to the leader, with regard to decision making? Do all members of the team need to be consulted? Perhaps people outside of the team must be included in some decisions.

(b)   How does everyone know that a decision has been made? In other words how are/will decisions be communicated? It may be that due to different roles within the team, and certainly as the team size grows, that not every member of a team needs to know the outcome of every decision. If consideration is not given to this with larger teams then individuals may suffer from information overload. In the more formal setting of meetings who attends and how are unavoidable absences accommodated? The team must also have an approach to meeting structure and process.

(c)   The leader is in a very different category within the team. Leadership styles may tend towards the autocratic or inclusive. Sometimes the fact that inclusive, participative leadership styles have become more common has led some to place less influence on the role of the leader. Group development is fundamentally influenced by the style of the leader and this in particular will affect the efficiency of processes. In a 'performing' team the leader is most likely to seek and accept feedback on two aspects of his/her leadership – fundamental style/approach and on the impact their role is having on the team.

Activity 1.5

Team process problems

Analyse a team meeting that you have attended recently in which decisions were arrived at. Answer the following questions which attempt to assess how many process problems you have.

- o How were decisions taken? How many participated in making the decisions? How was disagreement resolved? Did only one person make each of the decisions in effect?
- o Were you clear as to who had responsibility for each decision?
- o Did everyone have the same amount of information to support their contribution to decision making? Perhaps each team member had specialist information, however, did those bringing most information to the decision have greater influence?
- o Was influence purely on the basis of perceived or actual job role or perhaps on the basis of seniority in the team/organization?
- o How was the meeting structured? Was there a clear agenda? How was time keeping at the meeting?
- o Was there a lot of pointless debate? Was there a feeling that the meeting, perhaps only in places, was going nowhere?
- o What role did the 'leader' (however defined) take? To what extent did they let participants exert affluence or did the leader use an autocratic approach? Obviously the leader's approach may vary in the course of the meeting.

How many of the answers to these questions indicated the existence of process problems? If there are many, you must hold a team meeting specifically to address process problems, otherwise you can never become, or remain, a high performing team.

Relationship problems

Relationship issues may be considered as potentially the lowest level, or most detailed aspect, of potential team problems. They are in fact the most intractable and hardest to resolve as they operate at the most personal level. The other three areas of potential team problems (already discussed) are 'external' to the individual. Individuals are generally not affected fundamentally by changes in each of these. However relationship problems may be deep seated. They may arise from a lack of mutual respect or trust in technical competence or judgement.

Unfortunately 'relationships' may be regarded as an issue when in actual fact the problem is concerned with goals, roles or processes. For example, conflicts between individuals may be due to a failure to clarify goals or roles rather than any fundamental problem that individuals have with one and other.

We understand that teams generally go through various phases, ideally culminating in operating as a 'performing' team. The concept of an evolution of team performance suggests that sub-optimal performance may be different in each phase.

The application of the ideas of Irwin *et al.* (1974) to the different stages of team development is apparent.

Goals and priorities	Vital that goals and priorities are established at the *forming* stage. However the team leader may not have established his/her authority. In addition, often the team must construct their own goals and priorities. At this stage in development, team members may argue forcibly about these issues and it is vital that this is resolved and members come to an agreement on a shared approach or accommodation that they can work with.
Roles	By the time the team gets to the *norming* stage, roles should be established. Prior to this, especially if a new member joins the team, expectations about the non-specified aspects of the role have to be reconciled – an obvious potential source of conflict.
Processes	Meetings can be a very good indicator of performance problems. At the *performing* stage, team members listen actively to one and other, exhibit a high degree of collaboration resulting in rapid decision making. Process issues, especially with regard to meetings and decision making, will have been determined and members will be open to continuous modification and improvement. However, prior to this stage, e.g. at the *storming* stage, team members may be prone to talk and not to listen, time management may be poor with meeting time overruns and decision making may be fairly crude, simply through majority voting.
Relationships	In a *performing* group there will be a high level of trust and commitment between team members. Effective team functioning will build shared experience and engaging in co-operative behaviour will reinforce relationships and facilitate their development towards a deeper level.

Extending knowledge

Taking action to control sub-standard performance is the focus of the section in Brown (2002) on 'Controlling projects – taking action' pp. 74–87. Brown, M. (2002) *Project Management in a Week*, 3rd edition, London: Hodder & Stoughton.

Improving the team's performance, including plans to improve motivation, commitment and loyalty

Two general approaches to this may be considered. One is continuous, ongoing development of team performance on a daily and weekly basis. The other is to instigate specific team development events.

Both approaches require some form of review or assessment of the current situation before recommending further action. The general problem-finding approach of goals/roles/processes/relationships provides one suitable approach to improve team performance through team building and development.

The aim of team building may be stated as:

> *To help people who work together to function more effectively in teams and to assist the team itself to work more effectively as a whole.* (Moxon, 1994)

21

Ongoing development

Moxon (1994) suggests that teambuilding involves:

o Regular meetings to establish and review processes, procedures and objectives. Effectiveness will decline if this is not undertaken.
o Sessions specifically on addressing issues. Strengths and the causes of successes are examined rather than simply focusing on weaknesses and their causes. The focus is on workable solutions.
o Ongoing emphasis on encouraging open and honest discussion rather than superficial politeness. This requires the creation of a sense of security within the team where team members feel able to take risks and share their deeper and true feelings.
o A commitment to personal change and development and to change to improve team performance. Change will be detailed in action plans and these will also be subject to review.
o Frequent time away from the job, especially in the early stages of team formation, in support of team development.
o Openness of the leader to receive feedback from the team on leadership style and effectiveness.
o Development of interpersonal skills, especially with regard to processes (e.g. meetings) and relationships. This normally should take place as a team.

Formal workshops focused on team development

A more comprehensive and detailed approach to team development exists where a decision has been taken for a team-building programme or event (Figure 1.3).

Diagnosis	Data collection
	One-to-one interviews – provides very detailed contextual information although very time consuming and relies on an open and frank discussion by the manager
	Questionnaires – quick, less threatening than an interview and allows easy and rapid analysis
↓	Provides suitable information in order to arrive at a diagnosis of the problem(s)
Design and planning	Session design can be tailored to the particular problems that must be overcome
	Define objectives
	Broad design
	Exercise selection
	Administration (of session facilities and equipment)
↓	Pre-work (by the team before they attend the session)
Running the sessions	Introduction
	Discussion
	Action plans
↓	Summary and agreement
Follow-up	Write-up outcomes
	Review progress
	Future dates

Figure 1.3 An approach to team development
Source: Adapted from Moxon (1994)

Numerous diagnostic tools exist to establish particular problems and issues. By clarifying these, teams can then construct their own action plans to suggest how they may be addressed, use a facilitator or employ an external training organization. An example of a questionnaire on team effectiveness is given below (Figure 1.4).

Assess your team on each of the factors presented. Read the brief comment supporting the single word description before assessing your team on the scale of 1 to 9.

Group objectives
Well understood and accepted by all team members. These are reviewed frequently.

123456789

We are unclear about our objectives and there is frequent lengthy discussion on our priorities when we have achieved the latest working objective.

Atmosphere
Informal and comfortable with everyone at their ease. People are involved and even excited in their work.

123456789

There is a high degree of tension. The majority of people are overloaded or have insufficient work to do at times.

Communication
We are very good at communicating and highly focused on the task. We are sensitive to the views of one and other and listen in a non-judgemental way.

123456789

Communication appears to suffer from a few people dominating the conversation. We frequently go off the subject during meetings. It seems that we do not listen attentively to each other.

Conflict resolution
We handle conflict, such as exists, very well. People are prepared to disagree and these are debated openly rather than shouted down. The minority who sometimes do not agree with a decision accept the disagreement graciously.

123456789

People become highly charged during disagreements or seem not to let conflict arise, either through the role of the chairperson or because there is a concern about being perceived as negative. We tend to use majority voting and it seems that the more dominant group members get their way.

Decision making
This is consensual. Team members feel able to raise disagreements however we are good at laying bare the basis for disagreement especially where this is due to subjective weighting of influencing factors.

123456789

Decisions seem to be taken far too quickly without sufficient debate or consultation. The leader tends to dominate leaving many uncommitted to the final decision.

Criticism
Very open but certainly not personal. We find criticism to be well considered and delivered sensitively. Team members usually take it on board without feeling a loss of status.

123456789

It seems that we try and score points off each other. There is a certain pleasure by some in criticizing others and this creates a certain degree of tension.

Expression of personal feeling
Uninhibited and people do not seem to want to follow a personal agenda.

123456789

We are never usually clear about peoples' personal feelings. There is a reluctance to expose our personal feelings to group scrutiny because of the potential risk that this engenders.

Leadership

1 2 3 4 5 6 7 8 9

The leader is not overly concerned with exercising and demonstrating authority. In fact at times, group members appear to take on group leadership. We seem to be more concerned with completing the work rather than on the display of power.

It is obvious who the team leader is. Frequently we may discuss an issue and then the leader makes the final decision, even though the case for the decision is not apparent and perhaps many of us have argued against that particular decision.

Achievement of tasks

1 2 3 4 5 6 7 8 9

We operate with clear, mutually agreed action plans. We regularly review performance against these plans and indeed the plans themselves. Team members are highly committed to achieving the action plans.

We don't tend to know who is to do what and by when. We seldom review performance against plans or indeed the plans themselves. When people are given particular tasks these are often ambiguous. We are not good at following up who has done what.

Review of team processes

1 2 3 4 5 6 7 8 9

We are in control of our own processes. These are reviewed to see if they can be done better, from decision making to the way we run meetings and allocate tasks. We assess whether process issues are causing a reduction in the effectiveness of the team.

We do not really discuss team process issues and review these. Some team members like to talk about our failings in private, or outside of team meetings when only a few members of the team are present, but for some reason they do not raise these issues in team meetings.

Figure 1.4 Assess the effectiveness of your team
Source: Adapted from Moxon (1994, pp. 102–106)

Teams and their impact on corporate success

The role of teams is central to corporate success. They are in fact the vehicle for the initial creation, and implementation, of marketing plans. The work by Belbin (2004) clearly demonstrates a relatively strong association between team types and financial success in substantial numbers of management team simulations where 'real' managers competed in teams in realistic business simulations.

In developing Belbin's work further, there was a requirement to clarify teamwork responsibility, especially including autonomous elements. While in some countries this was considered, in others, e.g. the UK, there was resistance at senior levels within corporations. One explanation is that CEOs are paid very large salaries which are also linked to performance bonuses (and reputations). These people wish to lead from the top (see Adair, 2002, on leadership). They do not wish to place their personal fortunes in the hands of others, especially the many formal and informal teams within the organization. Their preference is to lead in effect by edict. In Belbin's analysis these amounted to hierarchical bureaucracies which somehow had to co-exist with established bureaucracies and this fundamentally unbalanced the organizational mode of operation.

Stacey (2003, p. 69) concludes that:

> *bureaucratic control is neither rational nor efficient outside certain limited conditions and that it produces a number of negative, limited ... undermining consequences.*

Bureaucracies have an alienating impact on the individual by too narrowly defining work roles which generate a feeling of powerlessness and isolation and prevents the individual from developing shared values and a sense of belonging in the organization. Bureaucracies, as rigid structures, cannot cope with adaptation to a dynamic environment. Consequently, informal groups inevitably form within the organization and operate to counter the sense of alienation, frequently in a way that runs counter to the aims and objectives of the bureaucracy.

Extending knowledge

Belbin (2004) Chapter 13: Where are we now, and Stacey (2002) Chapter 4, especially Sections 4.5–4.8 inclusive.

Summary

Organizational strategy is increasingly implemented in teams. These teams are no longer made of individuals with many years of experience working together. Instead team members may be drawn from across the organization for projects that may last only a few weeks to many years where new organizational structures are established. These teams may be made up of people from within the organization or from people taken from all stages of the supply chain. Team members can no longer rely on being located in close proximity to 'bump into each other at the coffee machine'. Instead they may be located across the globe or perhaps be located in the same building but due to a shift system be temporally separated.

Teams move through various stages as team members get to know other team members and develop and understand the role that the team has. To use the language of this subject area, teams must resolve and harmonize interpersonal relationships and task activities. Consequently this is a very dynamic process.

Effective teams take account of the need to consider not simply team tasks that must be completed but also the need for balance in terms of team roles. Team roles are determined by individual personality and result in characteristic behaviour patterns in the context of team work.

Teams are generally successful where people are emotionally engaged. Team members must be motivated and this creates loyal team members. Where problems exist, one perspective is to consider these as problems in setting and achieving appropriate goals, roles, processes and relationships.

Sample exam question

You have been promoted to General Manager of a poorly performing division of your company. After a few weeks in the role you realise that everything seems to be geared to cost management, there is no marketing function for example and you see this as critical to future progress. You are becoming increasingly concerned at the lack of customer focus and attention to revenue generation. Your Managing Director has asked you to summarise in a brief report to him what steps you can take in the short term to improve sales and how you would set about establishing a marketing function.

Discussion

Please refer to the syllabus, element 1 – Creating the Organizational Context for Effective Implementation of Strategy.

In considering this question first think through the circumstances this division is likely to find itself in. Poor and declining performance, lack of investment with question marks over things like product quality and customer service. The question asks you to consider short and longer term issues. Consider what might be appropriate in each of these circumstances, the underlying principles and concepts, and how this can be drawn together in a report to your Managing Director. You have just been appointed and he will be looking closely at your performance and plans for the future.

Bibliography

Adair, J. (1986) *Effective Teambuilding*, Gower: Basingstoke.

Adair, J. (2002) *Inspiring Leadership: Learning from Great Leaders*, London: Thorogood (ISBN 1854182072).

Ahmed, P. and Rafiq, M. (2002) *Internal Marketing: The Tools and Concepts for Customer-focused Management*, Oxford: Butterworth-Heinemann (ISBN 0750648384).

Belbin, R.M. (2000) *Beyond the Team*, Oxford: Butterworth-Heinemann (ISBN 0750646411).

Belbin, R.M. (2004) *Management Teams: Why they Succeed or Fail*, Oxford: Butterworth-Heinemann ((ISBN 0750659106).

Brown, M. (2002) *Project Management in a Week*, London: Hodder & Stoughton (ISBN 0340849371).

Davidson, H. (2002) *The Committed Enterprise: How to Make Vision and Values Work*, Oxford: Butterworth-Heinemann (ISBN 0750655402).

Irwin, I.M., Plovnick, M.S. and Fry, R.C. (1974) *Task Orientated Team Development*, New York: McGraw-Hill.

Katzenbach, J.R. and Smith, D.K. (1994) *The Wisdom of Teams*, New York: McGraw-Hill (ISBN 0875845819).

Moxon, P. (1994) *Building a Better Team: A Handbook for Managers and Facilitators*, Aldershot: Gower (ISBN 0566074249).

Pelled, L.H., Eisenhardt, K.M. and Xin, K.R. (1999) 'Exploring the Black Box: An Analysis of Work Group Diversity, Conflict and Performance', *Administrative Science Quarterly*, **44**(1), March, pp. 1–28 .

Piercy, R.M. (2002) *Market-led Strategic Change: A Guide to Transforming the Process of Going to Market*, Oxford: Butterworth-Heinemann (ISBN 075065225X).

Scholtes, P.R. (1992) *The Team Handbook: How to Use Teams to Improve Quality*, Madison: Joiner (ISBN 0962226408).

Stacey, R.D. (2003) *Strategic Management and Organizational Dynamics*, Harlow: Prentice Hall (ISBN 0273658980).

Tuckman, B.W. and Jensen, M.C. (1977) 'Stages in Small-group Development Revisited', *Group and Organizational Studies*, **2**(4), pp. 419–427.

Wheelan, S.A. (1999) *Creating Effective Teams*, Thousand Oaks: Sage Publications (ISBN 0761918175).

unit 2 organizational culture

Syllabus links

Learning outcomes

'Identify the barriers to effective implementation of strategies and plans involving change (including communications) in the organization, and develop measures to prevent or overcome them.'

Please see Appendix 4 for full details of the learning outcomes, related statements of practice and knowledge and skills requirements.

Information on the syllabus element (and its weighting) that is supported by this chapter can be found in Figure P.1, in the preface to this book.

Learning objectives

By the end of this unit you will:

o Understand the meaning of 'market orientation'

o Understand the meaning of culture in an organizational context

o Understand the meaning of 'environment' and how it influences organizational culture

o Be able to critically evaluate how organizations can become more market orientated

o Be able to critically evaluate the factors that constrain progress towards a more market-orientated organization

o Understand what is meant by 'change' in the context of an organization

o Be able to critically evaluate the main pressures on an organization to change

o Be able to critically evaluate the potential initiatives available to allow an organization to change

o Be able to assess pressure on the organization and suggest relevant change strategies.

Key definitions

Market Orientation – Market Orientation entails: one or more departments engaging in activities geared towards developing an understanding of customers' current and future needs and the factors affecting them, sharing of this understanding across departments and the various departments engaging in activities designed to meet select customer needs (Kohli and Jaworski, 1990).

Culture – Aaker (1998) suggested that organizational culture involves three elements: (1) A set of shared values or dominant beliefs that define an organization's priorities; (2) A set of norms of behaviour and (3) Symbols and symbolic activities used to develop and nurture those shared values and norms.

Strategic fit – This is where the organization's strategy is aligned with the marketing environment in which it operates. Many marketers use the analogy of the organization being like an animal that attempts to be in harmony with its environment. In the case of the organization this is aligned with the customers that it serves.

Environmental scanning – (A) 'The process of monitoring and analysing the marketing environment of a company' (Jobber, 2001, p. 142).

(B) 'The process by which environmental stimuli are selected and organised into patterns which are meaningful to the organisation in the light of its current and future needs and interests' (Brownlie).

Marketing environment – 'Consists of the actors and forces that affect a company's capability to operate effectively in providing products and services to its customers.'

Micro-environment – 'Consists of the actors in the firm's immediate environment that affect its capabilities to operate effectively in its chosen market. The key actors are suppliers, distributors, customers and competitors.'

Macro-environment – 'Consists of a number of broader forces that affect not only the company but also the other actors in the micro-environment. These can be grouped under economic, social, legal, physical and technological forces. These shape the character of the opportunities and threats facing a company, and yet are largely uncontrollable' (Jobber, 2001, p. 120).

Environmental scanning – 'The process of monitoring and analysing the marketing environment of a company' (Jobber, 2001, p. 142).

Study Guide

This unit will take you about 4 hours to work through.

We suggest that you take a further 4 hours to do the various activities and questions in this unit.

Introduction

Organizations are social structures in which people co-operate to achieve organizational objectives. In the first unit we considered the role of teams and the factors influencing team performance. In this unit we provide an understanding of how the strategic marketing manager can influence the organizational culture, in particular into adopting a stronger market orientation. The main pressures on an organization to change are considered and initiatives available to respond are discussed. Unit 3 goes on to address the planning and implementation of change, using the concept of internal marketing, to facilitate and manage the consequent change in the organization and marketing team. Units 2 and 3 together cover the part of the syllabus that draws on the theories of culture and change management.

Building blocks of organizational orientation and change

We must understand what an organization is before we can think about changing it in a particular direction. Stated simply we can consider the organization to be what the CEO says it is. This person simply, by edict, announces any intended change which they can personally direct in a relatively straightforward process. Alternatively, we can consider the organization as an entity in its own right into which any individual, including the CEO, must be socialized. These are two contrasting perspectives that may be taken as the basis for formulating an organization's strategy and how it may be implemented. Stacey (2003), in Unit 1, provides a detailed discussion of these divergent perspectives. At one extreme the organization may be seen as consisting of individuals who create the organization and its view of the world, i.e. the individual is primary. At the other extreme, the organization is considered as determining how the individual behaves, i.e. there is an organizational culture into which individuals are socialized: the group shapes the individual. The consequences of adopting either of these two extreme positions are fundamental in guiding our thinking about organizational change. If we assume that the individual is supreme, then we implicitly agree that the CEO, or whoever, follows a rational approach to strategy formulation and implementation and drives it through. However, if the group is supreme, then strategy formulation emerges through conversations within the organization in which many people participate. Linking these two extreme positions is a continuum in which both positions are considered to be relevant but in varying degrees. The main point however is on which of these two positions the greater emphasis is placed as this has fundamental implications for change and change management.

These polarized extremes of describing an organization, with an infinite amount of positions in between, are perhaps unsurprising. There is a large variation in organization type in terms of their size, structure (e.g. functionally based or regionally based), legal status (e.g. private family business versus publicly quoted on the stock market), market and geographical reach. For example, in a small family run business it is probable that the organization is the sum of the individuals where one or a few individuals in fact define the organization, i.e. not every individual has an equal weight of influence. In this case where the owner manager wishes to change any aspect of the business then this change will be implemented. In complete contrast are large international businesses that develop a self-sustaining organizational culture where the influence of any individual founder has become history. In this case the organization develops corporate memory and identity which is not simply a projection of one individual but of the 'group' (current and previous generations of employees as well as other stakeholders). Again, the influence of particular stakeholder groups, and perhaps individuals, will not be equal, but the distinguishing aspect is that there is an organizational identity that is independent from one individual. Change in this context is much more complex as this requires a change in group culture.

Market orientation

What is market orientation? A behavioural definition is provided by Kohli and Jaworski (1990):

> *The organization wide generation of market intelligence, dissemination of its intelligence across departments, and organization-wide responses to it.*

Several research studies have provided direct evidence for a link between market orientation and business performance, for example (Kohli and Jaworski, 1990). In a company that is market-oriented, all departments (not just the marketing department) would be customer-focused, and the aim of providing superior customer value would be seen as everybody's responsibility (i.e. that everybody is seen as a part-time marketer). Some authors refer to this as market orientation; others as marketing orientation. Often the two terms are used inter-changeably. However, Piercy (2002) argues that markets are what are important, not marketing and therefore more emphasis should be placed on 'market orientation'. Many studies have attempted to identify the key characteristics of market-oriented companies. Kohli and Jaworski (1990) identified that a market orientation entails:

1. One or more departments engaging in activities geared towards developing an under-standing of customers' current and future needs and the factors affecting them
2. Sharing of this understanding across departments and
3. The various departments engaging in activities designed to meet select customer needs.

In other words, a market orientation refers to the organization-wide generation, dissemination and responsiveness to market intelligence.

Narver and Slater (1990) considered market orientation in terms of organizational culture that resulted in appropriate staff behaviour resulting in superior value for buyers and consequently for the organization. They developed the following model that highlights the key components of a market orientation (Figure 2.1).

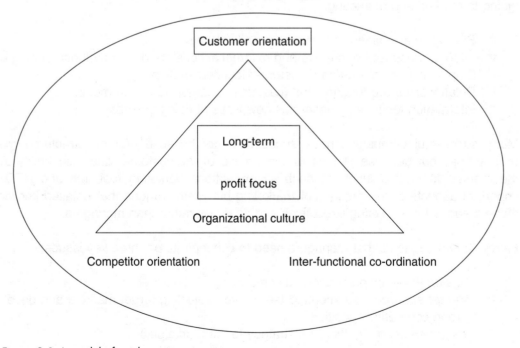

Figure 2.1 A model of market orientation
Source: Adapted from Narver and Slater (1990)

- o *Customer orientation* – concerned with understanding customers so that you can better meet their needs
- o *Competitor orientation* – having an awareness of competitors' capabilities
- o *Interfunctional co-ordination* – all aspects of the business striving to create value
- o *Organizational culture* – a culture that facilitates organizational learning
- o *Long-term profit focus* – as opposed to a shorter perspective.

A key theme is that of market-led strategic change. Piercy (2002) developed this phrase and places much emphasis on 'going to market' rather than marketing. Nigel Piercy (2002, Chapter 1) takes a very readable, yet authoritative and practical approach for using the term 'market-led' rather than marketing-led (similarly market rather than marketing-orientated). Rather than marketing residing in a specialist department in the organization it resides in everyone and in every place in the organization, and has the status of a sort of organizational soul. Part of everyone's job is to be a part-time marketer, with the marketing specialists designated as 'full-time' marketers.

To encapsulate this thinking he summarized effective comment from Anthony Brown of IBM in which Brown suggests that the new corporate philosophy of marketing will be achieved by clusters of teams who will be formed from individuals and groups within the organization and increasingly outside of the organization. The focus of the formation of these teams will be customers (see Unit 1). Such team networks will rely on, and be supported by, IT systems.

Consequently 'marketing-led' is an outdated term implying that somehow the marketing department leads the organizational direction. Organizations go to market and this is a process that is owned by everyone. Suddenly, by this shift in thinking, the reader will realize that the task of ensuring stronger market orientation becomes organization-wide and consequently potentially far more problematic to achieve in practice. Nigel Piercy advocates quite a fundamental change in thinking on what it is that marketing should deliver. Marketers still bring their knowledge and skills to the organizational table, just like accountants, engineers, general managers, etc. However, he advocates a different context for marketing as a philosophy rather than as a functional discipline located within, and only in, a marketing department. It may be argued that marketing departments could disappear in a truly market-oriented organization but going to market will always endure. Piercy (2002) identifies a number of important differences between 'going to market' and marketing:

- o Strategies are based on customers and markets
- o Internal processes of change and external actions are driven by those strategies
- o Emphasis is on delivering a customer-focused strategy
- o Relationships are fundamental (customers, competitors, intermediaries)
- o Information technology underpins new ways of doing business.

Many successful companies have succeeded, not because of their structured marketing programmes but because of their understanding of the customer and their ability to sense the market. Marketing functions such as promotion, marketing research and NPD are all important aspects of the process of marketing but Piercy argues that detailed knowledge of these areas is for marketing executives and agencies rather than managers.

Piercy (2002) suggests that managers need to concentrate on three key issues:

1. *Customers* – understanding customers
2. *Market strategy* – segmenting the market, selecting target markets and developing a strong competitive position
3. *Implementation* – getting the strategy to the marketplace.

Too often these important issues are not given priority because immediate problems get in the way. Managers should be concentrating on these strategic issues rather than getting involved in the tactics. Many strategies fail, not because they are poor strategies but because they have been poorly implemented. Managers need to focus as much on the implementation as they do on the contents of the strategy.

Piercy (2002) acknowledges that the process of going to market is not easy, may require substantial change in the way organizations are run and that a key role of marketing is to encourage and facilitate change so that employees are more likely to accept and embrace it willingly. Piercy acknowledges that the market is dynamic and that for companies to maintain their competitive advantage they will have to respond to the following new challenges:

○ *New customer demands and expectations* – customer expectations are increasing and they are less willing to accept second-class service
○ *New competitors* – competition is coming not just from established competitors but also from new entrants, such as the entrance of Virgin into financial services and EasyJet into car rental
○ *New types of organizations being established* – many organizations are downsizing and becoming more narrowly focused. Others (such as Time Warner and AOL) are entering strategic alliances and collaborative partnerships
○ *Whole new ways of doing business are being developed* – for example, electronic marketing.

It is imperative that marketers continually adapt and respond to these new challenges in order to gain/maintain competitive advantage.

Activity 2.1

How market-oriented is your organization?

Hooley *et al.* (1998) in their text, *Marketing Strategy and Competitive Positioning*, have developed a framework for evaluating market orientation. Complete the assessment presented on pp.11–13 of their book, by applying it to your own organization. To what extent do you think your organization is market-oriented, and how helpful is this framework in understanding the key components of market orientation?

Overcoming barriers to market orientation

In reviewing the barriers to market orientation, Harris (1999) concluded that these may be grouped into two categories: organizational culture, including organizational learning, and secondly, systems and structures issues.

Slater and Narver (1995) suggested that organizations had to maximize organizational learning on the continuous creation of superior customer value as one-off ideas could all too readily be copied. To understand current and future customer needs better than competitors was the long-term aim of every business. This requires a culture and climate within the organization to maximize organizational learning. Secondly, an ability to change and become more market orientated is linked crucially to organizational structures and systems. For example, Ruekert (1992) found a link between recruiting, training and reward processes and market orientation.

Piercy employed the term 'market-led strategic change' to encapsulate many of the ideas suggested to becoming more market orientated or as he terms it 'market strategy implementation'. He suggested that organizations should:

- ○ Follow more closely than anyone else the market requirements of customers.
- ○ Focus on factors that cause a lack of customer focus, namely the way the organization is run. Too often the focus is incorrectly on lack of information or insufficient technology investment which are rarely problematic.
- ○ Change the way the organization is structured and run and the way staff within the organization look at the world, to be more in tune with customer wants and demands. Customers must be the central focus of the organization.

Extending knowledge

See Piercy, N.F. (2002). *Market-Led Strategic Change*, Oxford: Butterworth-Heinemann, pp. 390–402. (075065225X). This is certainly a marketing practitioner-focused text. Read, in particular, Chapter 1 'Whatever happened to marketing?', which is devoted to a discussion of market orientation. Chapter 2 on customer-focused issues will also contribute to your understanding of this topic. Later in this unit other reading from this text will be recommended.

Stacey, R.D. (2003). *Strategic Management and Organizational Dynamics*, Harlow: Pearson Education Limited. (0273658980). A more theoretical approach to the subject which allows you to obtain a deeper understanding of underlying principles and dynamics within organizations. Read Chapter 1 as an introduction. Later in this unit other reading from this text will be recommended.

Case study

Achieving a market-led culture – Medical Instruments and Devices Inc.

A multinational medical devices B2B company operating in the UK was profitable and growing but considered itself to be confronted by several problems from the macro and micro environment. Problems in the macro environment arose from technological developments that resulted in change in the use of their products, changes in social expectations of healthcare systems and in legislation concerning regulation and trading. However of primary concern were political and economic forces which demanded demonstrable cost effectiveness.

In the micro environment market concentration was occurring. In each market sector there was competition from two sources: more highly resourced competitors who tended to have higher market shares and lower resourced niche players who appeared to be more aligned to customer needs for their specialist niches.

Organizational buying practices were also changing from a single clinician, to a decision making unit involving many people and with a formalized decision making process.

There was a further problem in terms of this international business attempting to adopt global strategies, especially with product development to obtain scale economies, but at the same time attempting to implement nationally based strategies.

Problem

The corporate culture itself was described as: 'product-orientated, technically focused, reactive rather than pro-active with a bias for immediate action over planning' (Rowland and Smith, 2001, p. 216). Rapid and substantial increases in product development times and costs, increased regulatory influence and activity and market maturity required comprehensive, systematic market analysis and planning rather than a simplistic and somewhat limited approach responding to customer feedback.

Solution – towards a market-led culture

- Adopt an incremental approach – no quick fix.
- Agreement from senior management team on a new approach.
- Increased time allocation and encouragement of strategic thinking rather than only operational management.
- Personal development supported by diagnostic tools (e.g. personal profiling).
- Formal skills training, especially of the key technical sales force product managers who had little marketing knowledge. They were given tailored training in market analysis, strategy development and tactical implementation which also directly supported their work.

Source: Adapted from Rowland and Smith (2001).

Market orientation in context

The core approach that companies should adopt is to focus on customers and markets. Piercy admits that he is simply refocusing people back to the core issues. His argument is that managers have been distracted to detailed considerations of techniques, for example, various strategy and planning models, various theories and models about the marketing mix and marketing research. In his perspective, managers are in danger of taking their eye off the ball. However, where he does add something is in the area of implementation, which he places within the top three areas on which to focus along with customers and market strategy based around conventional segmenting, targeting and positioning and maintaining sustainable competitive advantage. Implementation and change operate side by side to drive this corporate philosophy of marketing forward. He sees this as being put into operation by 'clusters of teams' who build relationships both within and outside of the organization supported by an IT function.

Case study

Ethical Market orientation – Baxter International

Baxters is a US medical-equipment manufacturer with a turnover of approximately $8 billion, for example for products such as filters used in dialysis. This is an organization which succeeds in achieving a balance for all stakeholders. While one perspective is to extract as much as is possible out of employees for shareholder value, this company takes a longer term perspective in which corporate productivity in this approach is seen as counter productive. The company believes that shareholders and the organization are rewarded when employees are motivated and committed. A central principle of this approach is: 'to do the right thing'. In August 2001, several dialysis patients died in mysterious circumstances in Spain, one possible factor could have been problems with the filters. This was followed closely by deaths in similar circumstances in Croatia. Baxter experts investigated the problem and eventually discovered that it was caused, not by their filters, but by a fluid, manufactured by another company, turned to gas when exposed to body temperature blood, causing a fatal pulmonary embolism. The chairman determined not to get

involved in an unseemly, public blame allocation with the testing company and made financial settlements with the families of the victims. In addition, the plants manufacturing the filters were closed down. The cost to the company was $180 million. In addition, the chairman recommended that his bonus be reduced by 40 per cent and that bonuses for other senior executives be reduced by 20 per cent.

The chairman's approach was to 'practise what he preached'. In so doing, he creates a stronger company, as stakeholders believe in its values, employees in particular are more committed to the organization, through its consistent behaviour and this ultimately provides long run improvements in shareholder value.

Organizational culture

Various definitions of culture and organization culture exist. Stacey (2003, p. 56) defines organizational culture as:

> that set of beliefs, customs, practices and ways of thinking that they have come to share with each other through being and working together. It is a set of assumptions people simply accept without question ... In order to determine whether a plan is likely to be acceptable in cultural terms it is necessary to analyse peoples' shared beliefs. Analysis of the culture is thought to reveal whether options being considered fall within that culture or whether they require major cultural change.

The culture of an organization often develops over many years and is influenced by a whole range of factors such as management style, organizational structure, the organization's history, chief executive leadership style, type of market, number and intensity of competition, location, PEST factors, union involvement and the nature of the business (i.e. traditional or based on new technologies). All of these factors will develop a culture that is unique to a particular organization.

Schein (1985) believed that it was possible to analyse an organization's culture using a perspective that views culture as an adaptive, learning process in which the organization communicates its culture to new recruits. His approach is to assess the values that govern behaviour through an analysis of the:

o Recruitment and induction process.
o Response to 'critical incidents' in the organization's history. These represent major events that help form behaviour, and behavioural responses, that are internalized into common 'organizational cultural' practice.
o People regarded as representing the organization's culture, for example long-serving staff and senior managers.

However, it is possible to identify various different organizational cultures. Deal and Kennedy (2000) identify four different cultures according to their attitude to risk (see Figure 2.2).

Speed of feedback

	Slow feedback	Fast feedback
Hard risk	'Bet your company culture'	'Hard Macho culture'
Attitude to risk		
Low risk	'Process culture'	'Work hard/play hard culture'

Figure 2.2 Corporate cultures
Source: Deal and Kennedy (2000)

Case study

A clash of two cultures

Mergers, partnerships and strategic alliances are becoming commonplace in the industrial landscape and yet research has shown that many of these relationships do not reap the promised benefits. According to a KPMG study, just 17 per cent of cross-border mergers and acquisitions from 1996 to the end of 1998 added to shareholder value. What so many acquirers forget is that while finance might propel the deal, its lack of marketing synergy will undo it. 'The hard stuff is relatively easy to calculate. But they usually haven't done their homework on the soft stuff, and so the integration fails because of a culture clash' says Anita Hoffman, business development director at management consultancy, Accenture. 'There is little discussion about how the two cultures will fit together in terms of how they go to market, how they sell and how they treat the customer' says Helena Rubenstein, managing director of branding consultancy, The Lab.

The potential for a culture clash was enormous when Unilever acquired Ben and Jerry's ice-cream. Ben and Jerry's distinctive ethically oriented culture and brand values are in stark contrast to the vast conglomerate's culture. There was a danger that Ben and Jerry's would be submerged in Unilever's culture and lose its uniqueness. In an attempt to retain its unique culture and the brand's ethical stance a clause that stated that 8 per cent of pre-tax profits should continue to go to charity was incorporated into the buyout agreement.

A major challenge for all parties involved in mergers, acquisitions or partnerships is how to effectively integrate disparate cultures. The importance of culture cannot be over-emphasized and companies should seek out partners that they believe will prove to be complementary and synergistic.

Source: Mazur (2001).

An organization's culture must support it in aligning with the environment if successful strategies are to be pursued. However, as organizations develop and evolve, they tend to progress through a cultural lifecycle. Stacey (2003) suggests that cultural evolution goes hand in hand with structural evolution. Initially a 'power' culture is appropriate when the organization is in its infancy. It then becomes more appropriate for a 'role' culture to be implemented to operate a functional structure effectively, and finally, as the organization grows and expands, a divisional

37

structure is used and in this context a 'task' culture is most appropriate. What are these cultural types? Handy (1981) cited in Stacey (2003, p. 65) provides a four-category organizational cultural classification.

1. *Power culture* – with the owner manager/entrepreneur acting with complete authority. Such people are risk takers and tend to see administrative processes and procedures as getting in the way. They are the source of power. They do not emanate from the organizational systems and procedures that legitimize action in larger, long-established organizations.
2. *In the role culture* – organizations are highly bureaucratic with people specializing on a functional basis. Order, predictability and hierarchy are important. Procedures, rules and regulations for them define the essence of the organization and adherence to these is the essence of 'good' management.
3. *Task cultures* – as the name suggests, are highly focused on work, whether it is in terms of general work function and/or particular projects with which people are involved.
4. *Person cultures* – are where personal goals, satisfaction and interest drive organizational behaviour. This is most commonly manifested in organizations and divisions where technical specialists predominate – e.g. engineers, accountants, lawyers, etc. They see their work as a vehicle for personal expression rather than simply getting the job done.

Handy's classification approach is useful when considering most western style business organizations, however, Burns (1996) suggests that it fails to accommodate Japanese organizations as their organizations contain elements of each extreme. For example, Japanese companies have very tightly defined and highly structured jobs and this is particularly evident at the more junior levels in the organization. Japanese organizations are very hierarchical, deferential, but in spite of this they exhibit initiative and creativity in problem solving.

Case study

Organizational adaptation to its environment – changing leader

The owner manager is characterized by creativity, risk taking and frequently a detachment from the day-to-day administration required of businesses. The latter was certainly not the reason for their interest in commercial activity. Consequently, as the business grows beyond operating as a niche player, the ideal profile of the leader often must change if the business is to continue to succeed and maintain a close strategic fit with its environment. When owner managers have led the business to a substantial size this change may be forced upon the entrepreneur by stakeholders in the business who realize the very different requirements of a larger, more complex organization in which achieving strategic fit requires active management of the organization itself. So it was the case when the founder of Apple Computers, Steve Jobs, an innovative and creative entrepreneur, was ousted from his leading position on the board by an 'administrator' leader – a leadership style more suited to running a large corporation.

Schein (1999) considered that corporate cultural values resulted in observable behaviour that could be described as being valued and encouraged by the organization as well as organizational structures and processes. This approach to the effect of culture on behaviour is summarized in Table 2.1 and describes the corporate culture of the case study 'Achieving a market-led culture – Medical Instruments and Devices Inc.'

Table 2.1 Organizational response to cultural values

Cultural beliefs	Rapid response to customer feedback	Personal employee commitment	Technical product superiority
Behaviour valued by the organization	Rapid new product development based on customer feedback	Individually tailored HR management	Processes to establish new ideas to incorporate into NPD
Tangible rules and response practice	Budget allocation to new product development rather than market research	Staff rather than process centred HR processes	Large proportion of budget to developing relationships with key decision makers – rather than Market Analysis

Source: Adapted from Rowland and Smith (2001).

Activity 2.2

Try and apply the ideas on behaviour manifestations of cultural beliefs summarized in Table 2.1. For your organization, or another with which you are familiar, try and establish a cultural belief that is implicit in your behaviour. Do this for two different examples and perhaps discuss your answer with a colleague. You can work through the table above in reverse order:

1. Identify a tangible rule by which you work.
2. What particular behaviour is valued by the organization?
3. What cultural beliefs do you believe Stages 1 and 2 indicate?

Culture plays an important role in intra- and inter-organizational communication. Large organizations tend to employ staff from a variety of national backgrounds. Naturally they bring their own national/cultural approach to communication. Doole and Lowe (2001) present a summary of Hofstede's cross-cultural analysis of the influence of national culture on communication within a single global organization. People from Northern European cultures (including people from English-speaking advanced industrial economies) communicate in a literal sense, i.e. what is said, or written, is what is meant, so-called 'low context' cultures. In contrast are cultures where the context of the message gives meaning to the message. Who said it, how it was said, the context in which the message was delivered, in combination must be used to decipher the meaning of a message, whether written or spoken, so-called 'high context' cultures.

Hofstede further researched the role of national culture within the organization and identified five dimensions which he argued largely accounted for cross-cultural differences in people's belief systems and values. These he termed: 'uncertainty avoidance' masculinity; individualism; 'power-distance' and Confucian dynamism.

Individualism versus collectivism
(Examples: Individualistic = USA, GB; Collectivistic = Pakistan, Taiwan)

Is the individual the basis of society or does society give meaning to the individual? The USA is the best example of a society in which individualistic traits are most pronounced. For example, differences are admired and the cult of individuals prospers most. Perhaps in direct contrast is the Chinese culture, where societies' rights and responsibilities are dominant and individual needs are subservient. Here conformity is generally considered the norm.

Masculinity versus femininity
(Examples: Masculine = Japan, Italy; Feminine = Denmark, Sweden)

Masculine cultures emphasize 'assertiveness' compared to 'nurturance' for feminine cultures. High masculine societies, whether individualistic like USA or collectivist like Japan, provide weaker people with, on average, less support whether from within the organization or from society at large. People learn to admire the strong and to have a relatively negative view of the weak and dependent.

Power–distance
(Examples: Low = Denmark, Austria; High = France, India)

Measures the extent to which individuals (society) tolerate an unequal distribution of power in organizations and in society as a whole. In high power–distance organizations, superiors display their power and exercise it. Subordinates expect this behaviour and feel uncomfortable if they do not personally experience their superiors displaying their status and power. In high 'power–distance' cultures, subordinates feel separated from one and other: it is not easy to talk with higher-ranking people and real power tends to be concentrated at the top.

In low 'power–distance' societies members of organizations, and of society, tend to feel equal and relatively close to each other at work. Power is much more likely to be delegated in low 'power–distance' cultures.

Uncertainty avoidance
(Examples: Low = Denmark, Sweden; High = Japan, France)

Measures the extent to which people tend to feel threatened by uncertain, ambiguous, risky or undefined situations. In cultures where uncertainty avoidance is high, organizations promote stable careers and produce rules and procedures, which staff must follow (and which staff find comforting to follow). Hofstede argues that uncertainty avoidance is about reducing ambiguity and should not be confused with risk avoidance.

Confucian dynamism
(Examples: Low = USA, Australia; High = China, Japan)

Measures the extent to which conformity according to 'position' is stable and elicits predictable behaviour between individuals. Behavioural attributes that are valued highly include obedience, deference, maintaining the status quo within organizational and social hierarchies and trouble free social relations. Where you are in an organizational hierarchy pre-determines the way you are expected to treat others and in turn the way you should be treated. Behaviour is much more predictable in Confucian cultures that exhibit high levels of Confucian dynamism.

The environment

An important part of the strategy development process is that of strategic analysis – i.e. answering the question 'Where are we now?' Without first understanding this question it is impossible for organizations to decide where they want to go. Strategic analysis consists of undertaking an audit of both the external environment and the internal corporate environment. Organizations do not exist in a vacuum and when developing their marketing strategy it is essential they take into account the changing external environment. Undertaking a strategic analysis will enable organizations to identify potential opportunities and threats that may arise from the changing environment and allow them to exploit potential opportunities and reduce the impact of threats.

Porter (1985) stressed the importance of analysing the external environment:

> *The essence of formulating strategy is relating a company to its environment. Every industry has an underlying structure or set of fundamental economic and technical characteristics. The strategist must learn what makes the environment tick.*

Activity 2.3

Contemporary examples

The Examiner is looking for evidence that students can apply theoretical concepts to practical situations. Scan the quality press such as *The Financial Times* and journals such as *Marketing, Marketing Week* and the *Economist* and search for articles that relate to the external environment, both macro and micro. Classify articles according to the type of external analysis they demonstrate. For example, an article on the impact of the Internet would be classified under the macro environment as a technological influence.

This portfolio of articles will provide you with a set of contemporary examples that you can use in the exam.

Environmental scanning/sensing

The environment is dynamic and it is often commented that the speed of change is increasing. This creates problems of uncertainty for managers and therefore the need to monitor these changes is of paramount importance to all organizations. The means by which information is gathered about the environment is often referred to as environmental scanning.

Fahey and Narayanan (1986) identify three basic goals for environmental analysis:

1. The analysis should provide an understanding of current and potential changes taking place in the environment
2. Environmental analysis should provide important intelligence for strategic decision makers
3. Environmental analysis should facilitate and foster strategic thinking in organizations.

Many organizations find it difficult to develop effective methods for scanning the environment. Probably more challenging is the task of converting this information into action. Information is basically a tool to reduce risk in decision making. Too many organizations collect information religiously without actually using it to help make decisions. Organizations must develop scanning processes that not only collect the data but also convert these data into useful information that can aid decision making. Information must then be transmitted to the right people, at the right time and in the right format. Scanning includes both directed and undirected searching as well as informal and formal processes. On the one hand scanning may involve formal analysis of the economic environment including interviews with industry experts; on the other hand it may include browsing the national newspapers in the weekend. Both forms of scanning can be of equal value.

Case history

Effective scanning leads to new opportunities for Iceland (or does it?)

Iceland, the frozen foods specialist, was thought to have effectively identified an environmental change on which they were able to capitalize. Iceland correctly predicted that there would be a growth in the market for both organic foods and genetically modified (GM)-free foods. They used their stance on GM foods as a key differentiating factor. The growth in organic and GM-free foods has been fuelled by consumers' concerns over food safety and many organizations, including Iceland, saw this as a great opportunity.

Iceland positioned itself as a 'wholesome' retailer, by removing all artificial colours and flavourings from its own-brand products and being the first supermarket to ban GM foods. It purchased 40 per cent of the world's supply of organic vegetables and attempted to widen the market for organic products by removing the traditional price differential between organic and inorganic foods. They sold their own-label organic frozen vegetables at the same price as other supermarkets' inorganic frozen vegetables.

On the surface this seemed to be an inspired strategy that capitalised on changes in the external environment. However, in reality Iceland's core customers were not interested in GM free foods and in fact complained that they could not get their 'normal products'. This example illustrates that it is not enough to identify market opportunities but these must then be matched with a company's core competencies.

Source: Adapted from Mutel (2000).

Environmental monitoring system

For environmental scanning to be effective it is important that organizations develop effective systems for managing the information generated from the process. Johnson and Scholes (1999) propose a framework for undertaking an environmental analysis (Figure 2.3). This model provides companies with a more formal approach to monitoring the environment.

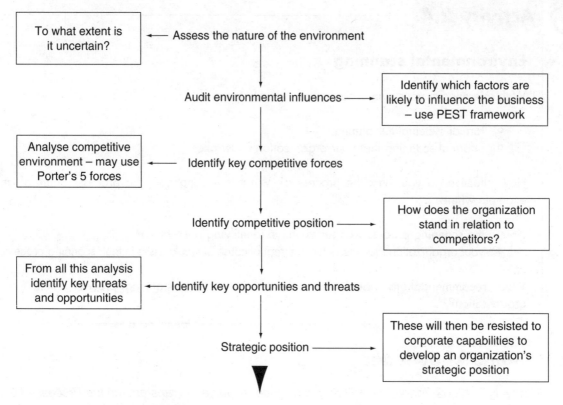

Figure 2.3 Steps in environmental analysis
Source: Johnson and Scholes (1999, p. 99)

There is almost unlimited information available, and organizations cannot hope to scan all of it. Therefore, organizations have to look at the return on investment of their efforts in terms of the contribution the information makes to the marketing decision-making process. Aguilar (1967) suggests that managers search for information in five broad categories:

1. Market intelligence (market potential, competitors, customers, etc.)
2. Technical intelligence (licensing and patents, new products and processes, etc.)
3. Acquisition intelligence (information on mergers, partnerships and acquisitions)
4. Broad issues (PEST factors)
5. Other intelligence (resource availability, miscellaneous).

The process of environmental scanning is of paramount importance when organizations are trying to identify the 'drivers of change' for their industry. Too often, companies fail to even identify major 'drivers of change' because they are looking backwards instead of forwards.

Activity 2.4

Environmental scanning

With reference to your own organization, identify types of:

- o   formal systematic scanning
- o   informal scanning that your organization undertakes.

How effective do you think the process is? What is missing from the process? Think of an example where:

- o   the scanning process was successful in identifying a threat
- o   your organization failed to detect a threat because of weaknesses in their scanning process.

What recommendations would you make to improve the scanning process within your organization?

Extending knowledge

Piercy, N.F. (2002) *Market-Led Strategic Change: A Guide to Transforming the Process of Going to Market*, 3rd edition, Oxford: Butterworth-Heinemann. 075065225X. Read pages 390–403, but especially the discussion in the section entitled 'Enhancing our marketing sensing capabilities'.

This is also a good time to review your understanding of environmental analysis using one textbook source. There is a chapter on this in any good marketing management or even marketing principles textbook.

Activity 2.5

PEST analysis

For your own organization examine the macro-environmental factors, using the PEST framework, that have impacted on your business over the last 5 years.

How has your organization responded to these threats/opportunities?

The organization may be considered as being buffeted by the environment in which it is located. Whichever direction the leaders of the organization are taking it, the environment itself will exert pressures on the organization. Stacey (2003, Section 5.3) summarizes ideas proposed by Weick in which he suggests that there are different ways of considering the impact of the environment. The general perspective discussed individual managers/workers as responding to the 'true' environmental forces in the cognitivist perspective. However, Weick suggests that people have selective perception of the environment and further modify the 'true' reality by selective memory about the impact of past forces. Consequently, people and organizations operate using their perception of the environment. This approach would suggest that two organizations could potentially perceive, and respond, to similar environmental pressures in very different ways. Consequently, predicting responses to environmental pressures becomes even more problematic.

Regardless of whether the reader considers that an 'absolute' or 'selective perceptual' view of the environment should be taken, it is presumed that the organization is conducting some form of environmental sensing as the basis of informing their particular view. Piercy (2002) provides a very practical perspective on market sensing in emphasizing its role in focusing on managers' understanding of the market. An important line of reasoning is that to get people to change in response to the environment you must let people take charge and discover this for themselves. Edicts from above simply do not work. However, they may cling to an outdated perspective of the environment, through selective acquisition of information and selectivity in emphasis and in memory.

Environmental analysis

A structured approach to environmental analysis is advocated by Piercy, who borrows on ideas from others, for example Kotler. In this approach the market sensor is encouraged to move beyond simply listing environmental threats and opportunities and to engage with the information on two dimensions. These take account of either risk/return and of the probability of the event occurring. It is obviously of some consequence to know whether the arrival of a new competitor is probable, for example, and whether this particular competitor is considered to pose a high-risk threat to the business. Simply to list the possible existence of a new competitor does not really progress our thinking towards action, i.e. marketing implementation. Piercy (2002) and Kotler (2000) consequently advocate that each environmental factor should be assessed on two dimensions: first according to the likelihood of the environmental factor arising and having some sort of impact and secondly on the magnitude of the impact. This could be positive (an opportunity) or negative (a threat). Both authors suggest rating the impact of environmental factors on these two dimensions using an assessment grid. Kotler advocates two different assessment grids, however, Piercy provides a more elegant approach in which the two are combined by adopting a rating scale which ranges from highly negative to highly positive impact. This general approach is similar to that adopted for the General Electric portfolio planning tool and is summarized in Figure 2.4.

Probability of the event

	High		Low
Highly positive		**Probable +ve impact zone** Plan to capitalize on these.	
Impact on the company	**Uncertain impact – close watch zone**		**Neutral impact zone**
Highly negative		**Probable –ve impact zone** Plan to take precautionary measures.	

Figure 2.4 An assessment framework for analysing the external environment
Source: Adapted from Piercy (2003) and Kotler (2000)

Interrelationships between organizational culture, the environment and market orientation

Organizational culture influences, and is influenced by, the beliefs, values and norms of each individual in the organization and is consequently relatively difficult to change. In marked contrast is the environment in which the organization operates in which quite profound changes can take place in a relatively short space of time. To operate effectively, Handy (1986) suggests that an organization's culture should match, or be suited to, its structure. Rapid changes in environment or organizational structure will consequently result in the culture being out of step either temporarily or permanently depending on whether measures are implemented to rectify this imbalance.

Dobson, P. (1988) in a survey of the UK's largest public and private sector organizations found that over a quarter of them had been involved in a culture change programme in the previous 5 years, due to culture being out of alignment. Dobson suggested a four-step approach to changing culture.

Step 1 – Change recruitment, selection and redundancy policies to change the composition of employees to reflect the new beliefs and values that the organization wishes to promote.
Step 2 – Change through promotions and job reviews the balance of employees to ensure that the most suited to the new culture occupy positions of influence.
Step 3 – Communicate the new values effectively – see Unit 3 on internal marketing and internal marketing communications plan.
Step 4 – Change organizational systems and procedures, in particular connected with staff appraisal and reward.

Influence of organizational structure

Structure is an influential factor on cultural change, however, various studies on the relationship between the environment and organizational structure concluded that there was no single most appropriate structure for a given environment. However, general principles were established linking environmental uncertainty (five categories from stable to least predictable) to two main forms of structure (mechanistic and organic).

Mechanistic structures included the following characteristics:

o Clear hierarchical structure
o Task specialization
o Highly defined duties and responsibilities.

In contrast, organic forms were characterized by the following:

o Network structure of control, authority and communication
o Commitment to the work group and its tasks
o Much greater flexibility
o Status and individual prestige and status linked to performance rather than seniority
o Continual redefinition of tasks.

General principles to arise were that mechanistic structures were more efficient in stable environments while organic structures operated with greater effectiveness in less predictable environments.

Success criteria

Strategic planning concerns the fit between an organization (including its culture) and the environment in which it operates. There is not sufficient to obtain a fit with the present rather the strategic planning process attempts to obtain a fit with the future environment. The future must be forecasted and required organizational change planned and implemented to ensure future strategic fit. Performance targets must be set to monitor progress both financial and operational. Criteria that must be satisfied include those of acceptability, feasibility and suitability (Stacey, 2003, Section 4.2).

Acceptability criteria

Stacey (2003, Section 4.3) argues that pressure on the organization arises from three sources, i.e. from three leading stakeholders. These are: *owners and creditors*; the most *important groupings within the organization* (undefined) and finally the *external groupings* on whom strategic change will impact. This creates financial performance pressures (from owners/creditors and discussed further in Units 5 and 8). Key internal groupings, and organizational staff in general, will be concerned about the consequences of change on the way they work, their relative power within the organization and whether planned change in any way is at odds with their personal ethical values. Consequently, the organizational culture must be understood as well as the power structure within the organization. External groupings must be considered where there is a direct consequence of the organization's strategy – whether noise and pollution from a new factory to spoiling the visual environment as a result of a new structure such as new electricity pylons, windmills, telecommunication masts/towers, etc.

Feasibility criteria

The possibility of plans being implemented require them to be feasible, i.e. not asking the impossible. Financial constraints, strategies appropriate to the relevant stage of the product life cycle, appropriate to the position of the firm on its experience curve, and maintaining a balance portfolio and ensuring sufficient numbers of people with the right skills mix receiving adequate training are the principal feasibility criteria.

Suitability

These criteria require that the organization's objectives can be delivered (i.e. the organization is capable of delivering (by virtue of possessing appropriate structures, control systems and culture). Particularly helpful techniques in support of this include SWOT analysis and Porter's five forces industry structure and value chain analysis.

Stacey (2003, Section 4.5) argues that *contingency theory* is useful in supporting the strategic planner in ensuring good strategic fit. This is a general theory about cause and effect. A given environment will determine the most appropriate organizational structure, for example. It does not give any credence to contextual factors. So small differences in two organizations operating in the same environment, e.g. one with slightly more advanced technological expertise, will not lead to substantially different outcomes in terms of their performance in that environment. A small difference in the cause (technology) cannot possibly lead to a proportionately larger difference in the effect (e.g. market performance and strategic fit). Examples of the types of pronouncements provided by contingency theory are provided by Stacey (2003, p. 61):

o Mechanistic bureaucracies are most suited to stable market environments.
o Organization forms are most suited to complex rapidly changing environments.
o Large organizations require divisional structures.

Change pressures on an organization

Pressures to change

Stakeholders

The main pressures on an organization to change arise from its stakeholders. They provide the mechanism that translates the impact of the marketing environment into pressure. Of course there may be some occasions when all stakeholders are unaware of these environmental pressures, however, such organizations do not tend to be around for long. Davidson (2002) suggests that customers are increasingly becoming more influential as stakeholders (while the influence of finance providers is still dominant) and that it is inevitable that eventually their influence will be pre-eminent. He suggests that in addition to identifying who the stakeholders are, CEOs are concerned with establishing their relative importance and linking their interests. He considers it a vital function of senior managers to resolve conflicts between stakeholders.

> *Robust linkages (exist) between customer commitment, employee motivation and share-holder value, something many business leaders already understood. However, under-standing stakeholder linkages is not enough. They must be managed and aligned. To successfully manage conflicting stakeholder needs, organization leaders need to unite them through strong vision and values.* (Davidson, 2002)

Davidson reminds us of the importance of the ongoing debate in service marketing of requiring ever higher levels of performance, i.e. to become an emotional organization and to strive to achieve this in order to be competitive in the medium term. Individuals who work within the organization work with customers and as customer loyalty declines due to more choice and more intensive competition among other factors, it becomes increasingly difficult to establish loyal customers. Consequently to do this on the basis of functional product/service attributes is increasingly less likely. However, by aligning the vision and values of the organization with those of customer groups, then links will be established with individual customers at an emotional level. These are the customers that are most likely to remain loyal. One vital source of change pressure is to move the organization in this direction to ensure that it is aligned with its environment in this key area.

Davidson proposes seven best practices to align the organization with all its stakeholders within the environment. He rarely, if ever, uses the word 'culture' to describe some of the issues he addresses. However, there are elements of culture that he proposes to change in the organization. On the basis of detailed interviews with many CEOs in high performing organizations (profit and not for profit, including educational institutions) he provides highly applied conclusions. These are especially valid as they are based on the experience of leading, currently successful practitioners. This discussion is not simply about writing vision and value statements but in getting them infused into the deepest recesses of the organization to actually get them applied. Some of the themes can be found in the marketing literature, however, Davidson is particularly successful in bringing together many of the themes in an original, as well as concise, high impact text with many illustrative and relevant quotes from leading practitioners. To use Davidson's terminology, seven best practices are advocated in the pursuit of change to achieve 'the Committed Enterprise' (Figure 2.5).

1. Define the organizational purpose and understand and link the needs of key stakeholders.
2. Establish a clear, distinctive vision that is customer related and is ambitious in terms of the organization's ability to achieve it.
3. Build strong values to support the vision based on key factors for success. It is essential that values are turned into measurable practices.
4. Communication is about leaders winning hearts and minds of senior managers who will then cascade this through the organization. This must ring true to the previous 'Best Practices'. For example, stating values as 'highest quality' or as 'teamwork' will not be embraced where people in the organization know and see 'average quality' as the accepted standard and a culture of 'blame' to be pervasive.
5. Organizational structure should facilitate vision and values and the latter should influence recruitment, training, reward and promotion, if this is to become 'embedded' in the organization.
6. Link branding to vision and values and ensure this addresses the needs of all stakeholders.
7. Measure committed customers, motivated employees and satisfied finance providers as a means of assessing how effectively visions and values are implemented.

Figure 2.5 Davidson's seven best practices in making vision and values work
Source: Davidson (2002)

Extending knowledge

Davidson, H., (2002). *The Committed Enterprise: How to Make Visions and Values Work*, Oxford: Butterworth-Heinemann. (0750655402). This is a very readable and practical text based on interviews with leading, successful marketing practitioners and certainly does not feel like a textbook. Read the preface to put you in the mindset of the author. It is a book that can be read fairly quickly.

Information communication technology (ICT) – a key driver of change

ICT has revolutionized the ways in which companies do business. For example, the Internet has produced new distribution channels, has enabled companies to enter new geographical markets with greater ease and has improved, if not replaced in some cases, ordering systems, customer service and purchasing. Intranets are increasingly being used to improve internal communications and the impact of digital technology will be immense. The case history below provides two very different examples of companies that have seen the development of the Internet as an opportunity and have successfully capitalized on its increased use.

Case history

EMI records

Many music companies, particularly retailers, have felt threatened by the onset of the Internet for two reasons. Firstly, there is a trend towards on-line buying, where fans no longer need to visit a store to buy CDs. Market Tracking International predicts that the global value of the on-line music market (including CDs sold over the Internet) will be $5.2 billion in 2005 (11.3 per cent of a forecasted $46 billion music market). Secondly, the main challenge facing the music publishing business is that more fans are downloading music directly from the Internet, sometimes illegally. These trends are a significant threat to record companies, which face the loss of their very healthy profit margins on CDs. The combined force of consumers empowered by this new technology and artists keen to use the Internet to sell directly to fans has led the record companies to realize that they will have to act quickly.

EMI has joined forces with Time-Warner and AOL in an attempt to develop their Internet business. Two main strategies are to sell their music on-line using free downloads as a promotional tool. EMI has taken equity in musicmaker.com, a site that allows consumers to custom-make their own CDs from a selection

of 100 000 tracks. The concept is proving popular – unusually for e-commerce sites it is making money! EMI is also digitizing its entire catalogue of music, making it possible to sell all its 'artists' music over the Internet.

Possibly one of the greatest opportunities arising from the Internet is the ability to target and develop stronger relationships with key customers through e-mail and the use of special promotional offers.

The Internet is changing the face of the music business and many believe that the record companies will have to concentrate on the skills of creating acts and marketing them, and leave the distribution to others.

Source: Adapted from Murphy (2000).

Case study

www.landsend.com: a new technology, customer-focused retailer

Technology provides new business opportunities for organizations with developed market sensing systems and abilities. For organizations who do not obtain first mover advantage, technology can be the cause of a new competitive threat. The amount of new business activities generated through the Internet has been overstated. Simply because services are delivered on the Internet does not mean that a profound change in a business model has occurred. Many businesses simply use the Internet as an electronic brochure.

In contrast Lands' End, the US clothing company, has used the Internet as a means of establishing a very different relationship with customers. Prior to embracing the new technology, they were essentially a catalogue retailer, offering everyday clothing targeted at reasonably affluent consumer segments. However they have used technology to establish one-to-one relationships with their customers, deliver a personalised service that is superior to many clothing retailers with a physical presence in city and shopping centres. They offer the services standard that rivals Hong Kong bespoke tailors but with a fashion catalogue that rivals the range of well-known high street clothing retailers.

In 1998, to stimulate demand for online clothing sales, they created a 'virtual model' (i.e. computer manikin). Customers, in many shopping centres throughout the USA, were invited to have their body scanned by a laser measuring 200 000 points on the body. Subsequently, scanners were installed in many shopping centres through the USA.

Shopping online both male and female customers can select clothes from the online catalogue, simply by selecting options for different styles and colours, from the on-screen menu. Customers who have had their bodies scanned, are able to see how different sizes, styles and material fit and hang on the body.

Customers using the website have built millions of virtual models since then, illustrating the customer interest in this service. Ongoing development now requests some simple information from customers on style preferences which is then used in subsequent online interactions with the Lands' End system. The system can then prompt the customer to try on (virtually) a selection of clothes. New high technology services are continually being added. 'Shop with a friend' is a service where two customers, at different computers perhaps located in different countries, can surf the website catalogue together via an online chat feature.

This company has therefore used the Internet to deliver a particularly customer focused service. It has achieved a highly market orientated approach in employing systems and processes to deliver customer valued products and services. Increasingly its competitors will be perceived as offering a dated approach to retailing as growing numbers of customers embrace this new business model in clothes retailing.

Source: www.landsend.com (Lands' end, 2004).

Globalization – a key driver of change

Globalization is the tendency for organizations to operate on a global level. The term should not be taken literally, as frequently 'global' organizations focus on supply bases and customers in the major centres of economic activity of North America, Europe, Japan, China and South East Asia and more recently India. The engine driving globalization is economies of scale. The size of global organizations gives them enormous economies of scale in manufacturing, in new product development and in market coverage. Global reach allows them to tap into new ideas and opportunities wherever they may occur. However, a major dilemma for global organizations is the extent to which local markets require adaptation of products and services, and/or marketing strategy and tactics, in order to meet the requirements of local consumers. For example, Hindus do not want to eat beef burgers, clothes for the American market must be adapted for the slighter Asian figure, and European and American cars must be adapted to meet stringent pollution limits in the Japanese market.

Case history

Wal-Mart – Conquering the World?

Wal-Mart was founded in 1962 it now has sales of £150 billion, 3400 American stores, 1200 international stores in nine countries and employs more than 1.3 million people. It is the world's largest retailer and has got an ambitious goal of doubling its sales in just 5 years. In order to achieve this goal Wal-Mart will have to enter new overseas markets. Last year 16 per cent of the firm's total sales were generated by their international stores. However, Wal-Mart encounters many challenges when entering new markets. In Europe and Asia transport systems are not as refined as in the US. This has made it more difficult to keep down supply chain and inventory costs.

Entry into China and Korea has been successful but Argentina and Brazil continue to be difficult markets. In Mexico they are now the largest retailer. The acquisition of the Asda brand in Britain is regarded as a success. The German market has proved more difficult primarily due to the cultural differences. For example, Wal-Mart employs 'greeters' to welcome customers to the store. German customers viewed the friendly door greeters with some suspicion and in some cases found them sickening. Wal-Mart also faced stiff competition from German chains.

Source: Adapted from Rossingh, D., Wal-Mart: A Retail Titan, http://news.bbc.co.uk/1/hi/business/2657089.stm, 14 January 2003.

Ethical concerns – a key driver of change

The concept of societal marketing suggests that marketing should be concerned not only with satisfying customers and achieving organizational goals but that companies should have a responsibility to society in general. Increasingly companies are coming under pressure to operate in an ethical manner. Issues such as environmental concern, human rights and fair-trading are increasing in importance in the political arena. This is a key driver of change in the current external environment and one that many companies are having to take into account. In fact, many companies are regarding the increased interest in ethical marketing as an opportunity rather than as a threat. As Vernon Ellis, international chairman of Accenture, said at the New Statesman lecture in 2002, 'Global business is not something apart from society; its health and even its long term survival depend on the global environment in which it operates' (Mason, 2002). Those companies that have not embraced ethical marketing are those that have yet to realize that it makes good business sense and can gain them a competitive advantage. Consumers are also becoming increasingly concerned about ethical issues. Research by

Business in the Community shows that, where price is equal, more than 80 per cent of Western consumers would change brands and have a better perception of a company that does something to make the world a better place (Mason, 2002). The Co-operative Bank is a good example of a company that has positioned itself on their ethical banking practices.

The following examples illustrate how two companies, keen to develop ethical business practices, have gained a competitive advantage.

Case history

The Day Chocolate company

An increasing number of businesses are winning the Fair Trade Logo for their products. This logo shows that the producers are receiving a fair price for their products. One such business is the Day Chocolate company which is part-owned by a co-operative of cocoa farmers formed in Ghana nine years ago. Originally the co-operative helped its members by organizing trading and ensuring that beans were weighed fairly, that they were paid promptly and they were offered credit facilities if they were in financial difficulties. However, the farmers only earned approximately £300 a year selling cocoa and they realized that they had to do more than just grow beans. They decided to make chocolate and so the Day Chocolate company was formed. The company manufactures chocolate bars under the brand name 'Divine'. Profits from the business are given back to the farmers in the form of cash bonuses and development grants for water wells and schools.

There are several ways in which the co-operative's members benefit. Producers receive a guaranteed price for their goods and the security of long term standing contracts. Minimum health and safety conditions are established and there are training opportunities for the producers, especially for women and children. However, just being a fair trade product does not guarantee commercial success. Divine is competing with some of the world's biggest companies. Customers will not necessarily buy the chocolate just because it is a fair trade product, it must be of at least equal quality. The Co-operative was one of the first stores to stock Divine and they have reported that sales have been very strong. The Day Chocolate Company is not only satisfying its customers, it is helping to improve the lives of people in more deprived areas of the world.

Source: Adapted from www.bbc.co.uk/workinglunch.

Case history

Tesco

Tesco have been involved in 'cause related marketing' initiatives for several years. One of the most well known is the 'computers for schools' scheme which has been running for ten years. This is where customers collect vouchers and give these to schools, who exchange them for computers. The programme has been very successful from Tesco's perspective, 538 000 of its 9 million shoppers showed a substantial increase in spend during the programme. Schools have also been able to purchase computer equipment that otherwise they would be unable to afford.

A further initiative by Tesco has raised substantial funds for the I-CAN charity for children with speech and language difficulties. Tesco is hoping to raise £125 000 to help fund 20 early years centres offering education and therapy to children and their families. I-CAN believe that the deal is important financially but also that the programme helps to raise awareness of the charity, due to the five million parents with children under five visiting Tesco stores each day.

These types of schemes are sometimes criticized because the sponsors are often seen to benefit substantially more than the causes they support. However, many of these schemes are supporting causes that would otherwise struggle financially. They have also been criticized for impacting on traditional ways of giving to charity. Research suggests that this is not the case and that 'cause related marketing' programmes reach people that do not traditionally give to charity.

Source: Adapted from Mason (2002).

Activity 2.6

Business in the Community

Business in the Community is an independent Charity that 'creates a public benefit by working with companies to improve the positive impact of business in society'. They are involved in numerous projects. Visit their website www.bitc.org.uk (Business in the Community, 2003) to collect examples of ways in which companies are implementing strategies that benefit wider society.

Extending knowledge

See also Johnson and Scholes, 1999, *Exploring Corporate Strategy*, Chapter 5 'Stakeholder Expectations and Organizational Purpose'.

Achieving stronger market orientation

Environmental forces exert pressures, which will result in a lack of strategic fit between the organization and the environment in which it operates. To achieve stronger market orientation requires overcoming the barriers to market orientation and maintaining a very clear market-led, customer-focused perspective achieved through effective market sensing and suitable organizational structure.

Organizational culture may become inappropriate which will result in ineffectual organizational behaviour and increasingly a lack of competitiveness in the market place. In addition to the formulation of learning/sensing capabilities within the organization, a market-driven, or orientated, culture supports and values systematic and thorough market sensing. This is combined with co-ordinated actions within the organization geared to achieving and maintaining competitive advantage.

Harris (1999) considered a few factors to be relevant in achieving greater market orientation; some of these have already been discussed in this unit:

1. Organizational cultural commitment to market orientation
2. Identification of particular organizational members
3. Power and control issues.

Cultural commitment to market orientation

Organizational members must understand market orientation and its true value. As marketing personnel are most likely to initiate market-led change, the use of internal marketing (discussed in the next unit) is the most likely vehicle for achieving market orientation.

Identification of particular organizational members

One common theme is that there should be a marketing champion of the market-orientated cause to drive this forward. This need not necessarily be the CEO. While it is essential to gain the support of the CEO, senior managers in the organization can drive the change programme, combined with middle and senior management training in the meaning and substance of market orientation, as they will facilitate changes in structures and systems. From a cultural perspective, they will re-specify the behaviour valued by the organization and the tangible rules by which it operates.

Power and control issues

Use of power and control mechanisms within the organization will facilitate the development of a market orientation. The central role played by marketing in many organizations and the ability now to measure market orientation provide increased power and control for those wishing to move in a more market-orientated direction.

Summary

In considering organizational change we must begin by clarifying our view on the fundamental basis of social systems that we call organizations. Do we believe that they are the sum of their individual parts, or do they exist as entities in their own right into which new members are socialized? In the former perspective a new CEO can change organizational culture by edict and ask people to change. In the latter perspective organizational culture resides deep within all employees, is difficult to define and locate in any particular organization and is consequently very difficult to change.

In organizations that are market-orientated or market-led, all departments and not simply the marketing department is customer-focused. Everyone's job is to be a part-time marketer, rather than this residing purely within the marketing department. To be market orientated requires more than simply information on customers, i.e. marketing research. A deeper understanding of the market is required and this can only be achieved through effective market sensing. This requires cultural and organizational systems and structures to be in place to allow effective and efficient market sensing to be achieved.

Organizational cultures are the shared beliefs, customs and ways of thinking that people within the organization share with each other. This common culture results in shared and agreed behavioural responses to given stimuli from the marketing environment that prevents everything being discussed from fundamental principles. Such shared cultural values evolve in organizations and are in part the reason why a particular organization has been successful. The type of organizational culture that is most effective changes as organizations evolve. In addition, people from different countries bring their own national cultural perspective to the organization. In effect they bring a particular, national cultural lens, and associated behavioural response, to their work within the organization. Account must be taken of this when managing employees from many countries, especially where these represent very different national cultures, e.g. using research perspectives provided by Hofstede.

Organizations must be aligned with their environment if they are to be competitive in the long term. However, organizational culture changes extremely slowly, while the environment is very turbulent and the organizational structure through which changes to the environment can be implemented may be changed fairly readily. Consequently it is likely that organizations will find their culture coming out of alignment with the environment. In assessing environmental impact various authors suggest a more

proactive approach in which the probability of the environmental factor is assessed as well as the magnitude of the impact and whether this will be positive or negative (opportunity or threat).

The main change pressures on an organization come from four main sources: (1) stakeholders (2) micro- and macro-forces in the environment (especially information communication technology) (3) globalization and (4) ethics. Organizational culture must adjust to accommodate these change pressures. Organizational structure in part acts as a mechanism to facilitate cultural change. In an increasingly turbulent environment, more flexible, organic structures are better suited to continual change and adjustment in contrast to mechanistic structures that are more suited to stable environmental conditions.

Sample exam question

How can brand value be enhanced and why is it important in the context of a fast moving consumer goods company?

Discussion

Please refer to the syllabus, element 2 – Managing change and internal marketing and element 3 – Implementing the business strategy through marketing activities.

The question suggests a relatively short timescale in which the preparations have to be put in place. A further clue in the question is with regard to the creation and fulfilment of demand, suggesting the need for external and internal marketing. Think through the range of topics that need to be addressed and then the means whereby these can be implemented.

Bibliography

Aaker, D. (1990) 'Brand Extensions: The Good, The Bad, And The Ugly', *Sloan Management Review*, **31**, June, pp. 47–56.

Aguilar, F.J. (1967) *Scanning the business environment*, New York, NY: Macmillan.

Burns, B. (1996) *Managing Change,* London: Financial Times Management, pp. 106–120 (ISBN 0273611186).

Business in the Community (2003) www.bitc.org.uk.

Davidson, H. (2002) *The Committed Enterprise: How to Make Visions and Values Work*, Oxford: Butterworth-Heinemann, pp. 241–242 (ISBN 0750655402).

Deal, T. and Kennedy, A. (2000) *The New Corporate Cultures*, Texere Publishing.

Dobson, P. (1988) 'Changing culture', *Employment Gazette*, December, pp. 645–650.

Doole, I. and Lowe, R. (2001) *International Marketing Strategy*, London: Thomson Learning (ISBN 1861527721).

Fahey, L. and Narayanan, V.K. (1986) *Macroenvironmental Analysis for Strategic Management*, Southwestern College Publishing.

Handy, C. (1986) *Understanding Organizations*, Harmondsworth: Penguin.

Harris, L.C. (1999) 'Barriers to developing market orientation', *Journal of Applied Management Studies*, **8**(1), pp. 85–101.

Hooley, G.J., Saunders, J.A. and Piercy, N.F. (1998) 'Marketing Strategy & Competitive Positioning', *Financial Times*, 2nd edition, London: Prentice Hall.

Jobber (2001) *Principles and Practice of Marketing*, 3rd edition, McGraw-Hill.

Johnson, G. and Scholes, K. (1999) *Exploring Corporate Strategy*, Hemel Hempstead: Prentice-Hall, pp. 97–111 (ISBN 0130807400).

Kohli, A.K. and Jaworski, B. (1990) 'Market orientation: The construct, research propositions, and managerial implications', *Journal of Marketing*, **54**, April, pp. 1–18.

Kotler, P. (2000) *Marketing Management Millennium Edition*, Upper Saddle River: Prentice-Hall (ISBN 0130156841).

Lands' end (2004) www.landsend.com.

Mason, T. (2002) 'The Importance of Being Ethical – a new breed of caring consumerism means companies need to consider ethical issues', *Marketing*, **26**, October, p. 27.

Mazur, L. (2001) 'Acquisition activity is on a high, but in most cases the deal fails to deliver', *Marketing*, 8 February, p. 26.

Narver, J.C. and Slater, S.F. (1990) 'The effect of a market orientation on business profitability', *Journal of Marketing*, **54**(4), pp. 20–35.

Piercy, N.F. (1997) *Market-Led Strategic Change*, Oxford: Butterworth-Heinemann, p. 7 (ISBN 075064382X).

Piercy, N.F. (2002) *Market-Led Strategic Change*, Oxford: Butterworth-Heinemann, pp. 390–402 (ISBN 075065225X).

Porter, M.E. (1985) *Competitive Advantage: Creating and Sustaining Superior Performance*, New York: The Free Press.

Rowland, K. and Smith, B. (2001) 'Achieving a market led culture: A case study', *International Journal of Medical Marketing*, **1**(3), pp. 215–223.

Schein, E.H. (1985) *Organizational Culture and Leadership: A Dynamic View*, San Francisco: Jossey-Bass.

Schein, E.H. (1999) *The Corporate Culture Survival Guide*, San Francisco: Jossey-Bass Inc.

Slater, S.F. and Narver, J.C. (1995) 'Market orientation and the learning organization', *Journal of Marketing*, **59**(4), pp. 63–74.

Stacey, R.D. (2003) *Strategic Management and Organizational Dynamics*, Harlow: Pearson Education Limited (ISBN 0273658980).

unit 3
planning and implementing change

Objectives

Syllabus links

Learning outcomes

'Identify the barriers to effective implementation of strategies and plans involving change (including communications) in the organization, and develop measures to prevent or overcome them.'

Please see Appendix 4 for full details of the learning outcomes, related statements of practice and knowledge and skills requirements.

Information on the syllabus element (and its weighting) that is supported by this chapter can be found in Figure P.1, in the preface to this book.

Learning objectives

By the end of this unit you will:

o   Understand and be able to critically evaluate the various theoretical approaches to change

o   Be able to explain and discuss the change process

o   Appreciate the reasons why many change programmes fail

o   Be able to identify and evaluate the sources and the techniques for overcoming resistance to change

o   Understand and be able to evaluate how developing a market orientation can help to overcome resistance to change

o   Understand the role of project management in the implementation of change programmes

o   Critically evaluate the role of internal marketing in facilitating change

- ○ Be able to develop an internal marketing plan for managing change

- ○ Be able to identify the appropriate skills and capabilities needed to meet new objectives

- ○ Critically evaluate the role and content of an internal marketing communications plan and its contribution to managing change in an organization.

Key definitions

Planned approach to change – This approach views organizational change as essentially a process of moving from one fixed state to another through a series of predictable and pre-planned steps (Burnes, 1996).

Emergent approach to change – Starts from the assumption that change is a continuous, open-ended and unpredictable process of aligning and realigning an organization to its changing environment ... views change as a process that unfolds through the interplay of multiple variables (context, political processes and consultation) within an organization (Burnes, 1996).

Project management – Project management involves achieving unity of purpose and setting achievable goals within given resources and timescales (Drummond and Ensor, 2001).

Internal marketing – Internal marketing is a planned effort using a marketing-like approach directed at motivating employees, for implementing and integrating organizational strategies towards customer orientation (Ahmed and Rafiq, 2002).

Has the goal of developing a type of marketing programme aimed at the internal marketplace in the company that *parallels* and *matches* the marketing programme aimed at the external marketplace of customers and competitors (Piercy, 2002).

Internal relationship marketing – An integrative process within a system for fostering positive working relationship in a developmental way in a climate of co-operation and achievement. Varey and Lewis (1999), cited in Little and Marandi (2003).

Study Guide

This unit will take you about 4 hours to work through.

We suggest that you take a further 3 hours to do the various activities and questions in this unit.

Introduction

This is the second unit of the two units focusing on Managing Change and Internal Marketing. Unit 2 focused on the importance of organizational culture in managing change and the importance of achieving/maintaining a market orientation. It also discussed the main pressures on organizations to change and the barriers to change that may exist. This unit builds on the material in the previous unit and discusses the types of technique that can be employed to try and overcome resistance to organizational change such as internal marketing and project management. It also evaluates the role of an internal marketing communications plan in managing change.

Change management is concerned with the proactive execution of change in a planned and systematic manner. Change may be a result of internal adjustments to business strategy or it can be a reaction to external events and pressures. The objective of change management is to move the business from the current situation to the desired new position, whilst at the same time maintaining focus, achieving business objectives, controlling costs and managing people effectively.

If any change is to be successful it is essential that organizations' management can clearly envisage and anticipate cultural resistance and develop appropriate change strategies. Traditionally strategic change management was regarded as a step-by-step process from one state of rest to another, which would inevitably become outdated. This philosophy has been replaced with the view that change is a continuous function of the organization (Drucker, 1993; Handy, 1995; Peters, 1992; Stacey, 1993).

'Nothing is permanent except change' – Heraclitus.

Evidence suggests that up to 80 per cent of company change initiatives fail (Bicker 1999 cited in Piercy p. 632). There is an assumption in many organizations that change programmes, new initiatives and marketing plans will sell themselves. This is not necessarily true as in the same way that products will not sell themselves to external customers.

When companies are faced with implementing a new strategy, or a change programme, it needs to ensure that employee's attitudes and behaviours correspond with the overall vision.

Marketing implementation is concerned with translating marketing plans into action and of course this results in change. The marketing plan is the vehicle for communicating the strategy within the organization and it addresses the issues of 'what' should happen and 'why' it should happen. Implementation is concerned with 'how' the strategy should be carried out, 'who' should be responsible, 'when' things will take place and 'where' things will happen. Too often in organizations the implementation stage is overlooked and as a result a 'good strategy' can fail. It is important that organizations devote as much time and energy to the implementation of plans as they do to creating marketing strategies.

Piercy (2002, p. 578) wrote:

> the most important and productive thing to focus on in planning is not the techniques and formal methods, it is quite simply 'commitment' and 'ownership' ... the rewards come from getting our marketing act together and getting people excited and motivated to drive the market strategy and do the things that matter to customers in the marketplace.

Piercy (2002) suggests that there are at least three dimensions of the planning process:

1. Analytical dimension
2. Behavioural dimension
3. Organizational dimension.

In the past many companies have focused on the analytical dimension, i.e. planning techniques and models, procedures and systems. More recently organizations have realized that without recognizing the importance of people – motivation, ownership, commitment, etc. and the organization culture, structure, etc. – many 'good' plans will fail.

Planning for change

The major problem with implementation of plans lies in the failure of companies to manage change successfully. Inevitably a new strategy is going to result in the need for change. Many people are resistant to change because they are familiar with the status quo and fear the consequences of change. Therefore any new marketing strategy is going to be met with suspicion, unless the company can engender a culture that not only accepts change but also welcomes it. Marketing managers need to be aware of the internal barriers that exist, and then need to develop strategies to overcome these barriers. Organizations need to learn how to effectively manage change.

Approaches to change

It is essential that in order to facilitate change it is necessary to have an understanding of how change occurs in organizations. The subject of change is extensive and many text books and articles have been written on this diverse and little understood subject. The purpose of this text is not to provide a detailed critique of all the available literature on change management but to highlight some of the key issues and refer you to further reading which will provide greater discussion of the subject.

Planned versus emergent change
It is generally accepted that there are two main approaches to the management of change: the planned approach and the emergent approach.

Planned approach
> this approach views organizational change as essentially a process of moving from one fixed state to another through a series of predictable and pre-planned steps. (Burnes, 1996, p. 186)

Within the planned approach to change management there exists a variety of models. Lewin (1946), cited in Burnes (1996), developed three alternative models of the change process: the action research model; the three-step model and the phases of planned change model.

The action research model
Action research is based on the proposition that in order to solve organizational problems a rational and systematic approach must be adopted. This would include collecting information, developing hypotheses, taking action in order to achieve the desired objectives and finally evaluating the action. It therefore follows that the change process is in fact a learning situation in which participants learn from the action research. Action research continues to be adopted by many organizations to help initiate change. However, one of its barriers to use is the need to gain commitment from the organization and the subject of the change. This becomes increasingly difficult when dealing with large organizations. Therefore action research is often used as a first step in a large scale change programme.

The three-step model
Lewin (1958), cited in Burnes (1996), suggested that in many cases change was very short-lived and after a period of time group-behaviour reverted back to its previous pattern. The idea of the three-step model is that change is regarded as permanent. The three steps include:

1. Unfreezing the present level
2. Moving to the new level
3. Refreezing the new level.

This model recognizes that in order for new behaviour to be accepted old behaviour has to be discarded. The first two steps roughly relate to action research and the refreezing can be seen as a logical extension to action research. Refreezing relates to the need to stabilize the organization following a period of change.

The phases of planned change model

The three-step model provides a general framework for understanding the process of organizational change. However, it still adopts a rather broad approach and therefore a variety of models of planned change have been developed by a number of writers. For example Bullock and Battern (1958), cited in Burnes (1996), developed a four-phase model of planned change. This model explains change in terms of two major dimensions: change phases and change processes. Change phases relates to the stages through which an organization moves in planned change. Change processes are the means by which an organization moves from one state to the next.

1. *Exploration stage* – this is the time during which organizations will decide whether to initiate any changes and if so allocate resources to the process. The *change processes* may include becoming aware of the need to change and searching for external assistance.
2. *Planning phase* – this involves understanding the organizations' problem. *The change processes* involved may include: searching for information to make the correct diagnosis of the problem, and establishing objectives and gaining support of key decision makers.
3. *Action phase* – at this stage the changes are implemented. The *change processes* relate to the establishment of arrangements to manage the change process, gain staff support, evaluation of implementation; and taking corrective action if necessary.
4. *Integration phase* – this relates to the development of a new status quo. The change processes include reinforcing new behaviour through reward systems, disseminating relevant information; and encouraging improvements in all.

This model is useful because it makes a distinction between the phases of change and the methods of facilitating change.

The planned approach to change is subject to criticism. One key problem with this approach to managing change is that it assumes that organizations exist in different states and that planned change management can move the organization from one state to another. However, in reality these assumptions are somewhat flawed because we are living in a turbulent environment in which it is difficult to control the status quo. Instead, organizational change is perhaps more of a continuous and open-ended process than once thought. This approach also assumes that common agreement can be reached and that all those involved are willing and able to adapt to the change. Therefore, this approach tends to ignore organizational conflict and politics. It also assumes that one approach can meet the needs of all organizations in all situations.

Emergent approach

Starts from the assumption that change is a continuous, open-ended and unpredictable process of aligning and realigning an organization to its changing environment ... views change as a process that unfolds through the interplay of multiple variables (context, political processes and consultation) within an organization. (Burnes, 1996, p. 187)

The emergent approach has developed out of the criticisms of the planned approach which tends to be heavily reliant on the role of managers. The emergent approach recognizes that the business environment is becoming increasingly turbulent and difficult to predict, and stresses the unpredictable nature of change. It regards change 'as a process that unfolds through the interplay of multiple variables (context, political processes and consultation) within an

61

organization' (Burnes, 1996). Therefore successful change is more reliant on reaching an understanding of the complexity of the issues involved rather than developing a detailed plan that moves through a number of different stages. According to the emergent approach 'Organizational change can be regarded as a continuous process of experiment and adaptation aimed at matching an organization's capabilities to the needs and dictates of a dynamic and uncertain environment.' (Burnes, 1996). This is most effectively achieved by a number of often small-scale incremental changes over time which can in turn lead to major transformations. The role of managers in this approach is very different to that of the planned change approach. Rather than being planners and implementers of change their responsibility lies in creating an organizational structure and climate which encourages staff to embrace and initiate change.

Both approaches have their uses and also their limitations in helping us to understand change. Both stress the fact that the change process is a learning process and both have been developed with particular situations and assumptions in mind. For example, planned change is based on the assumption that organizations are operating in stable and predictable environments. In this situation it is believed that change is about moving from one state to another. In contrast emergent change is built on the assumption that organizations operate in more turbulent environments that are more unpredictable and that change is a continuous process of adaptation. Burnes (1996) suggests that in fact planned and emergent change are two ends of the same continuum – Figure 3.1. This model then suggests that a range of approaches that are relating to the environment in which an organization is operating can be adopted.

Figure 3.1 The change continuum
Source: Adapted from Burnes (1996)

Extending knowledge

For an overview of the complexities of organizational dynamics read Chapter 1 of Stacey (2003).

 ## Activity 3.1

Planned versus emergent change

Using your own organization or one with which you are familiar. Critically evaluate the company's approach to managing change, i.e. Is a planned approach or emergent approach to change management adopted? Consider the type of environment in which they are operating, the factors driving change and the people involved in the change process. To what extent is this a successful approach to change management?

The change process

Burnes (1996) provides a useful framework for analysing the change process. This suggests that the change process consists of three interlinked elements: objectives and outcomes, planning the change and people. This approach acknowledges the multi-dimensional approach to change management that is necessary.

Objectives – it is essential that objectives and outcomes are explicit and open. Burnes (1996) suggests that initially there will be a trigger that prompts the needs for change. From this clarity, agreement must be sought about who has the responsibility and authority to initiate change. It will then be necessary to identify the assessment team who will clarify the problem/opportunity, investigate possible solutions, provide feedback and then present recommendations. If from this the decision is to go ahead, then it becomes necessary to begin the implementation process.

Planning the change – According to Burnes (1996) this involves six interrelated activities:

1. *Establishing a change management team*
2. *Management structures* – special structures may be necessary to facilitate the change process
3. *Activity planning* – constructing a schedule to the change programme
4. *Commitment planning* – this involves identifying key people whose support is necessary for the successful implementation of change
5. *Audit and post-audits* – it is essential that progress is carefully monitored to identify whether objectives are being met
6. *Training* – this may be necessary to provide staff with the new skills they will need in the new era or it may involve providing training to help them facilitate change in themselves.

People – this is probably the most overlooked part of the change process. For change programmes to be successful it is essential that all the people affected are involved and motivated and that their support is gained. This involves creating a willingness to change, involving people and sustaining the momentum:

o *Creating a willingness to change* – many people will resist change because of the fear of the unknown. It is essential that people are made aware of the need for change and also provided with regular feedback on its progress. In order to create a positive attitude to change, organizations should publicize successful change and the benefits this has brought to employees. It is also essential that the concerns and fears of people should be taken seriously and addressed.

o *Involve people* – In order for people to 'buy into' the change process they must be able to take ownership of the process rather than having it imposed upon them. This can be achieved through effective communication (two-way) and getting people involved.

o *Sustaining the momentum* – It is difficult to sustain the momentum of change particularly when those involved continue to be faced with the day-to-day pressures of meeting customer needs. It is essential that organizations sustain the momentum and this can be helped by ensuring that sufficient resources are available, support is given to the 'change agents' and desired behaviour is reinforced through rewards. It is likely that change will result in the need for new skills and competences and it is essential that staff are adequately trained, mentored, counselled or coached.

It is apparent that the change process is a complex blend of objective-setting, planning and people.

Activity 3.2

The change process

Using the company that was the focus of Activity 3.1 identify a change that has been recently introduced. Evaluate the extent to which the company considered the three elements identified by Burnes (objectives, planning the change and people), when introducing the change. In particular to what extent did the company acknowledge the importance of 'people'? If people were not involved and motivated what were the implications of this?

Robbins and Finley (1998) identify what they refer to as seven unchangeable rules of change:

1. People do what they perceive to be in their best interest, thinking as rationally as possible. Robbins and Finley refer to this as the law of push.
2. People are not inherently anti-change. Most will embrace change if it has a positive meaning for them. Referred to as the law of pull.
3. People thrive under creative challenge, but wilt under negative stress.
4. People are different and no one-solution will satisfy everybody.
5. Actions speak louder than words.
6. The way to make effective long-term change is to first visualize what you want to achieve and then live this vision until it comes true.
7. Change is an act of the imagination. Until the imagination is engaged no important change can take place.

It is useful to contemplate these when planning for change.

Why change fails

As stated previously up to 80 per cent of change strategies fail. Robbins and Finley (1998) suggest a number of reasons as to why change initiatives fail:

o It is the wrong idea – no matter how well-implemented it is not going to succeed because it is inappropriate.
o It is the right idea but the wrong time – maybe too soon after a failed change initiative, too few available resources, lack of top management support.
o You're doing it for the wrong reasons – usually money. For example, companies initiate change as a means of increasing efficiencies and saving money.
o It lacks authenticity – some companies are led to change not because it is inherently necessary but because it is in vogue, i.e. everyone else is doing it.
o Your reality contradicts your change – for example, a company may announce a flattening of the organizational structure to encourage a more egalitarian culture. However, the reality is far from that – the old practices such as separate dining rooms for managers and workers send out stronger messages that in fact nothing has changed. This often leads to cynicism and distrust in the organization.
o You have the wrong leader – one cannot underplay the role of a strong leader that inspires and motivates staff. It is essential that the leader is compatible with the culture of the company or else this may result in conflict.
o Change for changes sake – senior management initiate change to alleviate the boredom of everyday life. They thrive on creating turmoil and even gain personal satisfaction from this turmoil.

- ○ People aren't prepared or convinced – in the short term this suggests the need for training and communication to encourage people to buy into the new ideas. In the long term it is probably more of an issue of corporate culture.
- ○ Bad luck – contingencies that are not planned for. For example, terrorist attacks, natural disasters, death of a senior manager.
- ○ There is nothing you can do – in some cases there may be nothing anyone can do to stem the rising tide of failure.

Activity 3.3

Reasons why change fails

Thinking about your company (or one with which you are familiar) identify the change initiatives that have been unsuccessful and referring to the list above identify why this was the case. What actions could have been taken, if any, to facilitate the change process?

Many companies adopt textbook approaches to managing change – producing new mission statements, new organizational structures, 'corporate culture' programmes, training programmes, regular attitude surveys. Senior managers believe that these will transform the organization and that as a result employee behaviour will change. Beer *et al.* (1990) found that in fact the opposite is true and that the greatest obstacle to change is the idea that it is achieved through company-wide change programmes often led by HR. They believe that most change programmes do not work because they are based on the belief that the starting point is with the knowledge and attitudes of employees. The theory suggests that changes in attitudes leads to changes in individual's behaviour and if repeated by many people will eventually lead to organizational change. This suggests that change is like a conversion experience and that once people get converted, changes in their behaviour will follow. Beer *et al.* (1990) suggest that this approach to change is in fact back to front. They believe that individual behaviour is shaped by the organizational roles that staff perform. Therefore the most effective way of changing behaviour is to give people different roles and responsibilities, i.e. a different context and this then 'forces' new attitudes and behaviours on people. For change to be successful staff must see a real alignment between their day-to-day role and the values declared by management.

Beer *et al.* (1990) suggests that for successful corporate change there are three interrelated factors:

1. *Coordination* (teamwork) – within and between departments
2. *Commitment* – high levels are required to ensure co-operation and co-ordination
3. *New competencies* – such as analytical, interpersonal skills are essential.

They believe that many company-wide change programmes fail because they do not address all three factors. Companies can try and avoid the problems associated with pragmatic change by adopting a 'task alignment' perspective, i.e. 'by focusing on reorganizing employees' roles, responsibilities, and relationships to solve specific business problems'. This in turn will shape new attitudes and ideas.

Marks & Spencer – How not to manage change

In April 2000 M&S sparked protests from across Europe when it announced store closures, job losses and major restructuring. They were taken to court in France over plans to close its European operations because they were accused of failing to follow procedures when announcing job cuts. This one error of judgement threatened to destroy the company's excellent reputation for treating staff well.

Source: Adapted from Benady (2001).

Activity 3.4

Success of change programmes

Consider at least three changes that have been introduced in your company in the last 12–18 months. How successful have they been? Consider the reasons as to why they succeeded or failed.

Making time for change

All individuals are faced with change in all aspects of their life – home and work. Robbins and Finley (1998) identify three types of change that we are all affected by:

1. *Global change* – this type of change relates to changes in the macro-environment such as technological, social, political and economic change. It happens to us all and there is little we can do about it.
2. *Organizational change* – this includes all the changes that are initiated by companies, such as new working practices, new organizational structures and new pay structures.
3. *Personal change* – this encompasses all the micro-changes that influence us on an individual level such as relationships, home life, financial situation, health, etc.

These three types of change influence us all to a greater or lesser degree for the majority of the time. We all have a limited capacity to change and when this 'change space' is filled we prioritize the things that we are prepared to change and dismiss the rest. For example, an employee that is going through a personal crisis – difficult divorce, financial problems, illness, etc. will find it very difficult to embrace change at work when faced with the change they are facing in their personal life. Therefore, a key task when initiating change is to make space in others for change. How can staff take on board new practices and new philosophies if they are currently firefighting in their existing roles? Some organizational changes fail not because they are not worthwhile but because people in the organization are overwhelmed and distracted by other changes. They lose the mind space that is necessary to give the change initiative it deserves. Alvin Toffler acknowledged this:

> *Man has a limited biological capacity for change. When this capacity is overwhelmed the capacity is in future shock.*

The task of managers and team leaders is to know and understand the people involved so that they can try to help balance each person's change load to leave room for organizational change to take place.

Adapting to change

The development of a culture that embraces change is an essential ingredient in the successful implementation of marketing strategy. The transition curve can help in understanding how people adapt to change (Figure 3.2).

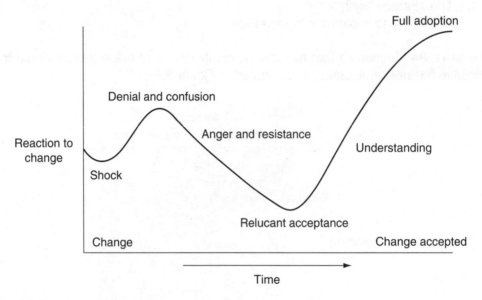

Figure 3.2 Reaction to change
Source: Adapted from Wilson (1993)

This model is useful because it illustrates that eventually people will internalize the new status quo (or will have left the organization). Adapting to change can be a very painful process and the expression of anger and frustration is a natural part of this adaptation. The implication for marketers is that the acceptance of major changes in working practices and responsibilities will take time.

Activity 3.5

Managing change

Select one example of change that has been instigated within your organization. To what extent did the model in Figure 3.2 fit your experiences of this change? How can managers use this model to their advantage?

Implementing change

The previous section discussed how companies could plan for change. This section focuses on how to achieve effective implementation of change.

Successful implementation

There are two factors that contribute to the success of a strategy:

1. The strategy itself
2. The ability to implement the strategy.

Bonoma (1984) suggested that the various combinations of these factors would lead to four alternative business outcomes, as illustrated in Figure 3.3.

Strategy

	Appropriate	Inappropriate
Good	Success	Chance
Bad	Problem	Failure

Execution skills (Good / Bad)

Figure 3.3 Strategy and execution
Source: Adapted from Bonoma (1984)

Success
This is the most desirable situation where an effective strategy is well implemented.

Chance
In this situation the strategy is weak. However, if the strategy was well implemented there could be a chance that it will be successful.

Problem
This occurs often. A strong strategy has been developed but is poorly executed, resulting in problems. It is interesting to note from this model that it is probably better to have an inappropriate strategy that is effectively implemented than a good strategy that is poorly implemented.

Failure
This is the least desirable outcome – a strategy is neither appropriate nor effectively implemented.

Obviously this is a simplified model that will vary depending on the specific situation and the degree to which strategies are inappropriate. However, it does present a graphical representation of the importance of implementation in the planning process. The next section will identify the reasons why strategies are often ineffectively implemented.

Activity 3.6

Success of plans

Refer to Figure 3.3 and consider which quadrant your organization's marketing strategies/change management programmes would normally fall into. Consider the reasons for your selection.

Assessing ease of implementation

The ease with which a strategy will be implemented can depend on strategic fit, i.e. the extent to which the strategy fits into current activities. The better the fit the more likely that implementation will succeed. The importance of the change and the degree of change will influence the extent to which implementation is successful. Figure 3.4 illustrates the relationship between change and importance.

Level of change in current operations

	High	Low
High	Overhaul	Synergy
Low	Overkill	Limited impact

Importance of change

Figure 3.4 Strategic fit

- ○ *Overhaul* – Implementation will have a significant impact and is likely to meet much resistance.
- ○ *Synergy* – The degree of change is low but it is very important. Resistance should be limited as long as the level of change required is minimal. Problems can occur if ultimately more change is required than first anticipated.
- ○ *Limited impact* – The importance of the change and the degree of change are both minimal.
- ○ *Overkill* – High degree of change to deal with relatively unimportant changes. This can alienate staff because they do not appreciate why change has to take place.

Factors critical for success

According to Stewart and Kringas (2003), the success of change programmes depends on a number of factors:

- ○ An appropriate change model
- ○ Effective leadership
- ○ Sufficient resources
- ○ Attention to communication.

Drummond and Ensor (2001) identify a number of factors that will contribute to the successful implementation of plans and can therefore be applied to implementing change programmes. This is illustrated in Table 3.1.

Table 3.1 Factors in successful implementation

Factor	Comment
Leadership	A strong and effective leader that is able to motivate and build teams is an essential ingredient for successful implementation.
Culture	Culture refers to the shared values and beliefs. If a plan goes against the dominant culture it is likely the plan will fail, unless support is gained via internal marketing.
Structure	Organizational structures not only denote levels of responsibility but also facilitates communication. Communication is a key aspect of implementation and organizations must ensure that the structures do not act as barriers to effective communication.
Resources	Appropriate levels of resources should be available – time, money and staff.
Control	Effective controls should be established to measure the progress and success of plans.
Skills	Skills necessary for successful implementation include: technical/marketing skills, HRM skills and project management skills.
Strategy	An appropriate and relevant strategy must be communicated to all participants.
Systems	Effective systems should be in place. For example, marketing information systems that generate relevant and timely information.

Source: Adapted from Drummond and Ensor (2001, p. 150).

These factors are embodied in the 7-S model developed by McKinsey & Co. as illustrated in Figure 3.5 This model consists of two categories of factors:

1. *Soft or HRM aspects* – style, staff, shared values and skills.
2. *Hard or process aspects* – strategy, structure and systems.

Implementation strategies focus all-too often on the hard or process aspects and ignore the very real 'soft' aspects that must be addressed if implementation strategies are to succeed.

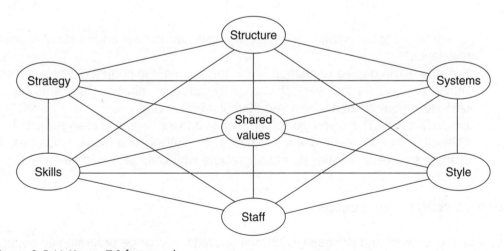

Figure 3.5 McKinsey 7-S framework
Source: Adapted from Drummond and Ensor (2001)

Techniques for overcoming resistance

There are various strategies that an organization can employ to try and overcome resistance to change. This section will discuss various techniques that can help facilitate the change process and hopefully overcome resistance to change. These include the development of a market orientation, internal marketing and the use of project management to facilitate the change process.

Development of a market orientation

The development of a market orientation can help facilitate the change process because staff become very much focused on the market place and it helps to develop a culture that embraces change rather than resists it. Without a customer-centred philosophy it is likely that any new strategy or change initiative will encounter problems. The development of a market orientation is a key task of the marketing department. However, this is often a difficult process due to the inherent conflicts that exist within organizations. Market orientation is discussed further in Unit 2.

Internal marketing

Internal marketing, discussed below, can be used to facilitate the change process and overcome resistance to change.

Project management

The ability to manage projects effectively is a key aspect of implementing plans and bringing about change. Project management is concerned with the achievement of predetermined goals within a certain timescale and with a limited amount of resources. The skills associated with project management are the same in whatever context they are being used. They are highly applicable to the implementation of marketing projects that are often complex, involve, and impact on, a wide variety of people from different areas of the business. It is inevitable that project managers will have to deal with 'opposers' and overcome other barriers to implementation. It is essential that project managers acquire the necessary skills to integrate activities, motivate participants, develop a sense of teamwork and monitor progress. Drummond and Ensor (2001) suggest five common tasks of project management Table 3.2.

 Definition

> **Project management** – Project management involves achieving unity of purpose and setting achievable goals within given resources and timescales (Drummond and Ensor, 2001).

Table 3.2 Common tasks in project management

Task	Comment
Objective setting	It is important that objectives are SMART (Specific, Measurable, Action, Realistic and Timebound).
Planning	This involves breaking down the project into manageable tasks, co-ordinating activities and monitoring progress.
Delegation	The key to successful management is the recognition that you cannot do everything yourself.
Team building	An essential skill for a project manager is the ability to build a successful team.
Crisis management	There will be times when things do not go according to plan and urgent action is required. In order to try to anticipate likely problems, scenario planning can be used.

Source: Adapted from Drummond and Ensor (2001, p. 262).

71

A useful way of viewing a project is as an 'instrument of change' (Brown, 2002). Therefore project management is a key skill that can be used to facilitate change in organizations. Projects vary considerably in terms of their focus, their timescale, cost implications and numbers of people involved. On the one hand you may be dealing with projects such as the Millennium Dome or on the other you may have been assigned the task of selecting a new photocopier for the office. Despite the myriad of different types of projects most projects have similar characteristics. According to Brown (2002) a project:

- Is an instrument of change
- Has a clearly identifiable start and finish
- Has a specific aim
- Results in something being delivered
- Is unique
- Is the responsibility of a single person or body
- Involves cost, resources and time
- Uses a wide variety of resources and skills.

In order to have a better understanding of what is involved in a project it is worth thinking about projects as all consisting of the same underlying structures:

- Initiation
- Specification
- Design
- Build
- Installation/Implementation
- Operation and review.

(Brown, 2002)

Adopting a systematic approach to project management ensures that the objectives of the project are clear and understood by all parties. It also encourages staff to take a logical approach to planning and provides a consistent means by which monitoring can take place. Despite taking a logical and systematic approach to project management the 'people' aspect cannot be ignored. Successful project managers need not only good organizational skills and a systematic approach to projects, they must also have good people management skills. Therefore, according to Brown (2002) project managers should have the following personal qualities:

- Motivating
- Delegating
- Communicating
- Leading.

These skills can be acquired through training and experience. Many organizations are now recognizing the need to equip their project managers with the necessary skills and are initiating project management development programmes.

Extending knowledge

For a practical and succinct guide to project management see Brown (2002) *Project Management in a Week*.

Cross-reference – Unit 6 Quality and Project Management discusses project management in further detail.

Internal marketing

According to Berry (1981), 'The most important contribution the marketing department can make is to be exceptionally clever in getting everyone else in the organization to practice marketing.' This is essentially what internal marketing (IM) is concerned with. It is more of a management philosophy and strategy than a marketing function.

Gronroos (1990) identified two separate but integrated elements of internal marketing: attitude management and communications management. Attitude management is associated with motivating employees to buy into the organization's goals whilst communications management involves providing and managing the information employees need to perform effectively.

What is internal marketing?

Definition

> **Internal marketing** – has the goal of developing a type of marketing programme aimed at the internal marketplace in the company that *parallels* and *matches* the marketing programme aimed at the external marketplace of customers and competitors (Piercy 2002, p. 592).

Internal marketing (IM) can play a key role in the implementation of plans. It is concerned with adopting the principles and practices of external marketing to the internal market. Figure 3.6 illustrates that in fact there are three types of marketing that occur within an organization. The success of external marketing lies in the ability of the organization to satisfy the needs of the customer. Organizations are dependent on their staff to achieve this, particularly in high customer-contact service businesses. Therefore, successful internal marketing is increasingly being seen as a prerequisite for effective external marketing.

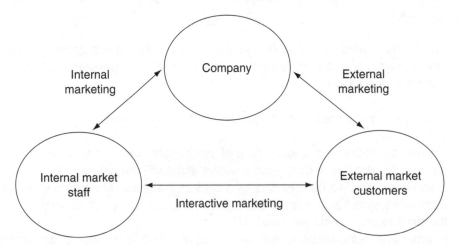

Figure 3.6 Three types of marketing
Source: Adapted from Kotler *et al.* (1999)

Internal marketing suggests that employees should be treated as internal customers and marketing plans need to be 'marketed' internally to gain acceptance and to ensure that employees understand the rationale behind the plans; can see how they can contribute to the success of the plan and importantly, 'buy into' the plan. This is not an easy task. A survey of employees in British companies with 1000 people or more, published by the Marketing & Communications Agency (MCA) and MORI, shows the scope of the challenge. The majority

of employees said they feel undervalued, uninvolved and lack confidence in their organizations' leaders and vision (Mazur, 1999). Employees that lack motivation and confidence in their organizations are unlikely to buy into new ideas readlly.

Internal marketing can play an important role in managing innovation. For further discussion, see Unit 7.

There fails to exist a single unified definition of what is meant by internal marketing. However, there is general agreement that internal marketing involves a planned effort to overcome organizational resistance to change and to align, motivate and integrate employees towards the effective implementation of corporate and functional strategies (Ahmed and Rafiq, 1993). It is likely that any change in strategy will require internal marketing to overcome organizational resistance and to help motivate staff.

Ahmed and Rafiq (2002) have undertaken an extensive review of internal marketing and from this they have identified five main elements of internal marketing:

1. *Employee motivation and satisfaction* – IM acts as a vehicle for staff acquisition, motivation and retention that in turn leads to increased productivity and external service quality.
2. *Customer orientation and customer satisfaction* – IM can promote customer-orientated behaviour among staff.
3. *Inter-functional co-ordination and integration* – these are key elements of a market orientation as identified by Narver and Slater (1999), see Unit 2. IM can be used to co-ordinate the efforts of the different functions in an organization.
4. *Marketing-like approach to the above* – other tools can be used to achieve the above. However, IM relies on achieving these through the use of marketing principles and tools.
5. *Implementation of specific corporate or functional strategies* – Piercy (2002) suggests that IM plays a crucial role in the implementation of strategic change by ensuring understanding and support for the strategies and also for removing barriers to change.

Ahmed and Rafiq (2002, p. 11) produced the following definition of IM that encompasses all of the 5 elements above:

> *Internal marketing is a planned effort using a marketing-like approach directed at motivating employees, for implementing and integrating organizational strategies towards customer orientation.*

Simms (2003) suggests the following guidelines on internal marketing:

- o Trying to communicate with internal customers using only external campaigns will merely alienate them. Employee surveys alone will not engage staff.
- o Employees need to be targeted as a distinct audience. Most companies would benefit from employing some form of internal communication specialist that can draw on both the disciplines of marketing and HR.
- o Internal communications should be part of corporate communications or marketing. If it is the responsibility of HR it can become a vehicle for communicating only HR issues and therefore fails to deliver wider messages.
- o Staff, unlike customers, are part of the brand and not just recipients. It is essential they are engaged and involved in the brand – they therefore have to be educated, motivated and measured in addition to being communicated with.
- o Make sure that staff know everything about your brand before the customers do.
- o Ensure that HR and marketing are involved.

Development of internal marketing

The notion of internal marketing traditionally evolved from the service sector where there was concern that contact employees were engaging in 'interactive marketing' and it was essential that they were responsive to customer's needs. It was also apparent that it was insufficient to have customer-conscious front-line staff but there also had to be effective co-ordination between contact staff and background support staff. Therefore internal marketing is also seen as a means of integrating various functions of an organization.

Ahmed and Rafiq (2002) have identified three distinct phases in the development of internal marketing:

1. *Employee motivation and satisfaction* – 20 years ago the majority of work on internal marketing, in particular the work of Berry (1981), focused on employee motivation and satisfaction and the impact this had on external service quality.
2. *Customer orientation* – the work of Gronroos (1990) developed the concept of internal marketing by advocating that staff are not only motivated to perform better but that they are responsive to customer needs and also that IM is a means of integrating the different functions of the organization that may have impact on customer relations.
3. *Strategy implementation and change management* – this recognizes the role of IM as an implementation mechanism and also that principles of external marketing could be applied internally to manage change in an organization.

Extending knowledge

See Chapters 1 and 2 of Ahmed and Rafiq (2002) for a more detailed discussion of: What is internal marketing and how it works?

Case history

Richer sounds

Julian Richer the founder of Richer Sounds embraces the concept of internal marketing wholeheartedly. He is probably unaware that this is what he is doing but the result is the same. Richer refers to this as the Richer Way: 'make sure your staff are happy in order to give good customer service, increase turnover, reduce complaints, cut theft and absenteeism'. Richer Sounds consists of 27 hi-fi stores located in the cheaper ends of towns and specializes in end of line equipment. In the London Bridge shop the average sales per square foot are £5500 compared with £630 at PC World and £520 at Currys. Richer Sounds has made the Guinness Book of Records for the last 10 years recording the highest sales in the world for stores of their size.

The general philosophy of these stores is to 'pile 'em high, sell them cheap but also have great customer service'. Richer Sounds' competitive advantage is its staff. Julian Richer realized that if staff were happy and motivated they were more likely to provide a better service to the customers. His methods of creating a happy workforce are numerous and legendary, including free access for staff to holiday homes in the UK and Europe (regardless of sales performance), trips on the Orient Express for staff who come up with the best ideas, a fiver every month to each employee so they can go down to the pub and brainstorm,

and use of a Bentley or Jaguar for a month for the best performing shop. The company annual attitude survey shows that 95 per cent of staff love working for the company, which speaks volumes about the success of Julian Richer's techniques.

Other companies, such as Asda and Halifax, are now recognizing the benefits of the 'Richer Way' and have employed Julian Richer as a consultant to advise them on staff motivation schemes and internal communication issues.

Source: Adapted from Beenstock (1998), Anon (2002).

The internal marketing plan

The internal marketing plan should take the same format as an external marketing plan with objectives, strategy, market segmentation, marketing mix programmes and evaluation.

Where are we now?

Market research is a key part of any external marketing campaign. In contrast companies seldom invest in research when conducting an internal marketing campaign. However, it can prove to be a valuable means of identifying the current situation with regard to employees' attitudes towards the company. Companies can use many of the same tools as for consumer research – survey, focus groups and in-depth interviews. The purpose of the research is to investigate issues such as attitudes to the organization, training, working conditions, opportunities for promotion, recruitment policies, etc. The research may also help to identify various segments of employees possibly with differing levels of resistance to change.

Where do we want to be? (Objective Setting)

It is essential that organizations are clear about what they want the internal marketing campaign to achieve and that senior management are committed to the programme.

Internal market segmentation

Internal markets could be segmented in a number of different ways such as by job function, role or location. However, these methods may not be the most appropriate. It may be useful to segment according to the extent to which people are likely to accept the proposed change. Jobber (2001) suggests that three different segments can be identified:

1. *Supporters* – likely to gain from the change.
2. *Neutrals* – will neither gain nor lose.
3. *Opposers* – likely to lose from the change or are traditional opponents.

Robbins and Finley (1998) categorize people according to their attitude to change. On one end of the scale there are those people that not only accept change readily but are naturally proactive and seek out change. This group of people help to drive organizations forward because they embrace change willingly as well as initiate it. On the other end of the continuum there are those people that are largely reactive and resist change. This group of people can be the death of any change initiative. This may be a useful way of segmenting employees. Organizations will have to expend differing amounts of resources and use different strategies for each group. These different segments can be plotted on a matrix relating to their attitude to change and their focus – Figure 3.7.

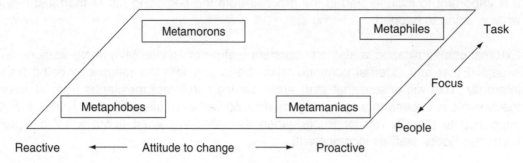

Figure 3.7 Segmentation based on attitudes to change and focus
Source: Adapted from Robbins and Finley (1998)

Metaphiles
These people embrace change willingly and are natural leaders and are focused on action. They are rather lacking in reflective skills but make up for this in their ability to get things done.

Metamaniacs
Metamaniacs tend to be highly creative, have great imaginations and some have to be changing to function. Like metaphiles they readily accept change, often initiating it, however they are not the most reliable people in terms of getting results because they are not task orientated.

Metaphobes
These people are generally averse to change. They display excellent 'people' skills and are generally good at relationships whilst being natural diplomats. They may have great ideas and opinions but they are often reluctant to share these because of the change that may result.

Metamorons
Like the metaphobes these people resist change, but to an even greater degree, and they are natural gatekeepers, stopping entry to the unknown. They are trustworthy and display perfectionist tendencies however their change mode is one of denial. They fear the unknown and will resist any change with great fervour.

A separate marketing mix can then be developed for each of these segments. It may also be possible to identify influential individuals that are opinion leaders.

Internal market positioning
The internal marketing mix can then be used to help position the internal 'product'.

Internal marketing mix
Product
The internal product can be viewed at a strategic level as the change programme or marketing plan, or even the company itself. At a more tactical level the product could be new procedures, appraisal systems or new ways of managing customers. At a more fundamental level the product can even be the individual's own job or function. Employees need the benefits of the 'product' communicated to them.

Promotion
This is a crucial element of the mix and refers to any medium that can be used to communicate with the target groups. The promotional mix could include newsletters, discussion groups, presentations, workshops, the use of the company Intranet, etc. It is also concerned with the message that is being transmitted. A key aspect of internal communication is that it is two way.

It is important to include staff in the process from the beginning rather than just telling them what is going to happen.

External communication is also an important feature of an internal communication plans. It is essential that any external communication be in line with the messages being transmitted internally. This will ensure that staff are receiving consistent messages from all sources. In the worse-case scenario external communication can even alienate staff. This is exactly what happened to the UK retailer Boots, when its staff complained about a TV campaign that portrayed Boots' staff as incompetent.

IBM successfully used external marketing in the form of their 1997 e-business campaign to not only position themselves as the leader in e-business with customers but to also align employees around the idea of the Internet as the future of technology. The campaign changed the way staff thought about the business and was successful because it gave employees a sense of direction and purpose and restored their confidence in IBM.

For further discussion of internal promotion, see the section on the Internal Marketing Communications at the end of the unit.

Distribution
This refers to the places where the product and communication will be delivered to internal customers such as seminars, meetings, away days, informal conversations, company Intranet, etc. There is some overlap between distribution and communication mediums.

Price
Price relates to the price the staff have to pay as a result of accepting the plan, new ways of working or new policies. Change may result in change of job role, loss of status, office moves, etc.

Physical evidence
This refers to the environment in which the product is delivered. In the context of internal marketing this may include documentation such as memos, training manuals, e-mails, etc. It also may include any conferences or training events that staff are asked to attend. These all send signals about senior management's level of commitment.

Process
Process can refer to the way in which changes are implemented. For example, is there any negotiation with unions or are the changes imposed? Process can also refer to the delivery method of the message such as video, presentation memos, etc.

People
'People' refers to those involved in both producing and receiving the 'product'. For example, changes should be delivered by someone of the right level of authority if they are to be achieved.

Internal marketing execution
Successful execution of the internal plan is reliant on three key skills (Jobber, 2001, p. 658):

1. *Persuasion* – the ability to develop a persuasive argument and to support words with action.
2. *Negotiation* – it is likely that some negotiations will have to take place so that all parties are happy.
3. *Politics* – organizations are made up of people, all with their own personal agendas. Therefore it is essential that the sources of power are identified and used to help implement the plan.

Internal marketing evaluation
In order to evaluate the success of internal marketing programmes appropriate measures have to be used, such as:

o The extent of support of key players
o Employee satisfaction levels
o Reduced customer complaints
o Higher customer satisfaction scores.

Many companies are now conducting regular surveys to monitor levels of staff motivation, acceptance of the marketing concept and perceptions of the organization. In addition, it could be argued that if internal marketing is being effective then it should be having an impact on external marketing. By measuring levels of customer satisfaction and numbers of customer complaints it may give an indication of the success of internal marketing programmes.

Potential problems
There are a number of potential problems associated with internal marketing. For example:

o Opposers create convincing counter arguments.
o Insufficient time to implement effective internal plans.
o High staff turnover that causes problems in ensuring all staff is involved.
o Low-paid shop (front-line) staff – this may result in a 'why should I bother?' attitude.
o Cost – internal marketing programmes can be costly and many organizations are still slow to recognize their importance. Staff training and other solutions can be very expensive and companies have to recognize that there may be diminishing returns on their investment in IM. It is essential that they recognize the optimal level not necessarily the desired level.

Extending knowledge

Piercy (2002) Chapter 14 'Implementing Market Strategies' provides an excellent discussion of internal marketing.

Activity 3.7

Ahmed and Rafiq (2002) suggest a multi-level model of internal marketing that provides a framework for understanding how implementation of strategy can be created by deploying the internal marketing mix using marketing research, segmentation and positioning. Ahmed and Rafiq (2002) present a case illustration of their multi-level model of internal marketing for Pearl Assurance on pp. 47–54. Read the discussion of this model on pp. 37–44 and then produce your own model for your own organization similar to that on p. 50.

It is also important to recognize that internal marketing cannot alone solve all employee-related and customer satisfaction problems. In some cases solutions lie more in ensuring that the right staff are recruited to the right positions in sufficient numbers and that they are adequately trained and motivated.

Merger of Lloyds Bank and TSB

The merger of Lloyds Bank and TSB could potentially have caused great problems with staff morale. In order to try and manage this momentous change an internal marketing campaign was carried out by Jack Morton Worldwide. Their task was to unite the 77 000 staff from the two companies and to rebrand the merged company as Lloyds TSB. The campaign consisted of two stages: firstly a trial of the jointly branded bank was established in Norwich and secondly an event to present the rationale behind the merger was held in Birmingham.

Many members of staff visited the pilot branch and feedback from this was used to help refine the messages to be used in the internal campaign. Over four thousand cash machines, 2300 branches and 40 000 uniforms then had to be rebranded.

It was realized that if the new brand values were to be communicated effectively to external customers that it first needed to communicate these to its employees to ensure they were delivering consistent brand images.

Five thousand members of staff, each representing 15 people, were nominated as 'pathfinders' and attended the live event in Birmingham – 'Your Life. Your Bank'. They were tasked with taking the message back to the branches. The presentation focused on explaining the rationale behind the merger, revealing the new blue and green corporate identity and explaining the new brand values with the objective being to gain staff commitment. The presentation culminated in a live concert by the Corrs, who also provided the music for Lloyds TSB's advertising campaign.

Afterwards the information was cascaded down through the entire organisation. Extensive research was undertaken by an external consultant to evaluate the process. According to the Managing Director of Jack Morton Worldwide 'the research concluded that the event was a huge success, that it met its objectives and that there was some change in all areas. Staff felt better informed about the changes, the values of the bank and had greater pride in it.'

Source: Adapted from Benady (2001).

Question 3.1

Answer Question 2 from the June 2001 Planning and Control Paper on internal marketing. Go to www.cimduhub.com to access specimen answers for this question.

Problems with the concept of 'employees as customers'

Viewing employees as customers and applying the tools and principles of external marketing to internal customers can be a very helpful approach. However, it must be viewed with some caution because the internal 'market place' is not an exact replica of the external one. For example, external customers receive products in return for payment of some sort. However, internally the products that employees are being offered may in fact be unwanted or even have a negative impact on them such as buying into new working practice, reorganizing/restructuring of the organization. In the external market place customers could choose not to buy or to buy other products. In contrast, internal customers must accept the 'product' or they can be forced into acceptance through the disciplinary action.

The idea of customer sovereignty does not apply equally to internal customers. Externally customers are viewed as 'king' and as always right. However, this does not apply internally because if they were to behave as external customers they would make impossible demands on their employers.

The suggestion that staff are the primary market of service organizations has major implications. For example, shop assistants would prefer not to work at the weekend however this is the time when a large proportion of customers wish to do their shopping. Putting employees' needs before customers' would be untenable.

These issues are largely resolved if a Total Quality Management (TQM) approach to IM is adopted. That is, the emphasis is on the relationships between staff rather than on the relationship between the organization and employees.

Extending knowledge

For further discussion of the tools of internal marketing, see Ahmed and Rafiq (2002) Chapter 3. This chapter includes interesting case studies of Sainsbury's and Pearl Assurance.

Activity 3.8

Internal marketing

To what extent do you think your organization has embraced the concept of internal marketing?

What impact does this have on their external marketing activities?

How has your company embraced technology, e.g. an Intranet in an attempt to improve their internal marketing/communications? How effective is this strategy?

IPC Media

Magazine publisher IPC Media received the Marketing Society Award for Internal Marketing in 2003. Its first internal marketing opinion survey in 2000 revealed low staff motivation, only 23 per cent of marketing staff were happy in their jobs and staff turnover was high at 28 per cent.

A new marketing structure was put in place with a group marketing director. A marketing executive was established comprising of all senior marketing directors across the company. An annual internal marketing budget of £75 000 was secured, a marketing vision, purpose and set of values were developed along with a marketing logo. Matrix, a toolkit for marketing staff, was launched setting out performance standards, training courses and self-appraisal data.

The first ever marketing conference and awards was organized; monthly learning lunches for all marketing staff were held and specific marketing areas were created on the company website and Intranet. Research in 2002 showed that 69 per cent of staff were now very happy in their jobs.

Employee branding

Increasingly, organizations are recognizing that one of their greatest untapped assets is their own employees and that getting staff to act as brand ambassadors is one of the few things competitors cannot directly copy. Research among marketers at last year's Marketing Forum found that almost half the delegates now had a dedicated budget for internal marketing (Mazur, 1999). Internal marketing is therefore not only important to ensure that staff buy into plans. It can also be used to transfer employees themselves into a source of competitive advantage.

> *Internal marketing helps generate higher levels of employee brand loyalty that can translate into incremental boosts in sales and profits. There's also significant potential for brand loyal employees to act as brand champions to families, friends and neighbours.* (Fram and McCarthy, 2003)

There is also the possibility that employees that use their own companies' products/services may stumble upon some unique product insights that may be of commercial value. There may also be a positive link between higher levels of employee brand loyalty and higher levels of employee job satisfaction.

Despite many organizations heralding that their employees are their biggest asset, they are often overlooked as a key target audience. Companies have spent millions on building their external brands and developing customer relationship strategies and yet have largely failed to explain to the very people they rely on to deliver the service, the rationale for the strategy and the important role they play. Internal marketing agency Enterprise IG Business and Brand Engagement (BABE) estimates that companies spend less than 1 per cent of their marketing and branding spend on internal communications. Therefore it is not surprising that even in the most customer-focused companies only one-third of staff act as 'brand champions'. Others add no value to the brand because they do not engage with it and the worse-case scenario is when staff actually act as brand saboteurs by actually criticizing the company publicly (Simms, 2003). Recently marketers have realized that staff need to buy into the brand and there has been an increased popularity in 'employer branding' where marketers 'attempt to adapt the tools and techniques traditionally used to motivate and engage customers, to secure the engagement and commitment of an internal audience' (Simms, 2003).

According to Terry (2003):

> *the toughest audience a company has is its employees. They know your brand, but the relationship an employee has with the brand is a bit like a marriage they see it unshaven, with bits of egg on its vest and endlessly hark back to that time when it was led astray by that bright young spark in the corporate communications department.*

There is evidence to suggest that many companies are not in a position to deliver their brand experience because of insufficient internal marketing. Intercommunic 8, an internal communications agency, conducted research with more than 1000 people in both the private and public sector. They found that there was a gap between what is promised to external customers via external communications and what is delivered by staff. This is particularly of issue, as we move further into a service-based economy. The research revealed that '37 per cent of respondents felt that the communication they received was inadequate in helping them to understand what their organization's values and brand meant. This 'yawning gap' between what is promised and what is delivered has a direct effect on a customers' relationship with that brand.' The research revealed that the value of internal communication in improving company performance is best implemented by the retail sector (Anon, 2003). Internal marketing should be seen as complementary to external marketing. The goal of an internal branding campaign is similar to that of an external campaign, to create an emotional connection with the company.

Companies that are good at internal marketing regard the external consumer brand and the employee brand as two sides of the same coin and ensure that all their communications are fully integrated and are sending out consistent messages.

Unfortunately in most companies, internal marketing is done badly, if at all. Most managers realize there is a need to keep staff informed of the company's strategy however few appreciate the importance of convincing them of the brand's uniqueness. Employees can enhance a brand's reputation with external customers and when employees also believe in the brand, customers are more likely to experience the brand in the way that the company has intended.

Extending knowledge

For further discussion of how to empower staff, read Chapter 5 of Ahmed and Rafiq 2002.

Case studies

Employee branding

Allied Domecq

Allied Domecq appoints 'employer brand managers' (usually marketers that are people orientated) to act as a bridge between HR and marketing. In an attempt to drive cultural change they have identified its 'people brand' as one of its nine core brands.

H-P Invent

H-P Invent, formerly Hewlett-Packard, utilise the skills of both HR and marketing to ensure the company communicates its brand values equally to both internal and external audiences. The corporate values of optimistic, inventive, trustworthy, inclusive and human are easily translated into the employer brand. Their 'Everything is possible' advertising campaign is as applicable and motivating for employees as it is for customers.

B&Q

An employer brand manager has been employed ('great place to work manager') to cut across HR and Marketing divisions. A distinct culture has evolved over the last 30 years that is built on its employees being brand ambassadors. Staff are used in all B&Q advertising and they have a well-known strategy of appointing over 50s. Each morning an 'Energize' session is held to encourage staff to work together and express their opinions about the store. At the centre of its business are 5 core values; a down-to-earth approach, respect for people, being customer-driven, being positive and striving to do better. These are the values that it wants its employees to work towards. Ensuring brand consistency is a huge challenge due to the size of the business and the geographical distance of its employees – 22 000 in 286 stores.

Carlsberg-Tetley

Marketing and corporate communications are responsible for the 'education and engagement of staff in the brands' at Carlsberg-Tetley. Consumers are particularly interested in their product range and it is therefore essential that the 2500 employees are well informed and act as brand ambassadors by communicating the right messages. Staff are regarded as a key target audience and have the opportunity to improve their knowledge and skills through an 'innovative and interactive' marketing-led training programme. 'Brand days' are held prior to the launch of new/revitalized brands where staff are given the opportunity to sample the products and enter competitions. Staff have the opportunity to see and discuss advertising campaigns and participate in internal promotions linked into key rugby or football sponsorships.

Source: Adapted from Simms (2003).

Extending knowledge

There is an interesting and extremely relevant discussion of internal marketing by Colin Mitchell in the *Harvard Business Review* (January 2002), pp. 99–105. This article outlines key principles of internal marketing and provides many relevant examples.

Internal marketing – whose responsibility?

There is much debate as to where the responsibility for internal marketing lies in an organization. Many Human Resource specialists argue that HR should have sole responsibility for internal communications because it is about people, not brands. However, others argue that marketing cannot effectively market the brand to external customers without first recognizing the importance of the internal customers, i.e. the employees. Marketers can adapt the tools and techniques they use to attract and retain external customers to gain the commitment of staff. The Chief Executive of BABE suggests that 'there should be someone in every marketing department specifically charged with the internal marketing of the brand ... they should be driving it and applying the same rigorous segmentation, measurement and investment disciplines to it as they do to the external brand'. The marketing department has the necessary skills and is also well positioned to ensure that internal marketing matches external marketing. There will probably be no agreement as to who should be responsible for internal marketing. However, what is more important is that both marketing and HR have an important role to play. 'Employee branding' may utilize many of the techniques used to motivate external customers however it is significantly different in that it involves 'not only communication but how the company interacts with its people, and that impinges on systems and processes' (Hail, 2003). Companies that successfully adopt a joint marketing and HR approach to internal branding are probably more likely to succeed in the longer term.

Extending knowledge

Ahmed and Rafiq (2002) Chapter 4 provides a comprehensive discussion of the relationship between HRM and internal marketing.

Internal marketing and relationship marketing

Varey and Lewis (1999), cited in Little and Marandi (2003) p. 115, developed the term 'internal relationship marketing' which they refer to as:

> *an integrative process within a system for fostering positive working relationship in a developmental way in a climate of co-operation and achievement.*

Little and Marandi (2003) suggest that internal relationship marketing involves blurring the internal–external boundaries of an organization by:

- Involving customers in product design, production and services
- Close partnerships between suppliers and customers
- Acceptance that relationships are organizational assets
- Exchange of ideas for mutual gain
- Collection and distribution of customer information.

Varey and Lewis (1999) suggest that internal marketing is not seen as a mechanism for encouraging change but is in fact an end in itself, i.e. the development of internal marketing relationships will encourage the conditions that are necessary for effective change to take place.

Little and Marandi (2003) identify a continuum of internal marketing from one based on transactions to one based on relationships (Figure 3.8).

Transaction-based internal marketing		Relationship-based internal marketing
One-way internal communication used to inform staff. Job design and development are viewed as the internal product and the price being the salary and training costs.	Some attempts at two-way communication between staff and organization. Management continues to make major decisions about strategy, albeit after considering staff views.	Two-way dialogue between management and staff. Role of senior managers is one of facilitator rather than leader or decision maker. The strategic direction of the company is developed jointly from the experiences and knowledge of staff and customers.

Figure 3.8 Continuum of internal relationship marketing
Source: Adapted from Little and Marandi (2003)

Relationship marketing relies on not only on getting customers, but more importantly on retaining customers and enhancing relationships. It emphasizes continuous long-term relationships that lead to repeat custom and customer loyalty which in turn leads to profitability over the lifetime of the customer. Relationship marketing takes an interactive approach to marketing and therefore relies on trust and commitment. The success of relationship marketing is therefore highly dependent on the attitudes, commitment and behaviour of employees, i.e. it relies heavily on ongoing internal marketing for its successful implementation.

Extending knowledge

For further discussion of internal marketing in the context of relationship marketing read Chapter 6 of Little and Marandi (2003).

ICT and internal marketing

Company Intranets can play an important role in internal marketing. They instantly and inexpensively connect all individuals within a company so that information can be readily made available and they also provide a great opportunity for the exchange of ideas. In the past, organizations were organized through hierarchies and bureaucracy because information was expensive, difficult and slow to obtain. Today Intranets have to some extent made obsolete the need for hierarchical structures. These have been replaced in many cases by cross-functional teams often virtual and have facilitated flatter organizational structures that are more cost-effective and more responsive. Intranets also encourage more informal networking and they have encouraged staff to engage in two-way communication with the company. They can be an extremely important and cost-effective internal marketing communications tool. According to Chaffey *et al.* (2000) Intranets can include the following information:

- Staff phone directories
- Staff procedures or quality manuals
- Up-to-date marketing intelligence such as competitor information
- Information that requires regular updating such as stock levels, prices and product specifications
- Staff newsletter or bulletin
- Training courses.

Developing appropriate skills and capabilities

In an era where companies face up to dealing with an ever-changing world, managers often find themselves unable to keep up with the pace of change. Traditionally people could learn faster than the world changed and could therefore anticipate and manage change. Today we are facing a new era where the world is changing at a faster pace and managers are faced with a situation where there is a lack of relevant skills and expertise to deal with the speed of change. Hunt (2003) suggests that the 'real challenge' associated with change 'is about people, aligning the business to meet the challenge'. He believes that too few companies have a workforce with the right skills to manage the 'new age' and this combined with continued under-investment in skills means that many companies are unprepared to deal with future challenges. According to Hunt (2003) most companies have older under-skilled workforces with 75 per cent over 28 years old and 58 per cent having left school at 16. The UK is currently facing a shortage of people with mathematics and IT skills in addition to people with good communication and problem-solving skills that are able to work effectively in teams. Within the senior management sector, Hunt (2003) suggests that there is a lack of relevant experience in three key areas; change management, international operations and the understanding of organizational paradigms. Companies will find that they are competing for the scarce resource of well-trained people.

It is essential that in order for companies to gain/maintain their competitive advantage they must ensure that they attract high-calibre staff and then hold onto them whilst at the same time equipping them with relevant skills and knowledge. For managers, it is not enough just to be a skilled organizer they must also be inspired and inspiring leaders. Successful change management is often due to the presence of a sound leader that helps to create the conditions for transformation.

Extending knowledge

Visit www.leadingtoday.org: This is the website of a non-profit organization WeLEAD that provides many insights about leadership, much of it thought-provoking and inspirational.

They publish a monthly online magazine that features book reviews, leadership tips and feature articles.

Skills audit

The first step in identifying whether or not staff have the necessary skills and capabilities to meet the changing needs of an organization is a skills audit. This will also identify any gaps in employees' skills or knowledge that can then be met with relevant training or even recruitment of staff with the necessary skills and capabilities.

Current skill and capabilities

According to Little and Marandi (2003) a skills audit can draw on several sources of information to form a picture of the current situation. These include:

- *External consultant* – the commissioning of a qualified external consultant to conduct the needs assessment will provide the organization with an independent view of the organization's skills gaps. However, the disadvantage of employing an external consultant is that they are unfamiliar with the organizational culture and their presence may be regarded with suspicion by staff leading to uncooperativeness.
- *Internal data* – data such as customer complaints, error data, grievance records and exit-interview information can reveal skills gaps. It must be viewed with some caution because it was collected for another purpose.
- *Managers' assessments* – input from managers is important. However, it must be handled carefully to avoid staff regarding it as dictatorial.
- *Analysis of Marketing Plans* – the sources referred to above are largely reactive and rely on identifying current training needs. By analysing future plans it is possible to anticipate future needs.
- *Employee feedback* – staff involvement in identifying skills gaps is essential not only because they may provide useful insights but also that any training is well received.
- *Customer feedback* – this type of information is not often used in skills audits. However, it can provide useful insights and also demonstrates a commitment to customer satisfaction.

Delivering the training

Once the needs assessment has been completed it is then necessary to deliver the necessary training. The major decision facing organizations is whether to rely on in-house training, on the job training or to take them out of their working environment. Internal training can be particularly useful in situations where skills or knowledge specific to the organization are being transmitted. For example, for staff that are involved in face-to-face contact with customers. For organizations that regard training as a means of generating organizational change, it is unlikely that internal training will bring about new ideas or practices. Therefore, external delivery of training allows staff to reflect on the organization, its culture and current working practices. It may also help to facilitate change.

Evaluation

It is surprising that considering the amount of resources many organizations devote to training that so little evaluation of its effectiveness takes place. According to Little and Marandi (2003) there are various methods of evaluation available such as trainee evaluations which can either take place immediately after the training or else after a time-delay to allow the trainees some time to reflect on the training. Productivity/financial measures can also be used to assess the tangible impact of training. Feedback from managers can also provide useful insights into the effectiveness of the training. The final type of evaluation is that of customer feedback which provides an external view of the impact of training.

Managerial skills

In order to execute strategies effectively managers must have the necessary skills and knowledge. According to Piercy (2002) managerial execution skills include:

- o *Interacting skills* – this refers to the manager's 'people' skills and their ability to influence the behaviour of those around him/her. These skills would include leadership, negotiating and using power effectively to achieve objectives.
- o *Allocating skills* – a key role of a manager is to delegate responsibility and to set out the ground rules for budgeting time, money and people to achieve implementation.
- o *Monitoring skills* – it is not enough to generate action but managers must also be able to develop and use feedback mechanisms that provide useful information.
- o *Organizing skills* – this may not necessarily be the textbook definition of organizing but a manager must be able to network, arrange things and fix things. It is increasingly being recognized that project management techniques are important skills that managers may require. For further discussion of project management, see Unit 6.

Internal marketing communications

The boundary between external and internal stakeholders is not as clear, as one may first think. For example, there has been an increasing trend towards more flexible working practices such as part-time workers, temporary staff, consultants, etc. and these people spread themselves across organizational borders. In addition, stakeholders may assume multiple roles in relation to the organization; such as employee, customer, financial stakeholder, etc. For example, an employee of Bradford & Bingley Building Society may also have a savings account or mortgage with them and in addition may also be a shareholder. This has major implications for the way in which organizations communicate with their various stakeholders. It is therefore essential that internal and external communications are compatible and communicate the same messages because internal stakeholders will also be exposed to external communications.

Role of internal marketing communications

Internal marketing communications is a key aspect of internal marketing and plays an important role in facilitating change. According to Fill (1999) internal marketing communications has several roles:

- o DRIP factors (**D**ifferentiate products and services, **R**emind and reassure customers and potential customers, **I**nform and **P**ersuade targets to think and act in a particular way)

  1. To provide information
  2. To be persuasive
  3. To reassure/remind
  4. To differentiate employees/groups.

- o Transactional

  1. To co-ordinate actions
  2. To promote the efficient use of resources
  3. To direct developments.

      o   Affiliation

            1.   To provide identification
            2.   To motivate personnel
            3.   To promote and co-ordinate activities of non-members.

This demonstrates the important role that internal marketing communications can play in helping to facilitate change management. However, internal communications cannot be viewed in isolation and must be viewed in relation to all external communication.

Internal marketing communication plan (IMC)

Internal marketing communication plans will vary considerably and there is no one standard approach to them. This section will highlight the key elements that should be addressed when preparing an internal marketing communications plan. The IMC plan is a key element of the internal marketing plan and therefore there is overlap in several areas with the IM plan as discussed previously in this unit. Also the IMC plan cannot be prepared in isolation and must form part of the wider external communications plan.

Communication audit

The audit is a critical stage of any plan and provides an evaluation of recent communications, both external and internal. This will provide an assessment of whether or not an organization is communicating effectively and efficiently with its various stakeholders such as:

      o   Is it transmitting consistent messages via all media and channels?
      o   Are internal and external communications compatible?
      o   Are the communications meaningful and understood by the intended audience?
      o   Are we reaching our intended audiences?

Competitors' marketing communication activity should also be evaluated because companies do not operate in a vacuum. All forms of communication should be evaluated including all printed and visual communications (such as advertisements, brochures, stationery, annual reports, point of sale, direct mail, logos, website, etc.). Internal communications should also be assessed such as internal newsletters, company magazines and notice board.) The communications audit should also include an investigation of staff attitudes to the organization and its communication.

The objective of the audit is to investigate whether the perceived image of the company reflects reality. It also evaluates the current messages being transmitted via various sources to assess whether they are consistent.

Communication objectives

It is essential that the goals of any communication plan are clear and internal communication plans are no exception. Objectives may relate to awareness, perceptions, comprehension/ knowledge, attitudes towards and perceptions of the change programme.

Communications strategy

A key aspect of the strategy is identification of the target audience. Previously in the internal marketing plan a number of methods for segmenting the market were discussed. It is essential that when developing an internal marketing communications plan it is clear which target audiences are being addressed. For example, a company may want to put more resources into targeting staff that are opposed to change or they may want to concentrate their efforts on particular parts of the workforce. It may be necessary to use different promotional tools to target

different segments. For example, personal selling may be necessary for opposers whereby more impersonal tools may be adequate for supporters of a programme. It is also necessary to consider the message that is going to be transmitted to ensure that clear positioning and message consistency is achieved across various media. Internal marketing communications should also be consistent with external marketing communications activity.

Promotional methods

There are a variety of promotional tools that can be used to inform and influence internal customers' attitudes towards change programmes. Many of these have traditionally come from the HRM department such as company magazines and newsletters. However, more recently it has been acknowledged that a more co-ordinated approach is necessary and that in many cases marketing departments can make a valuable contribution to this process.

Personal selling

Face-to-face presentation, to either groups or individuals, by managers can be an extremely effective means of communicating with staff. It not only provides the opportunity to inform, explain and persuade new policies but also provides the opportunity for two-way communication, i.e. staff can ask questions and seek clarification. These may take the form of formal presentations, workshops, discussion groups, conferences or meetings.

Advertising

Internal advertising can be in the form of broadcasting via the company Intranet. Some large companies have their own corporate television network such as Federal Express. This media allows companies to communicate in real time with all employees, even if they are geographically dispersed. Other types of advertising include posters on notice boards, company magazines and in-house newsletters. It is essential that external advertising is consistent with internal advertising because it is likely that staff will also be exposed to external messages.

Sales promotions/incentives

In order to encourage staff to change their behaviour they must be offered an incentive. Types of incentives may include bonuses, cash rewards, recognition schemes, prize draws and competitions. This technique can help to overcome resistance in the short term or can be used in the longer term to improve performance and encourage consistent behaviour.

Direct mail

In the context of internal communications this may include e-mails or letters sent directly to each member of staff.

Company Intranet

This is a cost-effective promotional tool that can reach all staff simultaneously if necessary. It can be updated in real time and gives everybody access to the same information. For further discussion, see the previous section on ICT and IM.

Sponsorship

Sponsorship could be used by companies to improve staff morale. For example, some companies support their employees in terms of sponsoring company teams such as football teams. This may include providing them with a football strip or supporting them in terms of funding other costs such as hire of equipment. Other companies choose to donate to charities of their employees' choice or support other initiatives that have been suggested by staff. These all have the effect of creating a positive relationship between the company and staff.

Timings

It is essential that a realistic schedule is drawn up and this must be co-ordinated with external communication. For example, a bank may be introducing a new type of savings account. It is essential that In this case internal communication precedes external communication to ensure that when new customers come into the bank asking about the new service that front-line staff are informed and knowledgeable about the product.

Budget

Many companies are increasingly recognizing the importance of internal communications and are allocating more resources to this key area. Previously most companies made only token gestures to IMC budgets and generally these would have been seen as HRM costs.

Evaluation

Evaluation of IMC is essential to ensure that it is in fact being effective. In order to measure the effect of IMC it is necessary to establish employee attitudes, perceptions and satisfaction levels through research.

Extending knowledge

Visit www.seraccom.com. This is the website of Serac Communications, an agency specializing in internal marketing and internal communications. It provides examples of some of the internal marketing campaigns in which they have been involved.

Activity 3.9

Internal marketing communications plan

Select one recent change initiative that has been implemented in the organization. Critically evaluate the way in which this was communicated to employees. For example, what was the objective? Who was the target audience? What was the message? What promotional tools were used? How was the success of the programme evaluated?

Produce an outline internal marketing communications plan for this change initiative that incorporates your ideas on how the process could be improved.

Summary

- ○ Change is inevitable in today's world. Organizations are having to adapt in order to remain competitive and capitalize on the new opportunities that are emerging from the changes in the external environment.
- ○ Many change initiatives fail because organizations do not implement the change programmes effectively. Many people resist change because they are familiar with the status quo and fear the unknown. A key challenge for organizations is to create a culture that welcomes and embraces change.
- ○ There are two main approaches to change. The planned approach that views change as a systematic process of moving from one fixed state to another through a series of predictable stages. The emergent approach views change as a process that unfolds through the interplay of multiple variables within an organization.

o There are many different perspectives on the change process. One useful way of viewing the process is by considering that the change process consists of three interlinked elements: objectives and outcomes, planning the change and people.

o Implementing change is concerned with translating plans into action. This is often overlooked by many organizations. In some case plans fail not because they are inappropriate plans, but because they are poorly implemented.

o The success of change programmes depends on factors such as adopting an appropriate change model, effective leadership, sufficient resources, a culture that embraces change, appropriate organizational structure and systems and attention to communication.

o There are many barriers to change such as staff attitudes, culture, lack of time and resources, processes and procedures. Organizations need to adopt strategies that can help to overcome these barriers such as the development of a market orientation, internal marketing and the use of project management techniques.

o Project management can be viewed as an 'instrument of change' and is a key skill that can be used to facilitate change in an organization.

o Internal marketing is concerned with applying the principles and practices used for external marketing to the internal market place. This will ensure that internal marketing campaigns mirror those of the external market place. Internal marketing plays a key role in facilitating change programmes.

o Staff are a key target audience because they generate powerful word of mouth. Ensuring that employees are committed to their company is one way of creating 'brand ambassadors'. Staff that are 'brand advocates' are increasingly being seen as a way of creating a sustainable competitive advantage.

o Both marketing and HRM need to be involved in internal marketing because marketing has the necessary skills and knowledge, and HRM has the responsibility for staff.

o It is essential that organizations continually review employees' skills and capabilities. The changing nature of business will inevitably result in the need for new types of skills and capabilities.

o Internal marketing communications plays an important role in helping to facilitate change. A key part of internal marketing relates to the need to communicate with internal target audiences.

Sample exam question

Your company, a consumer personal care products business, has just acquired a competitor. Your manager has asked you to prepare a report discussing the issues that need to be taken into account in order to integrate the two ranges of products.

Discussion

Please refer to the syllabus, element 3 – Implementing the business strategy through marketing activities.

The question clearly suggests that this is a project with a clear start and end point and an identifiable timescale. You should consider the range of issues that the question implies, this is a manufacturing business that produces consumer products, perhaps branded and in relatively high volumes. What are the implications for the type of activities that need to be undertaken, the decisions to be taken and the timescales involved?

Bibliography

Ahmed, P.K. and Rafiq, M. (1993) 'The scope of internal marketing: Defining the boundary between marketing and human resource management', *Journal of Marketing Management*, **9**, pp. 219–232.

Ahmed, P.K. and Rafiq, M. (2002) *Internal Marketing Tools and Concepts for Customer-Focused Management*, Butterworth-Heinemann.

Anonymous (2002) 'For richer for poorer, in sickness and in wealth', *Sunday Times*, 24 March.

Anonymous (2003) 'Survey reveals "inadequate" state of internal marketing', *Marketing Week*, 3 July, p. 8.

Beenstock, S. (1998) 'Ninety five per cent of this man's staff say that they love working for him. What's his secret?' *Management Today*, April.

Beer, M., Eisenstat, R. and Spector, B. (1990) 'Why change programs don't produce change', *Harvard Business Review*, November–December.

Benady, D. (2001) 'The inside story', *Marketing Week*, 6 September, pp. 30–31.

Berry, L.L. (1981) 'The employee as customer', *Journal of Retail Banking*, 3 March, pp. 25–28.

Bicker, L. (1999) Cited in Piercy, N. (2002) *Market-Led Strategic Change*, 3rd edition, Oxford: Butterworth-Heinemann.

Bonoma, T. (1984) 'Making your marketing strategies work', *Harvard Business Review*, **62**(2), pp. 68–76.

Brown, M. (2002) *Project Management in a Week*, 3rd edition, Butterworth-Heinemann.

Bullock and Battern (1958) Cited in Burnes, B. (1996) *Managing Change*, 2nd edition, FT Pitman Publishing.

Burnes, B. (1996) *Managing Change*, 2nd edition, FT Pitman Publishing.

Chaffey, D., Mayer, R., Johnston, K. and Ellis-Chadwick (2000) *Internet Marketing*, FT Prentice Hall.

Davidson, H. (2002) *The Committed Enterprise: How to Make Vision and Values Work*, Butterworth-Heinemann.

Drucker, P. (1993) *Managing for the Future*, Oxford: Butterworth-Heinemann.

Drummond, G. and Ensor, J. (2001) *Strategic Marketing Planning and Control*, 2nd edition, Butterworth-Heinemann.

Fill, C. (1999) *Marketing Communications Contexts, Contents and Strategies*, Prentice Hall.

Fram, E.H. and McCarthy, M.S. (2003) 'From employee to brand champion', *Marketing Management*, January/February, pp. 24–29.

Gronroos, C. (1990) *Service Management and Marketing*, Massachusetts: Lexington Books.

Hail (2003) Cited in Simms, J. (2003), 'HR or Marketing: Who gets staff on side?', *Marketing*, 24 July, p. 23.

Handy (1995) *Beyond Uncertainty*, London: Hutchinson.

Hunt, R. (2003) The Challenges of Change Management, *Focus*, October.

Jobber, D. (2001) *Principles and Practice of Marketing*, 3rd edition, McGraw-Hill.

Kohli, A.K. and Jaworski, B.J. (1990) Cited in Hooley, G.J., Saunders, J.A. and Piercy, N.F. (1998) *Marketing Strategy and Competitive Positioning*, 2nd edition, Prentice Hall.

Lewin (1946) Cited in Burnes, B. (1996) *Managing Change*, 2nd edition, FT Pitman Publishing.

Lewin (1958) Cited in Burnes, B. (1996) *Managing Change*, 2nd edition, FT Pitman Publishing.

Little, E. and Marandi, E. (2003) *Relationship Marketing Management*, Thomson.

Mazur, L. (1999) 'Unleashing employees' true value', *Marketing*, 29 April, pp. 22–24.

Mitchell, C. (2002) 'Selling the brand inside', *Harvard Business Review*, January, pp. 99–105.

Narver, J.C. and Slater, S.F. (1999) Cited in Hooley, G.J., Saunders, J.A. and Piercy, N.F. (1998) *Marketing Strategy and Competitive Positioning*, 2nd edition, Prentice Hall.

Peters, T. (1992) *Liberation Management*, New York: Macmillan.

Piercy, N.F. (2002) *Market-Led Strategic Change*, 3rd edition, Oxford: Butterworth-Heinemann.

Robbins, H. and Finley, M. (1998) *Why Change Doesn't Work*, London: Orion Business Books.

Simms, J. (2003) 'HR or Marketing: Who gets staff on side?', *Marketing*, 24 July, p. 23.

Stacey, R. (1993) *Managing Chaos*, Oxford: Butterworth-Heinemann.

Stewart, J. and Kringas, P. (2003) 'Change management – Strategy and values in six agencies from the Australian public service', *Public Administration Review*, **63**(6), November/December.

Terry, N. (2003) 'Marketers merit a greater role in internal activity', *Marketing*, 28 August, p. 18.

Varey and Lewis (1999) Cited in Little, E. and Marandi, E. (2003) *Relationship Marketing Management*, Thomson.

unit 4
strategic marketing managers' role

Objectives

Syllabus links

Learning outcomes

o 'Identify the barriers to effective implementation of strategies and plans involving change (including communications) in the organization, and develop measures to prevent or overcome them.'

o 'Initiate and critically evaluate systems for control of marketing activities undertaken as part of business and marketing plans.'

Please see Appendix 4 for full details of the learning outcomes, related statements of practice and knowledge and skills requirements.

Information on the syllabus element (and its weighting) that is supported by this chapter can be found in Figure P.1, in the preface to this book.

Learning objectives

By the end of this unit you will:

o Gain insight into why marketers need to relate their activities more directly to shareholder value

o Understand the common measures that are used when discussing value

o Relate the measures of added value to marketing activities

o Understand the principles of corporate social responsibility and business ethics

o Gain insight into how this relates to marketing activities.

Key definitions

Value added – the difference between the (comprehensively accounted) value of the firm's outputs and the (comprehensively accounted) cost of firm's inputs (Kay, 2003).

Shareholder value add – the discounted value of future cash flows over time (after Doyle, 2000).

Discounted cash flow – future cash flows multiplied by the discount factor to obtain the present value of the cash flows (Doyle, 2000).

Net present value – a net contribution of a strategy to the wealthy shareholders: present value of cash flows – initial investment (Doyle, 2000).

Corporate social responsibility – the social responsibility of business encompasses the economic, legal, ethical and discretionary (philanthropic) expectations that society has of organizations at a given point in time (Carroll and Buchholtz, 2003).

Ethics – a set of moral principles or values that deal with what is good and bad with respect to moral duty and obligation (after Carroll and Buchholtz, 2003).

Business ethics – is concerned with i.e., 'right' and 'wrong' behaviours and practices that take place within a business context. Often interpreted to include questions of fairness, justice and equity (after Carroll and Buchholtz, 2003).

Study Guide

This unit will take about 3 hours to work through.

We suggest that you spend additional time reflecting on the topics discussed and using the Internet to supplement your knowledge and understanding.

Introduction

Over the past 20 years the role of marketing in business has been increasingly questioned. Combined with which there have been significant and substantial changes in the business environment. Consumers are much more aware and demanding, and companies are utilizing their resources and capabilities in different ways in order to compete more effectively and perform against the relentless and increasing pressure to deliver profitability to shareholders. In this changing environment marketing has been seen to struggle as a function to maintain its position within the company and its status in the boardroom.

This unit will consider the nature of the changes concerned and then go on to consider two important factors which are shaping the changes in the way that marketing is practised; the need for marketing to be more accountable and to deliver value for shareholders and the importance of managing not just shareholder expectations but those of many additional stakeholders. Recent corporate scandals, such as those involving Enron and Parmalat, demonstrate the need for responsible corporate behaviour and ethical business practices.

Insight

The Economist has described Parmalat as 'Europe's Enron'. Enron, an American company, like Italy's Parmalat, went bankrupt and collapsed into debts with numerous accusations of false accounting and illegal practices. In the case of Enron the company's accounts had been audited by Arthur Andersen, an independent firm of auditors, which became so tainted by the association with the disgraced company that business fell away and the company was eventually taken over. In the case of both Parmalat and Enron very serious issues concerning corporate governance have been raised and legal action has been taken against company executives. These two cases highlight concerns over corporate behaviour.

Source: *The Economist*, and other published sources.

With respect to the 'Managing Marketing Performance' syllabus this unit addresses elements 3.1, 3.2 and 3.3. The module itself concerns the implementation of strategy and aims to develop appropriate knowledge and skills. The relevant statements of marketing practice include the ability to implement an integrated marketing communications strategy, the promotion and creation of customer orientation, the ability to establish and promote the use of metrics, the provision of professional leadership to develop a co-operative environment to enhance performance and the ability to promote cross-functional working linked to brands and the integration of marketing activities. Of course, with respect to the statements of marketing practice, there will be overlap between the various modules as they address these from differing perspectives and contexts.

The need for accountability

This section will consider the factors which have driven the way in which marketing is perceived within the organization and which underlie the current requirement for marketing to be seen to be more accountable and to deliver benefits to stakeholders.

Transaction marketing

Adam Smith (1776) illustrated how he understood markets to work by talking about the 'invisible hand' whereby supply and demand were equalized in the market place. The economist John Kay (2003) discusses how markets evolve from an economic perspective. In a market economy statutes or laws define issues such as the ownership of property, and contracts which are the agreements that exist between individuals and firms; this provides the framework within which trade can take place. In principle therefore it could be argued that this is what is required for a market place to work. Kay goes on to quote economists of the 'Chicago School' whose philosophy is defined as 'the combined assumptions of maximising behaviour, market equilibrium, and stable preferences, used relentlessly and unflinchingly, form the heart of the economic approach'. It is widely agreed that marketing could be explained by applying these economic concepts. Products are offered in the market place at a certain price and deliver benefits. By specifying a range of features and benefits, changing the marketing mix, a range of products can be offered at a range of prices. Hence this underlies the role of a Product Manager; to introduce products to the range, manage them over the life cycle for profitability and then eventually withdraw them.

Marketing originally developed as a business concept within the fast-moving consumer goods firms (Shaw, 1998). The objective of marketing 'to' customers in order to increase sales can be explained using this micro-economic perspective. Marketers will be familiar with the concept of the product life cycle, and this has been used to explain the role of marketing as a business function (Brookes and Palmer, 2004) (Figure 4.1).

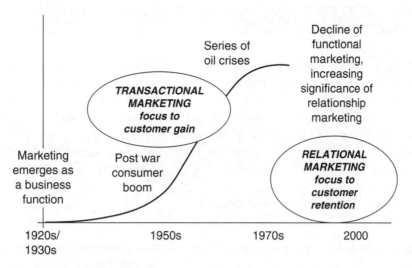

Figure 4.1 The life cycle of marketing
Source: Brookes and Palmer (2004)

Marketing developed rapidly during the 1950s and 1960s whilst consumers enjoyed relatively high levels of disposable income. There was strong pent up demand in this post-war period for a wide variety of consumer goods, such things as televisions, cars and the whole range of domestic items such as refrigerators and washing machines that nowadays are commonplace. In these circumstances of buoyant demand then a transactional approach was appropriate and successful. However, consumer attitudes and business perspectives changed significantly.

A number of triggers for this change can be identified. The oil crisis of the early 1970s, caused by rapid escalation of crude oil prices by Middle-Eastern countries, led to a slump in demand and a period of rapid inflation, and changed the balance between supply and demand. At the same time consumer attitudes were changing. Consumer awareness was being raised and this led to the start of the consumer and environmental movements. Organizations such as Greenpeace and Friends of the Earth became prominent and the power and influence of multinational corporations became a source of concern and even a focus of protest that still continues today.

Case history

The Ford Pinto

One of the early and very well-known examples of consumer activism and corporate social responsibility concerns the case of the Ford Pinto. This model of car was produced by Ford in the USA but developed a reputation for catching fire in rear-end collisions. These caused the fuel tank to rupture allowing the spillage of fuel. The Pinto had been quickly rushed into production in order to compete with smaller and more fuel-efficient European vehicles. Ford were keen to get the product to market as quickly as possible and although alternative designs of fuel tank were available the decision was taken not to change the design in order to save costs and time to market, even though pre-production testing had demonstrated this weakness. Ford then defended their position for eight years before eventually new legislation was brought in to enforce higher safety standards. The image and reputation of Ford were seriously damaged by the revelation that a cost benefit analysis had been conducted with respect to the cost of inserting a flexible liner into the fuel tank, at a cost of approximately $11 per vehicle, which was compared with the

costs associated with loss of life and injuries as a result of accidents. These figures showed that this modification would have saved on average 180 deaths a year. However, on this basis it had been concluded that it was not cost-effective to modify the fuel tank. The Pinto case is now regarded as a classic example of consumer rights and what is now known as corporate social responsibility.

Source: motherjones.com and published sources.

Relationship marketing

Changes in the pattern of demand, the balance between supply and demand, consumer attitudes, the rise of service businesses and changes in the technological and business environment generally led Wensley (1995) to say that 'the basic micro economic framework... Should not be seen as an adequate description of the analytical and processual complexities in specific situations'. This was echoed by other commentators (e.g. Brady and Davies, 1993) who were critical of the contribution that marketing was making to business success. The Contemporary Marketing Practice Group (see Brookes and Palmer, 2004) have been researching the nature of relationship marketing practices and have concluded that there are five major drivers of change (Brookes and Palmer, 2004):

1. The requirement for increased financial accountability, and focus to loyalty and customer value management
2. The increasing emphasis on service aspects of all products
3. Organizational transformation to reduce costs and increase service
4. Increasing retailer power and the role of systemic relationships within networks
5. The rise of interactive media, the need for mass customization.

These changes in the business environment have a wide range of implications for marketing practice (Table 4.1).

Table 4.1 Implications for marketing practice

Business environment	Customer
o Increasingly global nature of competition	o More sophisticated
o More demanding legislative requirements	o Lower brand preference
o Increasing social awareness	o Market saturation
	o Inelastic demand
	o Increased price sensitivity
Industry	**Company**
o Technology maturity	o Potential to maintain return on investment
o Overcapacity	o Limited resources
o Stabilization of production methods	o Little opportunity for differentiation
o Technology and cumulative experience common	o Increase in private label
o Stabilization and concentration of market shares	o Product modification rather than innovation

Source: Brookes and Palmer (2004).

Whilst relationship marketing exists as a number of different forms and ideas, as Buttle (1996) says, it has yet to acquire 'uncontested status and meaning', however there is widespread understanding of the definition proposed by Gronroos (1990):

The role of relationship marketing is to identify, establish, maintain and enhance relationships with customers and other stakeholders, at a profit, so that the objectives of all other parties involved are met; and that this is done by a mutual exchange and fulfilment of promises.

This definition introduces a number of important ideas. Firstly, that the role and purpose of the firm is to serve stakeholders other than just customers. Christopher, Payne and Ballantyne (1991) developed a multiple markets model and suggested that marketers should address the needs and requirements of each of these markets. These could include not just customers but consumer groups, pressure groups, consultants, financial analysts, journalists and many others who can influence the business environment in which the firm operates.

Figure 4.2 Multiple markets model
Source: Christopher, Payne and Ballantyne (1991)

The definition of relationship marketing also emphasizes the need to deliver profit. Finally, Gronroos's definition also discusses the exchange and fulfilment of promises. In other words, there are expectations placed upon the various participants or stakeholders in the rather more complex markets of today.

Marketing therefore has to address and resolve more complex problems in today's business environment, in particular, financial accountability and management of reputation in the wider community. The next sections will look at accounting issues, shareholder value, corporate and social responsibility (CSR) and business ethics and will also consider practical matters of implementation.

Accounting systems and value added

It is increasingly important, if not essential, that marketers are financially literate with a sound understanding of the balance sheet, profit-and-loss account and funds flows statement. If marketers are to demonstrate their accountability they must be able to communicate in terms that are relevant to other functional specialists within the company. This section discusses these terms and how they may be understood.

Performance and financial accounting

Whilst the primary tools of financial accounting – the balance sheet, profit-and-loss account and funds flows statement – must be understood together with how they can be used to generate insightful management information, these tools inevitably have some shortcomings.

Commonly business performance is judged according to 'profit', generally taken to be earnings before interest and tax (EBIT) as shown on the profit-and-loss account. Doyle (2000) discusses several reasons why measuring performance mainly or solely by earnings alone can be misleading, he distinguishes between earnings and cash generation.

Arbitrary figures

Whilst strict rules apply as to how the various elements that make up the statutory account can be treated there is nonetheless the opportunity to treat items in a number of different ways, by different but still acceptable accounting methods. Numerous items can be treated in such ways each of which may still be regarded as acceptable practice. These could include depreciation, valuations of stock and work in progress, and the treatment of items as either exceptional or extraordinary just as a few examples. Add to this the various incentives that may apply to managers via their bonus calculations, this can lead to alternative interpretations of earnings. Whilst earnings can be adjusted in these various ways, cash is much more tangible. As Doyle says, 'profits are an opinion, cash is a fact'.

Activity 4.1

Lucent Technologies was a dynamic growth stock associated with the dot.com boom of the late 1990s. The company reputation and share price was severely impacted by a profit warning that was not anticipated by analysts and brokers. Visit this website http://www.fool.com/specials/2000/sp000113lucent.htm which gives some insight into the 20 per cent decline in profits experienced by Lucent. This was largely associated with the difference between 'booked sales' and 'collected sales'. Whilst sales were reported, payment terms were such that the cash had not been received. With the extended payment terms offered this exaggerated the problems. Lucent had also seen an increase in the size of inventory, tying up working capital and reducing cash flow.

Capital

A surprisingly large proportion of newly established businesses go bankrupt not because of lack of profitability, but because of lack of cash. Earnings may be positive and indeed growing, but if in order to fund growth it is necessary to incur higher levels of fixed capital investment, in production capacity for example or working capital, perhaps in stock or trade debtors, then cash flow can become problematic and the company can experience reduced or negative cash generation and as a consequence liquidity problems. Earnings do not equate with cash generation.

Time value of money

Similar earnings over time can represent a reduction in value. This is because revenues generated over time have different values. A hundred dollars today is worth more than $100 in a year's time. To adjust for the time value of money interest is added on to current-day values, similarly future anticipated revenues are discounted back to give a present-day value. Whilst we might use the same unit of currency – the dollar or Euro for example – this can be quite deceiving as if the currency unit is the same we may be tempted to think that the value is also the same. If we were to use different currencies then we would apply an exchange rate as we compare one revenue stream with another. Similarly if we are to compare a year 1 dollar for example with a year 5 dollar then we have to adjust for the difference in value, not with an exchange rate but by means of interest or discount rates. Financial accounts do not take the time-based value of money into account and hence it is necessary to consider the anticipated future income stream that will be generated from a present-day investment in order to understand if the investment truly represents a sound return for shareholders. Discounted cash flow techniques are used for these purposes.

Return on investment

Clearly if earnings are subject to some arbitrary assumptions then any consequent calculations such as return on investment can also be misleading. This can be compounded by the fact that the calculation of the investment itself is also open to a degree of interpretation. The depreciation policy will affect the asset value and if assets are depreciated to a low level then the return on investment can look rather more attractive. However a competitor using similar equipment may in fact be performing to a higher standard yet show a lower return on investment due to differences in the way that assets are treated. This can be particularly problematical with companies that have intangible assets that cannot be valued for balance sheet purposes. These would include brands and intellectual property, or even the human resource of the business that walks out of the door every evening, hopefully to return the next day. Evaluating the performance of such businesses using conventional ratio and financial analysis becomes problematic.

Historical perspective

The financial accounts of the business are based on past performance and hence past decisions. The future value of a business will depend not on decisions that have been taken, but on decisions that will be taken now and in the future. Calculations based around historical earnings may not be in the least helpful in understanding future returns.

Value added

Using earnings as the primary measure of performance can be problematic. Its use encourages a short-term approach and does not necessarily give good insight and understanding as to the future potential for the business. Also a focus to earnings ignores to some extent the valuable role of cash and does not take into account the full cost of capital employed in the business. Tools such as the Boston Matrix help us to understand the importance of cash management, with the 'Cash Cows' generating cash for investment in the 'Problem Children' otherwise known as 'Question Marks'. When looking at the profit-and-loss account, we can see that interest on borrowings is allowed for but not the cost of shareholder capital. Shareholders will be evaluating investment alternatives in order to decide where to invest to get the best return on their funds compared to the risk involved. Hence greater insight into cash generation and returns after allowing for the full cost of capital is important.

If the results of marketing decisions can be expressed in these terms, then they are consistent with shareholder interests. Value-added techniques allow for a better understanding of these factors. This is important for marketers to understand; work by Richard Rumelt (1991), an American

academic, looked at how profitability could be explained. He found that the majority of variation in profit was caused by business unit-specific effects – the decisions that managers make within firms (Table 4.2).

Table 4.2 Sources of variation in profit

	% Variation in profit explained
Corporate ownership	0.8
Industry effects	8.3
Cyclical effects	7.8
Business unit effects	46.4
Other unexplained	36.7

Source: Rumelt (1991), see also Kay (1993).

This may seem odd at first glance as we intuitively seem to know that pharmaceuticals as an industry is more profitable than steelmaking. What Table 4.2 suggests is that within the industry there is much greater variation in profitability between pharmaceutical companies themselves than there is between these two industries.

There are a number of related ways to express the outcome of marketing decisions and actions, which will be considered in the next sections.

Cash flow

Cash flow calculations have been used for many years, for example when considering new product development or new business projects. Companies may well compare product or project potentials based on the anticipated net cash inflow. The future cash stream is discounted back using discounted cash flow (DCF) techniques in order to give a net present value (NPV). For example, a pharmaceutical company may discriminate between two potential new products based on their likely future performance. Hence strategic decisions are made by looking forward and using value-based techniques to guide management decision.

Economic value added

Whilst economic value added and cash flow techniques are very similar, indeed they can provide the same estimate of performance outcomes, they differ in detail. A particular problem with cash flow calculations is that they do not give easily comparable measures of performance. They may be useful to evaluate specific projects but managers may require a more universal measure of performance. It is also possible for a firm to be generating value whilst creating a negative cash flow. This would be the case for a new business start-up, for example, where high levels of investment are required in fixed and working capital.

Obtaining more capital, however, can compensate for the negative cash flow. Doing this increases the amount of capital used in the business, it also increases the cost of capital employed and hence can reduce the added value. Economic value added takes into account the cost of the capital used in the business and hence gives insight into whether value is created or not to give a measure comparable across businesses. As Doyle (2000) says, 'the level of cash flow does not provide information about whether a strategy has created value; economic profit does'.

103

Capital can be obtained from two main sources. Capital which is owned by the company is known as Equity. Most companies have to borrow additional capital as well and therefore incur debt. Borrowing money will require the company to repay the debt and pay interest. The interest rate will depend on the level of risk incurred and the lenders' expectations of returns, and this equates to the cost of capital. Interest is the cost incurred when borrowing money. Almost invariably the cost of debt will be higher than that for equity. Therefore it is necessary to calculate the weighted average cost of capital (WACC) in order to take account of the differing proportions of debt and equity funding and the different rates of interest that would apply.

Economic value-added calculations are often used to look at year-on-year changes in value generation. These calculations also have a role to play in determining executive remuneration packages. Hence in this way managers are motivated to create value rather than increase earnings.

Activity 4.2

EVA is the acronym for economic value added, and is also the registered trademark of Stern Stewart, an American firm of consultants. Visit their website http://www.sternstewart.com/evaabout/whatis.php to find out more about economic value added.

Shareholder value added

This is another variation on the theme of managing value creation and future expectations rather than by using historical earnings, and is closely related to the previous techniques discussed. The late Professor Peter Doyle contributed greatly to our understanding in this area and his book is an invaluable source of reference (Doyle, 2000). In calculating shareholder value, this can be considered as a combination of the cash flow and economic value-added techniques. Shareholder value considers the discounted cash flow of the future income stream of a marketing strategy and considers its economic value by allowing for the cost of capital. A strategy will create value by producing returns that exceed the cost of capital. We can make above average returns by offering products to customers that give a differential advantage. Whilst the term 'sustainable competitive advantage' is often used, it does beg the question as to how long the advantage can be sustained for? As a consequence, an important aspect of calculating shareholder value added concerns the period for which we can expect to obtain an advantage. This period is known as the forecast period, and subsequently when the advantage diminishes we can then expect returns beyond this to return to levels set by market competition. This is known as the continuing value period. This occurs when competitors have reduced our returns to around the cost of capital. This means that even if we make further investments whilst we might increase revenues, it will not necessarily increase value. If the firm cannot recover through the price mechanism, any increases that are due to inflation or other cost increases, then shareholder value will actually decrease in the longer term.

Strategies to develop shareholder value

Product

Peterson (2004) tells us that there are six sources or drivers of added value:

1. *Economies of scale* – as output increases this introduces efficiencies in production and also learning effects whereby better techniques and processes are developed.
2. *Economies of scope* – this is where an investment, such as a research laboratory, for example, can support not just the original activity but others in addition.

3. *Cost advantages* – sometimes known as first-mover advantages, where those who are first into a market have the opportunity to build brands and relationships, gain best access to distribution channels, etc. and hence increase the cost to others who wish to enter the market and compete.
4. *Product differentiation* – the more effectively a product can be differentiated, perhaps by the use of patents or brand name, the greater the opportunity to increase revenue and sustain margins.
5. *Access to distribution channel* – when product differentiation diminishes, particularly in mature markets, then access to and control of distribution channels is an effective form of competition.
6. *Government policy* – changes or increases in regulation can affect the perceived attractiveness of a market and may act to reduce the number of competitors.

It is these drivers of value that enable firms to develop differential and even sustainable competitive advantage. Without a source of competitive advantage a company will find it to be extremely difficult to develop and sustain value generation above the average weighted cost of capital. When considering the development and implementation of marketing strategy, Doyle (2000) identifies a number of different types of drivers. These form the basis on which enhanced cash flow and value added can be generated (Table 4.3).

Table 4.3 Devising and implementing marketing strategies

	Financial value drivers	**Marketing value drivers**	**Organizational value drivers**
Use these drivers to	Set objectives around:	Devise strategies based on:	Implement in practice using:
	Sales growth	Selecting attractive markets	Skills
	After tax operating margin	Opportunity to create differential advantage	Systems
	Level of investment needed	Ability to build on assets, brands, customer loyalty and relationships	Motivation
			Leadership

Source: After Doyle (2000).

This insight and understanding of shareholder value added complements our current understanding of marketing strategy development. In practice, most companies will have a range or perhaps several ranges of products, with managers striving to improve both profitability and value generation. If we consider the well-accepted portfolio management tool, the Boston Matrix, it can be seen how the concepts of shareholder added value can be interpreted in practice (Figure 4.3).

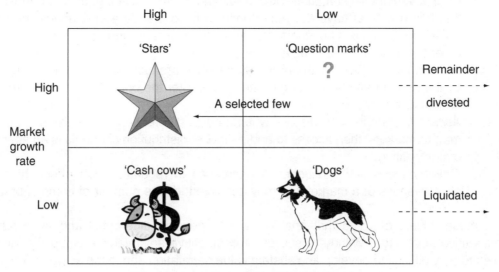

Figure 4.3 The Boston Matrix and shareholder value

The Boston Matrix enables the application of the principles discussed above to be applied in practice:

o *Question marks* – these are products that are approaching commercialization or have just been launched. In considering these products we are interested in the opportunity to generate revenues which can then be discounted and considered in terms of NPV. However the relative size of NPV for products competing for investment purposes is just one factor. We also need to consider the timing, degree of risk and duration or sustainability of competitive advantage to enable premium margins. Another important factor is the degree of investment that is required to bring the product to market. Whilst the shareholder value generated may be attractive, the amount of investment required may suggest that an alternative product requiring a lower initial level of investment is more attractive. Similarly, the earlier, higher and more reliable the income stream from products coming to market, the more attractive they become.

o *Rising stars* – these are products that have gone through the early phase of the life cycle and are rapidly gaining market share. It is important that these products establish early and high levels of market share, as when markets mature and become more competitive market share is generally more difficult to gain. Investment will still be required, perhaps brand support, the development of the product range or additional routes to market. Products in this phase of development are regarded in portfolio theory as being cash neutral.

o *Cash Cows* – as their name implies these mature products have a valuable role to play in generating cash to reinvest elsewhere in the business. In principle, investment should be minimized as differentiation diminishes and the value generated from these products approaches the cost of capital.

o *Dogs* – within the product portfolio dogs need to be carefully managed in order to avoid dilution of earnings. This occurs when the value added by the product falls below the cost of capital and acts to dilute overall returns. In practice many companies define a required rate of return known as the 'hurdle rate', below this level value generation is regarded as unacceptable. Eliminating dogs from the range poses many practical problems as by this stage they are very familiar to customers who may buy these types of problem together with others that generate greater value.

Price

The price at which products are sold is the means whereby the added value, so carefully generated by marketing strategies, is divided between the buyer and the seller. Price is the means whereby that division of value is made. Higher value generally means that a higher price can be achieved. Price can be considered in two main ways:

1. *Perceived price* – this reflects the positioning of the products in the market place. By understanding how the brand or reputation of the company is understood by buyers, products can be appropriately positioned to capture value. For example, the Swatch Group has a number of different brands of watches, e.g. Swatch, Tissot and Omega, that are positioned at different price points in the market to match the perception of the product generated by the communications strategy.
2. *Value in use* – commonly seen as a factor more often associated with business-to-business markets where buyers make trade-offs between the value offered by the product and the price at which it is sold. A buyer may well be prepared to pay a higher price if, consequently, greater value is offered.

In order to optimize the pricing decision it is important to know the characteristics of the customers who purchase the products, the circumstances surrounding its use and the value they obtain from it. Our understanding of the market is usually derived from segmentation, where we divide the market place into groups of customers with similar characteristics. For example, business travellers may be prepared to pay more for airline flights that offer greater convenience and higher levels of in-flight service at higher prices, whilst families who are travelling on holiday may look for a cheaper price. If we can understand the circumstances of use concerning how products and services are used, then this helps us to improve the value that we are able to offer customers and capture for ourselves. Airlines now have sophisticated yield management software programmes in place in order to enable them to optimize the match between capacity and demand.

Activity 4.3

Visit the websites of some of the well-known, low cost airlines such as easyJet (http://www.easyjet.co.uk/en/book/index.asp), Ryanair (http://www.ryanair.co.uk) and Air Berlin (http://www.airberlin.com/site/index.php?LANG=eng). Investigate the cost of travelling to a popular weekend break destination, such as Barcelona, at a weekend and during mid-week and at less popular and convenient times. Also visit the websites of several of the 'flag carriers' or national airlines, such as British Airways (http://www.britishairways.co.uk/travel/globalgateway.jsp/global/public/en_) and Lufthansa (http://cms.lufthansa.com/pre/de/en/homepage_Noframes/0,4449,0-0-605242,00.html), and compare prices.

Promotion

Those managers who are not familiar with the practice of marketing may ask how promotional expenditure, often a substantial element of the marketing budget, can be reflected in sales. This subject does not resolve itself into simple cause-and-effect relationships, and it is difficult to provide such categorical assurances and explanations. This is an area that requires skill and judgement and in attempting to forecast financial outcomes the only certainty is that the forecast is likely to prove wrong. However this does not mean that promotional spend should be incurred without a clearly defined understanding of what is to be achieved and how this leads to greater value.

In recent years there has been a significant trend from above-the-line promotion (advertising, posters, etc.) to below-the-line activities (sales promotion, direct mail, etc.). Following this trend it is now easier to devise a series of measures of the effectiveness of the expenditure. For example, in the mid-1990s, Porsche Cars Great Britain Ltd directed their spend into well-targeted activities based around a deep and insightful understanding of the customer buying process. Each element of the promotional activity was designed to develop and qualify the prospective purchaser. By adopting a process-orientated approach it was possible to measure each element of the process and then seek to improve it. In this way the cost of a direct mail campaign could be understood and the value gained from it tracked through to the number of replies and ultimately sales achieved.

Wherever possible the objectives for promotional activity should be stated in quantifiable terms and linked through to improved value. Doyle (2000) summarizes these linkages in this way (Table 4.4):

Table 4.4 Promotion and added value

Improve value added by	Demonstrate how promotional activity influences
Increased cash flow	Sales growth
	Price premium
	Increased brand loyalty
Accelerated cash flow	Faster market penetration
Extended duration of cash flow	Brand loyalty and premium
Reduced risk to cash flow	Brand loyalty

Source: After Doyle (2000).

Place

Distribution channels, routes to market and supply chains have changed dramatically in recent years, particularly since the use of the Internet has become more widespread. This has enabled many companies to streamline their operations by bypassing or removing inefficient supply chain intermediaries and to move directly to consumer level, even bypassing the retailer. Airlines now routinely sell tickets via the Internet, negating the role of the travel agent who previously enjoyed a commission of up to 10 per cent of the ticket price.

Techniques such as value chain analysis enable managers to make decisions about sourcing and distribution based on the opportunities to create value. By analysing the entire value chain or network of relationships it is possible to take out the cost that does not add value.

Case history

Monsanto and value capture

Monsanto have an outstanding track record over many decades for the development and successful commercialisation of agricultural chemicals for weed, pest and disease control. A more recent discovery is a product for controlling an otherwise uncontrollable fungal disease of cereals commonly known as 'take-all' – even its name indicates the severity of the disease. The product is highly effective but must be applied to the outside of the seed before planting, and this inevitably means a further processing step in the route to the farmer. Sophisticated fungicides are normally available from specialist advisors, whilst seed treatments have long been regarded as near commodities.

The supply chain suffers the near universal problem of maturity, demand has declined but supply chain members overhang their excess capacity and competition is reduced to a bitter price war. Even innovative new products are quickly discounted and profitability is reduced as it is negotiated away by price orientated end users, and value is destroyed as the technical service package that supports optimum product usage is discounted away. Monsanto's insight told them that processors within the chain were frustrated by their inability to achieve even minimal levels of profitability, yet end users needed their expensive technical advice, provided by field staff employed by processors and retailers. This posed a conundrum as to how to achieve these contradictory objectives. Low prices, minimal margins and poor results in use meant that every participant in the supply chain was dissatisfied to a greater or lesser extent.

Monsanto's response was to fully investigate and understand every element of the supply and value chain, what was valued and where value was created and destroyed, and the route by which products reached the farmer as the final end user. They used a range of sophisticated qualitative and quantitative research techniques and continually reviewed and revisited the data to ensure that their understanding was correct. In addition detailed studies were undertaken to understand the economics of wheat production and take-all infection at the farm level, in the process building up a valuable resource of technical information.

Building on this understanding Monsanto then took responsibility not just for the next step in the supply chain, the conventional supplier/buyer relationship, but for incentivising the whole network to help end users to obtain the best performance from the product. Specialist sales agents used sophisticated computer models to diagnose the optimum treatment taking account of soil, weather and farm conditions; processors were audited to ensure that the product was appropriately applied to the seed, and financial incentives were offered to motivate members of the network to ensure best results. To achieve this the product was sold directly to farmers complete with the technical advice package, network members received fees in return for their achievement of objectives. The overall focus to value generation at the end user level meant that farmer satisfaction with the product was high as excellent results were achieved, and the extra value generated could be divided as incentives between all the network participants.

Initially sceptical of the changed terms of business, but seeing the opportunity provided by a genuinely innovative product, the traditionally conservative supply trade has been remodelled as a result of this customer and value led initiative.

Source: Brookes and Palmer (2004).

Value chain analysis

In principle, Monsanto, the subject of the case study above, pursued the following steps in order to analyse the network of relationships within which they were operating. Then they used this analysis in order to synthesize appropriate solutions. Of course, each case will be different and finding some of this information will pose particular challenges. In some cases there is little transparency with regard to cost, and there may be a reluctance to discuss such issues. However, it is possible to gather information from a variety of sources and to at least estimate the sums involved so that an approximation sufficient for our purposes can be obtained. In principle the process steps are (Brookes and Palmer, 2004):

- *Input cost* – at the beginning of the chain identify raw materials and other costs entering the chain.
- *Process steps* – estimate the costs associated with each process step.
- *Output cost* – ascertain the cost of price at which the products will service is transferred from all leaves that part of the supply chain.

o   *Value creation/destruction* – add up all costs incurred in and subtract from the output cost/price to ascertain the value created or destroyed.
o   *Frictional costs* – as products and services are transferred between supply chain members this may involve transport and storage/processing/administration costs. Identify these frictional costs associated with moving products and services through the supply chain and cross check against input cost to the next supply chain member.
o   *Iterate* – continue until each of the elements of the chain has been analysed.
o   *Identify* – product volumes associated with each step in the chain to give an understanding of the value build by unit and in total.
o   *Review* – findings to identify:

   1.   Alternative, cheaper methods of processing.
   2.   Supply chain members adding more cost than value.
   3.   Alternative or cheaper routes to market.

o   *Estimate* – value capture compared to net value created

   1.   Consider reconfiguration to improve value capture.

This is demonstrated in the following diagram and an example is given in the case history 'Cleaning Up in the Bathroom Sector'.

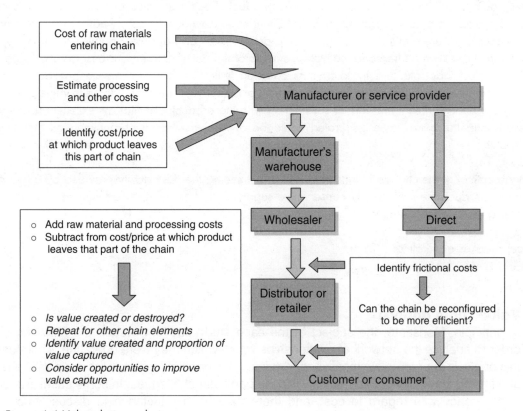

Figure 4.4 Value chain analysis

Case history

Cleaning up in the bathroom sector

A manufacturer of bathroom suites was experiencing unsatisfactory performance when compared to competitors. An analysis showed that this company was more effective at selling their products to builders of new houses, due to their presence in the large builders' merchants route to market. At the same time competitors were better positioned to access the faster growing do-it-yourself bathroom replacement market, due to their strong relationship with the retail 'sheds' – retailers such as B&Q in the UK and Home Depot in the USA. Sheds are a form of 'category killer' in the home improvement sector, so called because they are based in very large warehouse-style buildings. The analysis also highlighted a new, emerging channel – the complete installer. These companies had some high street presence and also advertised in magazines, etc., offering a complete bathroom replacement service including plumbing, redecoration and, of course, the bathroom suite itself. The bathroom suite manufacturer developed new products with greater appeal to the do-it-yourself installer, including such things as high quality taps and complete packs of fittings, and sold these into the appropriate channel – the retail sheds. The retail sheds are large and aggressive buyers and in return for the volume they offer, margins are quite slim. The attraction of the small but growing complete installation channel is the opportunity it offers for enhanced margins. By understanding costs associated with each of their product ranges, the margins available by each of the channels and the volume trends in the market, the company was able to map volume and value by channel and position itself for shareholder value growth.

Corporate and social responsibility

As we have seen with the chapter so far, marketing as a business function must be more accountable within the company and be seen to be delivering improvements in shareholder value. Similarly companies themselves now have to be much more accountable within society as a whole. In this part of the chapter we will understand what is meant by corporate social responsibility and ethics, consider the reasons why this has become such an important issue and finally consider ways in which these principles can be incorporated into our everyday business practice.

Business and society

As with the life cycle of marketing in business (Figure 4.1) we can also see an evolution in the way that business and society interact. At one time consumers may have been regarded simply as passive purchasers of the products that businesses chose to sell. The interface with society was managed by a part of the marketing mix known as public relations. That situation has now changed dramatically, this section will discuss the drivers of these changes, but first we will define these issues in more detail.

A business is a distinct legal entity, businesses exist in their own right and can own assets and incur debt. Businesses exist in all shapes and sizes, from small 'one-man bands', owned and managed by the proprietor himself, to more formally managed businesses that are managed by managers rather than the owners themselves. We can also identify the large multinational corporations, some are now so large that their turnover exceeds that of many nation states. The common thread that links all of these businesses is that they exist to provide a return to the

owners of the business, if the business is incorporated then we refer to these owners as shareholders. Within society some businesses attract a higher degree of interest than others. A nuclear waste processing plant or a manufacturer of cigarettes is likely to attract a higher degree of public interest than a hotel chain or a shoe manufacturing business. However each of them exists in the wider society and it is now generally acknowledged that such businesses have not just a responsibility to shareholders but to stakeholders as well.

Activity 4.4

Several years ago McDonald's took action for libel against protesters who were distributing leaflets outside McDonald's restaurants, which alleged shortcomings in McDonald's products and corporate behaviour. As a consequence McDonald's decided to sue for libel. Several of the protesters apologized and proceedings were discontinued, whilst two did not and a full-scale series of trials ensued. This became celebrated as the 'McLibel' case and the protesters were held up almost as crusaders against the overwhelming power of a multinational corporation. When the verdicts were handed down the judge found that some of the comments which were said to be libellous were actually true, causing great embarrassment to McDonald's. The full story is documented on this website http://www.mcspotlight.org/. The website has now developed a sophisticated focus on discussion and debate by consumer activists addressing not just McDonald's but other multinationals such as Coca-Cola as well. Visit the website and read the story of the libel case. Consider how effective McDonald's were in handling this case; should they have taken the two protesters to court in the first place? How should they have subsequently handled the negative publicity about the case? How can they now manage their relationships more effectively? This also demonstrates how effective the Internet has been in enabling very low cost but highly effective communications, largely uncontrolled and uncensored.

Society can be defined as a broad group of people having common traditions, values, institutions and interests (Carroll and Buchholtz, 2003). But within that society there may be interest groups that represent certain sections of society. With the rise of consumerism in recent decades we can see that these groups have developed significant power as society has become more pluralistic. According to McGuire (1963), 'a pluralistic society is one in which there is wider decentralisation and diversity of power concentration.'

Corporate social responsibility reflects the way that organizations manage and interact with the expectations of society. This applies not just to businesses but also to not-for-profit organizations such as government and charities. The Watergate scandal of the Nixon presidential era in the United States is an interesting early example of this. Numerous models exist to describe these complex relationships, Figure 4.5.

The Business in Society

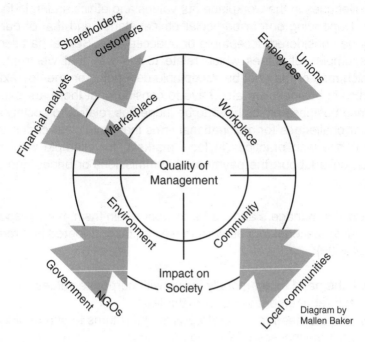

Figure 4.5 Business and stakeholder relationships
Source: www.mallenbaker

Ethics

For the purposes of this discussion ethics can be considered as the discipline that deals with what is good and what is bad. This is closely aligned to morals and moral conduct, which relates to our behaviour and whether it is ethical or not. There is clearly a close relationship between what is ethical and what is legal, but ethical practices may well differ from legal ones and are usually considered to override them. Also the law does not provide definitive guidance about every circumstance in which we might be involved, and then we have to make a decision based on our ethical perspective.

Question 4.1

You have been successful in obtaining an unexpectedly large order for roofing materials for your company, which supplies a wide range of building products. The customer is one who you have dealt with for a number of years and this large order demonstrates their commitment to you and a real chance of getting similar large orders in future providing you deliver on time. The warehouse manager tells you that the product is actually out of stock but he does have a very similar product that would substitute for it. This product is not of such high quality and has a design life of twenty years, whilst the product you sold will last for at least 30 years. The products look the same and the margin on the substitute product is much higher. Your boss says that the customer will never know and that as the product is in stock then simply send it along to the customer. If the customer raises any concerns you only need to say that a mistake was made and that the price will be reduced. This is much preferable to having the product sent back, but it is very unlikely that the customer will express any concern and the company makes a higher margin and the customer gets the product on time. What's wrong with that? What other options are there?

From an individual point of view ethics relates to our core values – the concepts we believe in, the standards that we live by and the views that we hold (Grayson and Hodges, 2001). So when dealing with colleagues in the workplace our values and ethics underpin the way that we relate to each other. Depending on our particular ethical stance and that of our colleagues, certain practices may be considered acceptable or unacceptable. Sexual harassment and workplace bullying are examples of issues which relate to the way that we treat each other, certain aspects of which may or may not be acceptable depending on the context. When considering the role of ethics in business we also have to consider that there are expectations placed on them, and hence business ethics have to be judged as relative to society's expectations. This poses particular challenges for multinational firms that have clear codes of conduct but which may be at variance with practices in local markets, for example with respect to issues of workers' rights; child labour; the payment of commissions or bribes and the use of business gifts and hospitality.

Businesses, and the managers and staff who work within them, have responsibilities not just to shareholders but to stakeholders as well; these can be considered in three main ways (Carroll and Buchholtz, 2003):

o   *Ethical* – the need to act morally in line with corporate values
o   *Legal* – the requirement to observe the law
o   *Economic* – the need to generate profits and returns to shareholders, or in the case of not-for-profit businesses to achieve objectives.

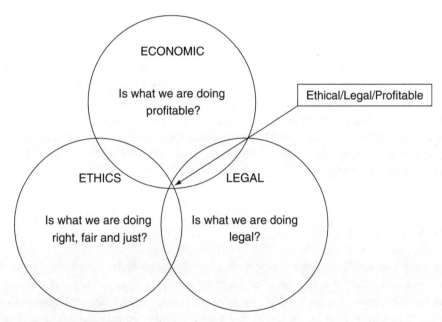

Figure 4.6 Ethical management
Source: After Carroll and Buchholtz (2003)

When considering our business strategy and the actions that we take to implement it, then this serves as a useful framework in order to test the integrity of our actions. Sometimes organizations make this explicit as part of their business processes. For example, a pharmaceutical company will have strict protocols in place to guide experimental procedures with respect to the development of new drugs. These are monitored by external agencies, such as the Food and Drug Administration (FDA) in the USA, who decide whether the proposed experimentation is acceptable or not. Universities and professional bodies often have codes of conduct and ethical committees who oversee and approve the various proposals that are put to them, perhaps with respect to research work or business practices.

Activity 4.5

If you have access to the Internet conduct a search, via Google, using the terms 'code of ethics' and 'code of professional conduct'. From this you can see how professional bodies accept self-regulation by the development of these standards. Consider the similarities between the various codes despite the differences in profession and industry and what this says about the types of behaviour required in professional life. Visit http://www.cim.co.uk/cim/abo/html/memCod.cfm and review the CIM code of conduct.

Each of us as individuals need to consider our own particular perspective on these issues. Here we are not guided by the law or by others, but by our conscience. Family, friends, work colleagues and the requirements of our employer, together with the influence of society and religious or spiritual beliefs, will certainly influence our views. If our own personal view of what is ethical and moral places us in a contradictory position to that of our employer then we face a moral dilemma. Do we conform to the rules and procedures of the organization, which in turn may well prevent us from speaking out on the issue of concern, or do our personal values and beliefs override our commitment to our employer? Those who do speak out in this way are often referred to as 'whistleblowers', some organizations now have a policy in place to enable individuals to express their disagreement or concerns with the policies and procedures of the business.

The increasing importance of CSR

There are many reasons that can be identified as to why corporate and social responsibility has risen so quickly up the business agenda, these can be summarized as:

○ *Technology* – information and communications technology has developed exponentially in recent years. This has not only enabled the rise of the global, multinational corporation but also given individuals unprecedented access to information by means of the Internet. There is a much higher degree of visibility and exposure of business actions. Now it is even possible to observe military action by means of video cameras showing what is happening in real time. Technology has delivered similar advances in the areas of production, manufacturing, medicine, transport and in many other ways that affects the lives of individuals.

○ *Globalization* – the rise of technology, the lower cost of international communications, travel and trade and changes in the world order together with the collapse of communism has seen globalization and liberalization develop alongside each other. Some brands are now truly global in their reach and provide icons of desire or disgust depending on your perspective. This has enabled the trend for manufacturing to move from high wage, Western economies to lower-cost Pacific rim countries and China. India is rapidly emerging as a services provider with a high level of education and English widely spoken.

○ *Affluence and education* – has led to a society that is much more questioning of business and demanding of rights with clearly communicated expectations. Pressure groups now have the power to confront the largest companies in the world and the purchasing power of individuals can be used to directly influence companies alongside other forms of direct and indirect action.

○ *Rights and entitlement* – there is now an increasing trend for society to be aware of its rights, with numerous pressure groups representing increasingly fragmented groups. Each of these groups considers that they have an entitlement to certain privileges. At the same time it has been suggested that those who do not receive their anticipated entitlements are therefore victims giving rise to the victimization philosophy.

The case for CSR

If we are to consider whether the issues of CSR are relevant to a particular organization, this can be considered from two perspectives. First, the degree to which the organization, or rather the people employed by the organization, feel that there is a requirement to acknowledge their moral and ethical status. Secondly the factors which could be taken into account when considering the importance and relevance of the issue to the organization.

The managerial drivers of ethical behaviour can be considered as spanning a continuum from on the one hand the fear of punishment for acting inappropriately to the other extreme of doing right because it is fair and just to do so (Figure 4.7).

Figure 4.7 Continuum of moral behaviour

Kohlberg (1973) developed a stage analysis of moral behaviour from his research into the area. He identifies three levels of development and two stages at each level. This is summarized in Table 4.5.

Table 4.5 Levels of moral development

Level	Stage	Description
Preconventional	'Reaction to punishment'	Conformance to norms in order to avoid punishment
Largely self interested	'Seeking of rewards'	Conformance to norms in order to gain reward
Conventional	'Good boy/girl morality'	Conformance to norms rewarded by acceptance, trust and loyalty
Conforms to social norms	'Law and order morality'	Conformance to wide-ranging social conventions
Postconventional or Autonomous	'Social contract'	Actively seek and work towards individual and social standards
Above social norms to reach an idealised view	'Universal ethical orientation'	Act for social good above conventional norms, enhance awareness of justice, rights and welfare

Source: After Kohlberg (1973) and Carroll and Buchholtz (2003).

According to Kohlberg's theories, the pre-conventional level is the type of behaviour that would typically be considered as immature. Most managers would fall into the central, conventional category where they would understand and want to respond to not just legal requirements but social conventions as well. This would include, for example, observing the common practice of not smoking in public environments or switching off a mobile phone in order not to interrupt a meeting. The post-conventional autonomous level describes the sort of behaviour that might be seen in thought leaders and those acting from a high set of principles. For example, Anita Roddick of the Body Shop is somebody who has built her business around the values that she espouses.

This provides us with a tool to understand where we can position our organization on the continuum, the second issue to discuss and summarize is whether the organization needs to consider its position and more actively manage the issue of corporate and social responsibility. The arguments for and against this are summarized in Table 4.6.

Table 4.6 CSR – A cause for concern and action?

Why not CSR?	Why CSR?
The purpose for a business is to reward shareholders and not to be involved in wider social issues	Wider social issues in society exist because of the existence of businesses, which have a responsibility to assist in addressing them
Business is not the appropriate vehicle with which to address the wider issues in society	Business is a part of society and it is in the long term interest of the business to be socially responsible
Engaging in wider issues takes managers away from the primary purpose of business	By not being seen to act responsibly society will impose constraints on business by means of regulation and other actions
Business already has significant power and influence in society and should not be allowed more	Businesses employ skilled and capable people who have the capability to address wider social issues
By becoming involved in wider social issues the business takes on costs which should be borne elsewhere and is therefore disadvantaged relative to competitors	By anticipating and managing potential social issues this is a cheaper and more effective way of dealing with them
Managers are employed because of their functional skills and are not primarily suited to engagement in wider social issues	All stakeholders, including business, take responsibility to at least try to address social issues

Source: After Carroll and Buchholtz (2003).

Grayson and Hodges (2001) propose seven steps that managers can use in order to minimize risk and maximize opportunities, this is a useful checklist for practical management purposes:

1. *Recognizing the trigger* – triggers can be gradual or sudden. Perhaps as a result of an ongoing concern becoming gradually more high profile or by a more dramatic circumstance such as an environmental pollution incident. By monitoring the internal and external business environment, wherever possible, triggers can be identified and even anticipated and appropriate safeguards put in place.
2. *Making a business case* – this is based on an analysis of the risks, opportunities, costs or savings. This is then presented as a basis for management decision as to whether action is required. Such decisions should be taken not simply on the basis of financial cost but also consider wider issues such as reputation, employee morale and the effect on relationships within the community. Regular environmental scanning and the assessment of opportunities and risks can assist in alerting the organization to potential issues and in preparing appropriate responses.
3. *Scoping the issues* – following the identification of opportunities and threats these can then be evaluated to judge their importance to the organization. Research and other intelligence can help to inform the assessment of the issues. If these can be expressed in some form of matrix or diagram, this helps to visualize the relative importance ratings (Figure 4.8). This is a useful tool for communication within and even outside the organization. Having identified relative risk this should then be monitored to determine whether it is increasing or declining. It may be helpful at this stage to consult other stakeholders outside the company as their insights and understandings may give a different perspective. Scenario analysis may also help to envisage the consequences of risks increasing.

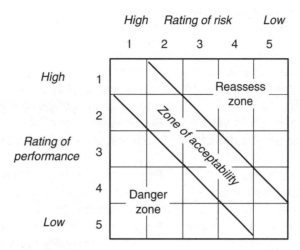

Figure 4.8 Risk/performance matrix
Source: After Christopher *et al.* (1991)

To use the risk/performance matrix:

Identify the risk and score its importance based on a weighting and ranking of individual factors, similarly identify the company response by weighting and ranking each of the various actions that have been taken with respect to their ability to counter or manage the risk. Plot on the matrix. Competitors can also be assessed to give a picture of relative performance. Additional risks can also be added to give a more complete picture.

4. *Committing to action* – once the decision has been taken to commit to a course of action this has the important effect of signalling the intentions of the organization to employees, customers and other stakeholders. It is essential therefore to ensure that appropriate oversight is in place in order that the intended, positive outcomes are realized. This could be by means of cross-functional task forces, involvement of directors and senior managers, use of external auditors and the involvement of other stakeholders; it can even include pressure groups themselves.

5. *Integrating strategy* – by a programme of continual improvement and process development it is possible to integrate what might otherwise be regarded as exceptional project-based activities into routine management procedures. This can eventually become proactive by the adoption of compliance and risk management procedures, regular policy audits and the demonstration of best practices.

6. *Engaging stakeholders* – regular communications with stakeholders should take place, rather than exceptionally when high profile issues arise. In this way relationships and routes of communication are established and understanding is built. This can develop into mutual respect as a consistent and credible policy is implemented. It can even develop into joint activities whereby a range of stakeholders address issues of concern in order that everybody's objectives can be met more effectively.

7. *Measuring and reporting* – developing a number of appropriate measures is an important way of demonstrating progress with respect to an issue; responding to questions that are raised and identifying adherence to appropriate standards and expectations of performance. Appropriate data can also help to differentiate the organization from competitors. Defining what to measure and how it should be measured will depend to a great extent on the context and position the organization finds itself to be in. A number of different codes of practice could be consulted and measures could be set according to the business principles or codes of practice that the organization might have. It may also be worthwhile to involve independent third parties to act as verifiers of the data and to demonstrate honesty and transparency in the reporting.

Summary

Significant and rapid change in the external business environment has changed the way that marketing is perceived and practised in business.

With respect to the internal business environment, marketing must be seen to be accountable for its actions and, more directly, demonstrate the ways in which it contributes to profits and shareholder value.

Profit, as determined by conventional accounting practice, is a relatively unsatisfactory measure of business performance. It is difficult to determine and is open to manipulation, it is also a short-term measure and does not necessarily demonstrate how future profits can be generated.

Shareholder value is a technique that takes into account the cost of the capital used in business and provides a measure by which the economic value added can be determined on a longer-term basis.

Changes in the external business environment mean that businesses must be more accountable for their actions and recognize their responsibilities to stakeholders in addition to shareholders.

The concept of corporate social responsibility recognizes that businesses have wider responsibilities and that society also places expectations on those businesses.

Ethics are determined by values that help individuals to decide what is good or bad, and this in turn guides behaviour which is either moral or immoral. Our own sense of ethics guides us in our everyday actions, but at times conflict with business ethics creates a moral dilemma.

It is advisable for businesses to incorporate principles of ethics and corporate social responsibility into their everyday business practice so that they may better anticipate and manage issues that can arise when differences of opinion and interests assume a higher profile and may affect the responsibilities of the company.

Sample exam question

A division of your company has suffered substantial loss of business due to a fault with a product that has led to the death of a customer. What will you do to ensure sales of your own products are not affected? You have been asked to advise the division concerned on how they should manage this issue. A TV company has just been in touch and asked to conduct an interview.

Discussion

Please refer to the syllabus, element 3 – Implementing the business strategy through marketing activities.

This question suggests that there are significant legal, ethical and economic implications for the business, combined with urgent short and medium term implications. It is likely that the involvement of the media will mean that you have to act positively in the very near future. If the product was at fault and was responsible for a death, how would you establish this? How should the company respond? What assurances and safeguards can be put in place with respect to the associated products? This question calls for urgent action and there is little time for meetings, discussion of alternatives or prevarication. Once immediate actions have been carried out, it would be useful to consider how such a situation could be better managed or avoided in the future.

Bibliography

Anonymous (2004) Leaders: The pause after Parmalat; European Corporate Governance, *The Economist*, London, 17 January, **370**(8358), p. 13.

Brady, J. and Davies, I. (1993) 'Marketing's mid-life crisis', *McKinsey Quarterly*, **2**, pp. 17–28.

Brookes, R.W. and Palmer, R.A. (2004) *The New Global Marketing Reality*, Basingstoke: Palgrave.

Buttle, F. (1996) *Relationship Marketing: Theory and Practice*, London: Chapman.

Carroll, A. and Buchholtz, A. (2003) *Business and Society: Ethics and Stakeholder Management*, 5th edition, Cincinnati, Ohio: South Western College Publishing.

Christopher, M., Payne, A. and Ballantyne, D. (1991) *Relationship Marketing*, Oxford: Butterworth-Heinemann.

Doyle, P. (2000) *Value Based Marketing: Marketing Strategies for Corporate Growth and Shareholder Value*, Chichester: Wiley.

Grayson, D. and Hodges, A. (2001) *Everybody's Business*, London: Dorling Kindersley.

Gronroos, C. (1990) 'Marketing redefined', *Management Decision*, **28**(8), pp. 5–9.

Kay, J. (2003) *The Truth about Markets: Their Genius, Their Limits, Their Follies*, London: Penguin Allen Lane.

Kohlberg, L. (1973) Continuities and discontinuities in childhood and adult moral development revisited, *Personality and Socialization*, In Baltes and Schaie (eds), 'Life-span developmental psychology', New York: Academic Press.

McGuire, J. (1963) *Business and Society*, New York: McGraw-Hill.

Peterson, P. (2004) Economic Value Added, A Resource Site prepared by Pamela P. Peterson, Florida State University, <http://garnet.acns.fsu.edu/~ppeters/value/>

Rumelt, R. (1991) 'How much does industry matter?' *Strategic Management Journal*, **12**(3), pp. 167–186.

Shaw, R. (1998) *Measuring Marketing Effectiveness*, London: Economist Books.

Smith, A. (1776) *The Wealth of Nations*, <http://www.bibliomania.com/2/1/65/112/frameset.html>

Wensley, R. (1995) 'A critical review of research in marketing', *British Journal of Management*, 6 December, pp. 63–82.

unit 5
implementing business strategy through marketing activities 1

Objectives

Syllabus links

Learning outcomes

1. 'Demonstrate an ability to manage marketing activities as part of strategy implementation.'

2. 'Assess an organization's needs for marketing skills and resources and develop strategies for acquiring, developing and retaining them.'

Please see Appendix 4 for full details of the learning outcomes, related statements of practice and knowledge and skills requirements.

Information on the *syllabus element* (and its weighting) that is supported by this chapter can be found in Figure P. 1, in the preface to this book.

Learning objectives

The content of this unit includes topical, management issues in managing marketing, some of which are new to the CIM syllabus at Diploma level. This unit addresses element 3 of the Managing Marketing Performance syllabus, on implementing business strategy through marketing activities. The topics of this unit inter-relate with those in the previous and following Units. At the end of the content on each topic, you should reflect on how this fits with the other topics in element 3 of the syllabus. This unit focuses on elements 3.4 to 3.6, and 3.8 of the syllabus, on brand valuation and brand equity, crisis management, and managing 'moments of truth' and service quality.

After completion of this section, you will be able to:

o   Critically appraise methods available for valuing brands and building brand equity, and recommend an appropriate approach for the organization

o   Propose a contingency plan and procedures to be taken in the event of a 'crisis' or threat to the reputation of the brand or the organization (including communications with the press and stakeholders)

o   Identify 'moments of truth' in delivering a service and activities that may add further value, and assess their likely impact on customers and intermediaries

o   Establish and apply techniques for managing and monitoring service quality, including the use of specific measures.

Key definitions

Brand equity – a set of assets and liabilities linked to a brand's name and symbol that add to or subtract from the value provided by a product or service to a firm and/or that firm's customers (Aaker, 1998, p. 173).

Contingency planning – the advance preparation of a course of action to meet events that are not expected, but will have a significant impact on the organization if they occur (O'Connor, 1978).

Service encounter – service encounters take place whenever customers, whether end consumers or intermediaries, come in contact (or interact) with the organization or its people.

Service quality – the consumer's overall impression of the relative inferiority/superiority of the organization and its services (Bitner and Hubbert, 1994, p. 77).

Service quality is when service delivery (i.e. the perceived service) meets or exceeds customer's expectations.

Study Guide

This unit will take about 4-5 hours to work through.

We suggest that you take a further 3-4 hours to do selected activities and reading in this unit.

Introduction

Marketing has never been more accountable than it is today. Yet the competitive challenges and customer expectations are ever increasing. This unit reviews four topics that address ensuring and delivering marketing effectively.

There are links between these topics. Brand reputations can be damaged by crises. Lack of integration in marketing communications can devalue brands. Service quality depends on service delivery, both in the core service and in any 'moments of truth'.

The linking feature is that these help or hinder marketing performance, and the successful implementation of marketing strategy. Sadly, few organizations can claim competence across the board.

Brand equity and its valuation

During the early days of own labels, commentators forecast the 'death of the brand'. This was rather premature, as brands have continued to flourish. Brand strength is increasingly seen as a function of good brand management. This relies on understanding the value of brands. This section addresses element 3.4 of the Managing Marketing Performance syllabus:

> *Critically appraise methods available for valuing brands and building brand equity, and recommend an appropriate approach for the organization.*

Activity 5.1

Imagine you have been offered the chance to have either the Coca-Cola brand or Coca-Cola's tangible assets.

Which would you choose, and why?

Now try this with your organization.

What does this tell you about your brand equity?

Brand valuation

Interest in brand valuation grew in the late 20th century, mainly as a result of large acquisitions. Companies bought organizations with strong brands for substantially more than would appear fair on the basis of reported assets. Most notably, Nestlé's purchase of Rowntrees, which owned brands like KitKat, Quality Street, After Eight, Smarties and Yorkie, attracted the attention of the media and the financial community. These takeovers showed two key issues:

1. Brands are assets, i.e. something that has a financial value
2. The financial value of these assets can be substantial.

Shareholder value from companies like Coca-Cola comes largely from brands and other intangibles. Yet, the annual accounts of brand owners typically fail to show this. Brand Finance (2000) found that 72 per cent of the value of sampled FTSE companies was not reflected in the balance sheet, and this figure rose to 78 per cent of S&P 500 (the largest US companies) (2002). The growing awareness that this needs to be valued led to interest in brand equity measurement. In some countries, such as Australia, brand valuation is now being introduced into the financial reporting system, although often reflecting financial analysts' requirements.

While brand valuation is essential for takeovers and recommended for annual financial reporting, it is critical for brand managers to improve the performance of brands. Marketers need this data to manage various aspects of the brand as indicated in Figure 5.1. These requirements are different from those of accountants and stockbrokers. Various approaches to brand valuation have emerged to meet these diverse needs.

Case study

Orange

In 1999, the German organization Mannesmann paid nearly £20 billion for Orange, a mobile phone brand that had only been around for five years. Less than a year later, the brand was again sold on, to France Telecom, for £25 billion. In 2004, Swedish/Finnish telecom TeliaSonera acquired Orange and its 605 000 customers from France Telecom for 600 million euros. This demonstrates how the brand value varies, based on an expectation of the anticipated future sales.

Other factors contribute to brand value. In the UK, Orange has high levels of customer awareness, higher customer acquisition rates, higher customer retention rates and higher usage rates than its rivals. Orange is distinctive and differentiates itself from its competitors through high reliability and higher innovation. It is hip and cool for the consumer market, but professional and competitive in the industrial sector. Orange has boosted its brand value by developing attributes and capabilities.

The value in brands

Choosing an appropriate approach to brand valuation needs an understanding of how brands add value and the purpose of brand valuation.

- ○ *Organization value* – Brands add value to companies as they enable them to charge premium prices and to achieve consistent sales volumes. Coca-Cola is not high-priced overall, but it is sold at a premium to own label or minor brands. Customer loyalty is relatively high and has reasonable stability in the market so the urgency (and costs) of finding new customers and channels is diminished. Coca-Cola's volume allows it to achieve experience curve effects, such as having lower cost of sales per unit, and having a strong bargaining position when negotiating prices for ingredients, cans, etc. A good brand has higher trade and consumer acceptance, and so is easier to sell. The top brands find it easier to recruit and keep staff, which reduces costs. All these factors create barriers to entry against competitors, and so give organizations time to respond to new products launched by competitors.
- ○ *Consumer/customer value* – Brands add value to consumers as it makes it easier to choose products. Anyone who has moved abroad how difficult it is to find replacement products for those they valued at home (even in increasingly global markets). Brands help us identify products, and assure the product quality. We know that Coca-Cola will taste similar in different markets, and we know that it will be an acceptable quality. Brands help consumers through their intangible attributes – the beliefs that brands have and that are shared by consumers. For example, there are thousands of pairs of jeans on the market, but many people select between brands on what they believe best fits them, not just physically but emotionally. These attributes give them satisfaction in using the product.

These comments identify core aspects of brand value. Keller and Lehmann (2003) develop this, commenting on the importance of understanding the brand value chain. Marketing programmes aimed at developing the brand have a direct influence on key brand measures such as awareness, associations, attitudes, attachments, activities. Success with the customer is not guaranteed in isolation, as factors such as competitors and channels impact on success. These

factors are called the market place multipliers. These impact on the brand performance, in terms of price premiums, market share, etc., which in turn influences the attitudes of investors. This builds on the importance of brands for investors. According to Kapferer (1997, p.31), financial analysts see that:

> *The brand removes the risk. The certainty, the guarantee and the removal of the risk are included in the price. By paying a high price for a organization with brands, the financial analyst is acquiring near certain cash flows.*

The overall outcome for this brand value chain (Figure 5.1) is shareholder value.

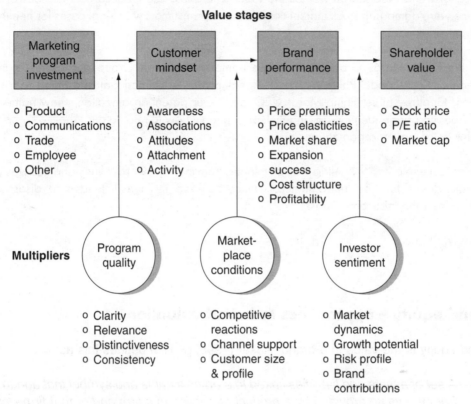

Figure 5.1 The brand value chain
Source: Keller, K.L. and Lehmann, D.R. (2003) 'How Do Brands Create Value?' *Marketing Management*, May/June, Vol. 12, Issue 3, p. 29

Extending knowledge

The Keller and Lehmann article details useful measurement approaches for monitoring brand value chain approaches. Check out the article to add depth to your knowledge.

Case study

Philip Morris/Altria

Some companies share their brand and organization names, such as Kodak, Polaroid, Martini and Coca-Cola or even use their corporate name prominently in their brands.

Philip Morris offered a cigarette brand called Philip Morris, but its best known brand is the market-leading Marlboro. Philip Morris is the largest consumer product organization in the world, owning brands Kraft, Jacobs, Suchard and Nabisco as well as the tobacco brands. The tobacco connotations of the Philip Morris name were damaging stock market confidence, as consumers won legal cases for health damage resulting from smoking.

In 2003, the Philip Morris Group changed its name to the Altria Group, Inc. Altria is the parent organization of Kraft Foods, Philip Morris USA, Philip Morris International and Philip Morris Capital Corporation. Geoffrey Bible, Philip Morris CEO, said 'Our parent organization's new name...should help clarify our corporate identity, making it clear to people how to refer to our tobacco companies and how to refer to the parent organization.'

The organization explained that Altria was developed from the Latin word 'altus', and this was chosen to represent the desire for best performance. Cynics believed this was intended to disassociate the organization from the tobacco brands.

Source: www.altria.com.

Brand equity – approaches to brand valuation

Brand equity is the value in a brand. Aaker (1998, p. 173) defines this as:

> *A set of assets and liabilities linked to a brand's name and symbol that add to or subtract from the value provided by a product or service to a firm and/or that firm's customers.*

In addition to the brand name and symbol, brand managers refer to the brand's personality and values as being central to its brand equity. Apple, for example, is as much about the organization's personality as it is about its products or even its name or symbol.

Aaker's definition is not on the financial value of a brand, showing that there is a difference between corporate or financial views of the brand equity and that of marketers using brand equity to measure and monitor organization brands.

Various models evaluate brand equity. This section reviews these, starting with general models, and moving to more detailed review of proprietary models offered by consultancies and agencies.

Basic classifications of brand valuation identify:

- ○ *Cost Approaches* – fit with financial and accounting views of valuing assets. The essence of valuing assets is normally based on depreciation, i.e., declining value over time. This contradicts the idea that a brand asset is one which appreciates, and does not recognize the investments in the brand over time. These methods commonly use rather simplistic measures of brand equity, such as stating that brand equity is a function of the

age of the brand, when it entered the market relative to competitor brands, how much has been spent on advertising throughout its life, and the brand's current share of industry advertising.

o *Market Approaches* – reflect what the brand owner is prepared to sell the brand for, and a new brand owner prepared to pay for it. This usually takes into account some future earnings that the brand can capture. Alternatively, a market valuation can be determined for public companies through the identifying the market capitalization that remains after subtracting value of assets from total market capitalization. This assumes that you can separate out brands in the organisation's financial statements. A third approach involves benchmarking against another brand for which a valuation has been set. Published brand valuations are relatively rare, and marketers would find it difficult to compare two brands in one market.

Activity 5.2

Assume a soft drinks organization wished to value its cola brand. What are the problems associated with using the cost and market based approaches for brand valuation?

o *Income Approaches* – take the view that brand value is the ability to produce income after tax. Methods in classification include value-added models, where brand equity is defined as the extra that a consumer will pay for a branded product over an own-label brand. This illustrates the power of brand's added value, but is not really valuing a brand asset. Brand licensing valuation details what a third party would be prepared to pay, and the brand owner prepared to accept, as an annual royalty to license the brand.

o *The Economic Use Methods* – vary, either forecasting brand earnings back to a NPV, focusing on the economic value of a brand to the current owner in its current use, which does not address the return to the owner from owning the brand. As such, this does not value the brand for a different owner or any future value in the brand, including brand extensions. An alternative view is a financial forecast, assessing brand earnings, and the application of a discount rate.

o *Brand Strength Assessment Approaches* – are approaches that address a range of factors that reflect the brand's strengths within its market. These are mainly proprietary methods developed and offered by researchers, consultancies and advertising agencies. Interbrand is the most famous of these. These approaches grew in favour as they reflected marketing issues, as well as financial issues.

Interbrand

Interbrand's brand-valuation analysis is reported in the *Business Week*. Its approach, which they claim is the world's most widely used method, is based on an economic model. Many major brand names are its clients.

Extending knowledge

Check out the list of clients and projects on the Interbrand website (http://www.interbrand.com). Also have a look at the articles in its http://www.brandchannel.com publication to gain current insights into branding issues.

The Interbrand approach is based on the analysts' approach of future earning potential. The projected profits are discounted to a present value, on the assumption that the earnings will materialize.

This approach starts by determining the percentage of an organization's revenues from a brand, whether this is almost the entire organization, e.g. McDonald's, or part of this, e.g. Marlboro. Interbrand uses financial analysts' reports from major financial institutions, such as J.P. Morgan Chase, Citigroup, and Morgan Stanley, to project brand earnings and sales for the next five years, and deducts any costs (operating costs and capital) and taxes to determine the intangible earnings.

Other considerations on market leadership, brand stability, and global reach are applied to brand earnings to get a net present value. Interbrand developed a three-year average of after-tax profits to set 'Brand profitability' as a single measure, or as a measure to be factored by a Brand Strength Multiple.

The results of this approach are shown in Table 5.1.

Table 5.1 Business Week/Interbrand brand valuations 2004

Rank			2004 Brand value $millions	2003 Brand value $millions	Percent change %	Country of ownership
2004	2003					
1	1	COCA-COLA	67394	70453	–4	US
2	2	MICROSOFT	61372	65174	–6	US
3	3	IBM	53791	51767	4	US
4	4	GE	44111	42340	4	US
5	5	INTEL	33499	31112	8	US
6	7	DISNEY	27113	28036	–3	US
7	8	McDONALD'S	25001	24699	1	US
8	6	NOKIA	24041	29440	–18	Finland
9	11	TOYOTA	22673	20784	9	Japan
10	9	MARLBORO	22128	22183	0	US
11	10	MERCEDES	21331	21371	0	Germany
12	12	HEWLETT-PACKARD	20978	19860	6	US
13	13	CITIBANK	19971	18571	8	US
14	15	AMERICAN EXPRESS	17683	16833	5	US
15	16	GILLETTE	16723	15978	5	US

Source: http://www.interbrand.com

The *Business Week* brand listing examines brands with a value in excess of $1 billion, and earning a third or more of their earnings outside its home country. It uses publicly available data, excluding some key brands, such as Visa, Mars and CNN, because of availability of unique brand data. This approach is not used for parent companies.

Activity 5.3

Looking at the *Business Week*, Interbrand valuation listing, what factors may account for the growth or decline in brand value from the previous to the current year?

Research International Equity Engine

Research International (RI) is a research agency, whose Equity Engine model identifies brand equity as being a function of the inter-relationship between affinity and performance. These dimensions represent the emotional and functional benefits of a brand to its customers. These result in customers being prepared to pay a price premium and brand value for the brand owner. This model is presented in Figure 5.2.

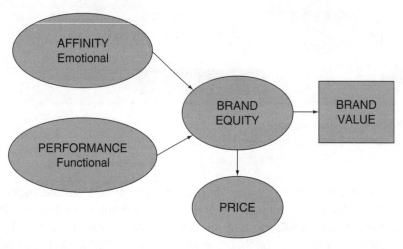

Figure 5.2 RI brand equity engine
Source: Research International

In this model, affinity is defined as: 'the "closeness" of a brand to a person, together with its authority and potential for the individual'. This is measured using traditional brand survey approaches across three basic dimensions:

1. *Authority* – which includes the brand heritage, the trust in the brand, and brand innovation (i.e. whether it is at the forefront of new developments).
2. *Identification* – which looks at the emotional bond that consumers have, whether the brand is caring (i.e. understands the consumer) and nostalgia (associated with happy personal memories).
3. *Approval* – the extent to which the brand is viewed as being prestigious, how acceptable the brand is (in terms of peer views) and endorsement by reference groups of opinion leaders.

Performance relates to functionality, and identifies core and augmented product features, relevant for the category.

RI store results on this in a database, which is analysed and use to predict brand performance.

Extending knowledge

Check out Research International's website at http://www.research-int.com. They publish short summaries of key studies which explain the use of their various brand models in practice.

Young & Rubicam (Y&R) BrandAsset Valuator

The BrandAsset Valuator (BAV) is Y&R's approach to measuring brand equity. This is shown in Figure 5.3.

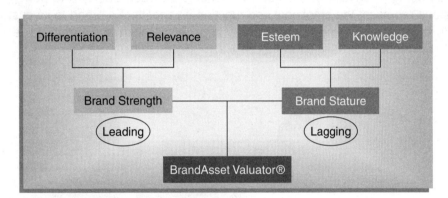

Figure 5.3 Y&R's brand asset valuator
Source: www.valuebasedmanagement.net

The model plots brand stature against brand strength. Brand stature represents the current brand strength, while brand strength is the brand's potential for growth. Brand strength is formed by analyzing differentiation and relevance, and relates to the brand's ability to charge price premiums and fend off competition. Brand stature is identified by combining Esteem and Knowledge, Brand stature declines if brand strength falls. Through analysis, the BAV determines likely future revenues and profits.

The four pillars of this analysis are:

1. *Differentiation* – The ability for a brand to stand apart from its competitors. This builds on the knowledge that a brand should be unique and distinctive, and that brand strength is built and maintained by making and delivering differentiating promises to leverage value.
2. *Relevance* – The brand's actual and perceived importance to a large consumer market segment is termed as brand relevance. This focuses on match of a brand to consumers. This is largely based on household penetration (the percentage of households that purchase the brand).
3. *Esteem* – The perceived quality of a brand and consumer perceptions about the growing or declining popularity of a brand are addressed in its esteem value. Esteem is thus linked to two factors: quality and popularity. This factor varies by culture and country.
4. *Knowledge* – The extent of the consumer's brand awareness and understanding of its identity defines brand knowledge. Brand awareness shows the extent of intimacy that consumers share with the brand. Brand knowledge is built through building awareness of brand values and identity.

Unit 5 Implementing business strategy through marketing activities 1

Case study

Applying the BrandAsset Valuator to Hong Kong

Hong Kong is seen as a brand in Y&R's BAV global database. International business audiences see Hong Kong as having high differentiation, but this is seen as low relevance (as locations are different by their geography and culture). These audiences viewed it to have only limited esteem, as there is only moderate knowledge of the Hong Kong brand in international markets. Proximity to Hong Kong increases familiarity with these attributes, with the highest scores coming from people in the Asia-Pacific region, who rate Hong Kong as a strong brand. People in regions such as Eastern Europe and Latin America consider Hong Kong to be a niche brand.

Favourable brand attributes are that people believe Hong Kong to be innovative, dynamic, intelligent, glamorous, progressive, trendy, prestigious, high performance, but it lacks the friendly attributes that New Zealand and Canada have.

Source: Brand Hong Kong, accessed at http://www.brandhk.gov.hk/brandhk/eresea3.htm.

Extending knowledge

A white paper on the use of the BAV is available at http://www.landor.com/pdfs/bav/BAV_whitepaper.pdf

Millward Brown's BrandDynamics™

BrandDynamics is the first of two brand equity measurement approaches from Millward Brown. It is designed to give a snapshot of current brand equity, data on ROI on past brand marketing investment. This uses the Millward Brown pyramid (Figure 5.4) as a basis of illustrating the strength of relationship between consumers and brands. It has a BrandSignature metric to identify the priority areas for marketing, and a BrandVoltage measure to determine a brand's growth potential.

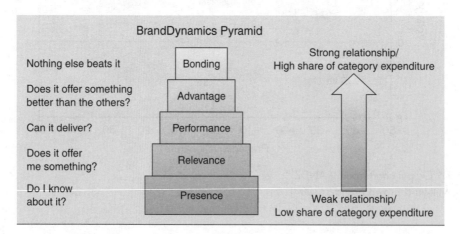

Figure 5.4 Millward Brown BrandDynamics Pyramid
Source: Millward Brown, BrandDynamics

131

Millward Brown's BRANDZ™

Millward Brown launched BRANDZ™ in 1998 to help WPP Group clients analyse and develop their brands. BRANDZ™ is a diagnostic and predictive tool for analysing customer loyalty, and can predict likely changes in market share, based on this. The research basis for this is global, featuring 3500 corporate and product brands, and is based on interviews with consumers across major world markets, including United States, UK, France, Germany, Brazil, Japan and China.

BRANDZ™ seeks to quantify the brand's strength, based on consumers' familiarity and loyalty, based on the brand pyramid, as identified in Figure 5.5. It identifies the factors behind consumer loyalty to determine customer preference and its impact on purchasing behaviour or 'share of wallet'. It allows 'benchmarking' of brands, and brand attributes, so can be used to evaluate co-branding partners.

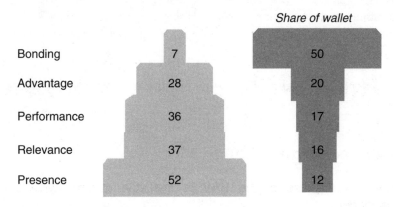

Figure 5.5 Loyalty and the brand pyramid

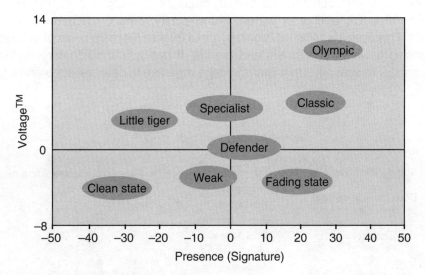

Figure 5.6 Output chart from BRANDZ™
Source: Millward Brown BrandZ (2004)

Extending knowledge

The brochures for Millward Brown's brand evaluation methodologies are available on their website http://www.millwardbrown.com.

Have a look at these to see the benefits and applications of each approach.

Activity 5.4

Using available data, or the criteria identified above, how strong is your organization's brand equity?

How can you improve your brand equity?

Activity 5.5

Millward Brown, Research International and Y&R are all owned by the WPP group. Why do you think these different methods exist?

Using brand equity

Brand equity identifies brand strength, brand potential, brand staying power, what will add to brand value, what will detract from it.

Financial uses

Brand equity measures guide the levels of investment required and its allocation, comparable to that for other business assets. This prioritizes brands, segments, geographic markets, etc., and offers a basis for comparison between investment in marketing, and investment in other areas of the business. Marketers show their contribution to business performance through relevant metrics. The brand value can help gain financial support or funding, or to support share prices.

Marketing applications

Brand equity management allows organizations to check the impact of the changing environment on their brand performance, so enable allocation on those brands with most need or most potential. Organizations can consider their brand architecture (e.g. corporate, product, subsidiary brands) according to the value and customer perception of the brand. Managing brand equity helps determine the answers to a range of business issues. For example, it suggests ways of managing brand values between different regions or subsidiaries, such as internal brand licensing agreements. It can determine which brands should be kept and how these should be managed after a takeover. It can help determine the value of co-branding opportunities.

Evaluating these approaches

The choice of brand equity measure is fundamentally based on the reason for measuring the brand equity. Measures of brand equity based only or mainly on financial measures are limited in their ability to understand, measure and report the marketing aspects of brand value, and vice versa. Choosing the wrong approach would not offer any assistance with managing marketing tasks.

The 'economic use' approaches provide a financial value for brands that is consistent with the principles of current corporate finance theory, and this helps analysts understand the value of brands along with other business assets.

The fit with financial reporting makes these approaches the most common measures of brand valuation. Interbrand has become the most widely recognized and accepted methodology, used in more than 3500 brand valuations worldwide.

The availability of market data and of the brand evaluation measures limits the value of these approaches. Marketing forms of brand valuation require adequate market data, which may not exist in some markets. For example, some service sectors lack such comparative data and some countries do not have sufficiently sophisticated data. This is less appropriate for small companies and many non-profits. The advertising agency models are commonly restricted to agency clients, although other organizations offer similar processes.

Activity 5.6

Which methods of brand evaluation are appropriate, and why, in the following situations?

o An accountant in an FMCG organization has asked you for advice in recommending a measure of brand equity as he believes the organization will be liable to a takeover in the near future.
o A marketer in the same FMCG organization has asked you for advice in recommending a measure of brand equity to help improve the brand strength in the market.
o A IT services provider serving B2B customers wants to see where to invest effort and money to improve the brand.

Case study

Unilever's brand 'cull'

In the late 1990s, Unilever announced the unthinkable – many best loved brands were to go, as Unilever's 'Path to Growth' strategy sought to improve profitability by improving the ROI on its assets, including its brands.

After reviewing its brands, Unilever announced that it would reduce the number of its brands globally from 1600 to 400 and to concentrate marketing and other investment on what it termed as Power and Jewel brands. Focusing on Power brands enables Unilever to improve margins against the other consumer companies against which it benchmarks itself, such as Colgate and L'Oreal. This was deemed an appropriate strategy for profitable growth in maturing markets.

Unilever have not disclosed all criteria for prioritizing its brands, but company reports show that the 400 brands were chosen as they provided 90 per cent of Unilever's turnover, were in categories that were central to Unilever's corporate ambition, were profitable and had future potential for profit (either through the brand or brand extensions).

Categories with high growth potential included tea, ice cream, hair products, skin products and deodorants. Steady, but less dramatic growth was expected in spreads and cooking products, oral products, laundry and household products.

In 2004, the organization announced that it had made significant progress towards its strategic ambitions. The brand approach had resulted in a focused brand portfolio and faster growth in leading brands and it achieved reductions in costs. The total benefit was higher margins and improved capital efficiency.

Initial results were promising, with leading brands accounting for 93 per cent of business in 2003. Unilever now has 12 brands with sales of over €1 billion, while in 1999 there were only four of those brands, and in 1993 there was only one. Unilever has sold 140 businesses with proceeds of €7.3 billion.

In 2004, Unilever reported in 2004 that 'Path to Growth' produced a stronger brand portfolio, with stronger geographic and category positions, markedly more focus and better cost base. Unilever failed to adjust its plans quickly enough, lacked competitiveness focus, and had weaker implementation than was required. Much of this was linked to the popularity of the Atkins Diet, which resulted in 11.4 per cent decline in quarter 4 sales in 2004 in health and wellness category products.

Source: http://www.unilever.com. Wllman, J., 'Unilever thinks the unthinkable to accelerate its growth prospects', *Financial Times*, 24 September 1999, p. 27.

Contingency planning for crises

Organizations increasingly face threats that could damage or destroy their business. The September 11 tragedy showed that organizations need to prepare for the unexpected, and the responsibility for managing many crises is within the marketing function. This section addresses element 3.5 of the Managing Marketing Performance syllabus:

> *Propose a contingency plan and procedures to be taken in the event of a 'crisis; or threat to the reputation of the brand or the organization (including communications with the press and stakeholders).*

Planning for crises

From a marketing perspective, planning for crises is closely linked with protecting the value of an organization or a brand's reputation. The term 'reputation' is critical in managing crises, and this has been defined as:

> *The loss of common estimation of the good name attributed to an organization.* (Booth, 2000)

The good name of an organization is largely based on external perceptions. Routinely, effective organizations monitor and manage of this throughout the multiple market domains. However, crises change perceptions.

A crisis is:

> *an event, revelation, allegation or set of circumstances which threatens the integrity, reputation, or survival of an individual or organization. It challenges the public's sense of safety, values or appropriateness. The actual or potential damage to the organization is considerable.*

Companies manage potential damage to reputations in several ways. First and foremost, they prepare for this by strategically by taking a proactive view that prepares for potential crises:

> *Crisis management is a mindset and process that, on a daily basis, drives a organization's decisions and actions... the goal of crisis management is to help organizations avert crises or more effectively manage those that do occur.* (Pearson et al., 1997, p. 52)

Operationally, crises are managed through contingency planning. According to O'Connor (1978), contingency planning is:

> *the advance preparation of a course of action to meet events that are not expected, but will have a significant impact on the organization if they occur.*

Case study

Yorkshire water

People in developed countries, especially those with relatively high rainfall levels, expect their water to be available from their taps. But, in 1995, not long after UK water industry was privatized, some UK households found themselves without water. A major factor in this was 'leakages' in pipes, especially in Yorkshire. The water shortage resulted in some communities being served by neighbourhood stand-pipes for water.

Local press rounded on the newly privatised Yorkshire Water. MPs debated this issue in Parliament criticizing Yorkshire Water for responding to this crisis in a way that was reflective of a nationalised industry, trying to control demand, when its obligation was to manage supply effectively. MPs commented that people must come first – above profit - and the supply of water must be guaranteed. Their conclusion was that 'All in all, the record of Yorkshire Water is a shambles and a disgrace.'

The company's reputation was severely damaged. Since then it has prioritised managing stakeholder trust (i.e its reputation). From its lowpoint in 1995 when it was considered arrogant and greedy, it has moved gradually to being seen as confident, professional and customer-focused in 2004. Its goals are to move to being viewed as responsible and an industry leading company in the future.

Sources: Hansard, http://www.parliament.the-stationery-office.co.uk/pa/cm199596/cmhansrd/vo951122/debtext/51122-11.htm, and http://www.keldagroup.com/kel/investors/reports/presentations/pres2004/analystvisit/analystvisit.pdf.

Growing importance of crisis management

Crises are occurring increasingly and their potential to occur is constant. Environmental factors, such as the growth of consumer groups and the improvements in communications which mean that news spreads quickly, are adding to this prospect. Poor practices and standards are no longer acceptable, and damage the reputations of organizations.

Crises are a feature of our modern society. Some major commercial crises are detailed in Table 5.2. This table shows the range and scale of crises. Many organizations do not survive such crises, or lose market position. Those which manage crises well may even grow brand strength. Not surprisingly, a key measure used to determine the success of a crisis management approach is a comparison of the organization's financial performance with the overall market for the crisis period (Siomokis, 1992).

Table 5.2 Crises

Date	Organization	Crisis
1978	Ford	A design fault in Ford's Pinto car led to fires, resulting in around 100 deaths and many more injuries. Ford knew of the fault before production, but calculation of the costs of recall vs the costs of paying damages. In 1980, following media criticism, it recalled 16 million cars at a cost of $200 million.
1984	Union Carbide	Thousands died in 1984 and for years after following a leak at Union Carbide's chemical plant in Bhopal. In 1989, Union Carbide agreed a $470 million legal settlement with the Indian Government, settling claims arising from the incident. In 1999, Dow Chemical bought Union Carbide. In 2004, anniversary coverage criticized the company's failure to understand and empathize with the results of this leak.
1987	Townsend-Thorenson	Ferry accident resulted in 187 deaths, after the ferry left Zeebrugge with its bow doors open. The inquest verdict identified that there was 'a "disease of sloppiness" and negligence at every level of the organization's hierarchy'. Townsend-Thorenson is now part of P&O.
1988	Perrier	Perrier's purity was challenged globally, when the product included Benzine. Perrier reacted differently to the crisis in different markets, and gave out inaccurate information in some markets. Later, when the full problem was identified, Perrier recalled product, and reputedly lost $200 million.
1989	Exxon	Exxon's *Valdez* oil tanker ran aground off Alaska, spilling approximately 11 million gallons of oil. The captain was accused of causing the 'world's biggest drunk driving accident', although he was later cleared of this. The *Exxon Valdez* spill is not one of the largest internationally, but had massive global media coverage. Exxon Shipping was renamed the Sea River Shipping Organization and the repaired *Valdez*, *Sea River Mediterranean*, was banned from entering Alaskan waters.
1991	Ratner's	In a recorded and televised presentation to the UK's Institute of Directors, Gerald Ratner compared the cost of his chain's jewellery products to that of a prawn sandwich and stated that the latter would probably last longer. Ratner's chain was renamed as Signet after sales fell and Ratner left the company.
1995	Pepsi	Claims of tampering, with syringes supposedly found in Pepsi cans in US.
	Intel	Flaws found in the new Pentium processor resulted in the organization having to set aside $475m for the costs of replacing flawed Pentium chips. This exceeded its earnings in the previous quarter.
	Persil	New Persil Power detergent criticized for damaging clothes. Unilever paid compensation to claimants in return, and the product was withdrawn.
2000	Coca-Cola/ Belgium	Coca-Cola withdrew products from the Belgium market, amid allegations of poisoning in its products.
	Ford–Firestone	Over 100 people died (with views that the real total could be 250 deaths) and more than 3000 injured by defective tyres on the Ford Explorer, which rolls over when a tyre bursts. Bridgestone (Firestone's parent) insisted their tyres were not faulty, but that the car was unstable; Ford did not share this view. Subsequently, the two companies stopped trading, after 100 years.
2003	SARS	SARS illness had substantial effects on tourism to Asia, and to Toronto. Business and the local economies in these areas were badly affected.
2004	Coca-Cola	Coca-Cola's Dasani brand recalled in the UK, following a controversial launch. Traces of carcinogenic chemicals found in the water brand. Planned launches in other countries were postponed.

Types of crises

Mitroff and Alspaslan (2003) identifies three generic types of crisis:

1. *Natural accidents*, which are outside the organization's control.
2. *'Normal' accidents*, such as those caused by unintentional human errors. These may be in the organization's control.
3. *Abnormal accidents*, which are external actions of evil intent, such as sabotage, kidnapping, theft, bombing, etc. These are outside the organization's control.

A second way of evaluating crises is whether they are:

○ *Discrete events* – such as sabotage or contamination episodes or natural circumstances
○ *Continuous cases* – resulting from bad management or ethical decisions with consumers or the wider community view as being inappropriate, which develop over time (Siomokis, 1992).

Crisis management must prepare for all crises, but the level of contingency planning differs depending on whether these can be anticipated and predicted. Mitroff and Alspaslan (2003) identified that crisis-prepared organizations face fewer crises than the crisis-prone – the former group averaged 21 crises between 1998 and 2001, while the latter averaged 33 over the similar period. Crisis-prepared organizations focus on creating a corporate culture of preparedness for crises, built on trust with stakeholders.

Activity 5.7

Refer to the Yorkshire water case.

Classify the Yorkshire Water crisis using the above categories. What lessons can be learnt about managing this crisis from these classifications.

Case study

Travel crises

In November 2004, an article appeared in *Travel Trade Gazette*, the trade paper for the UK travel industry, entitled 'Prepare for natural disasters or perish'. Little over a month later, the tsunami struck Asia in the middle of a peak period for European holiday visitors in this region.

Many people said that this event could not be predicted, but the idea of crises affecting tourists was predictable. Even so, many companies had no mechanisms in place to deal with customer problems.

Days after the tsunami hit, major airlines were offering tickets to affected areas and some tour operators offering holidays there, without mentioning the disaster. Only a few tour operators, such as Intrepid and Imaginative Traveler, had taken proactive stances, reflecting their involvement in responsible tourism. Online travel agents Expedia and Travelocity gave information about disaster resources and/or donation appeals.

These businesses are less affected than the devastated regions, although some will fail following the tsunami. Destruction of facilities restricted business, but damage to the reputations of these resort areas is potentially longer-lasting. Key resorts are no longer viewed as being as safe, and many believe that all resorts are destroyed. The result is that the tsunami will have an ongoing impact, until tourists' confidence returns.

The crisis life cycle

Crisis development has been compared to a life-cycle, showing changes as the process develops, as indicated in Figure 5.7 below (Gonzales-Herrero and Pratt, 1996). Management's aim is to stop the crisis before birth or prevent it moving to growth (called 'crisis killing'). Failing this, management should seek to prevent a crisis from developing fully, or to bring about a premature demise of a crisis (called 'crisis control'). Contingency plans are required for each stage as crises escalate (Table 5.3).

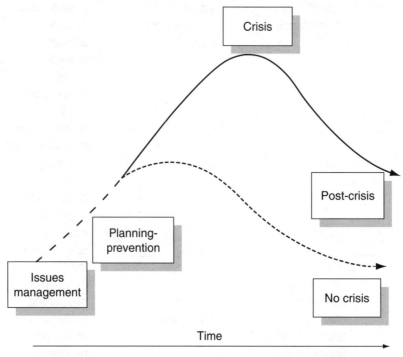

Development of issues with or without management intervention

Figure 5.7 The crisis life cycle
Source: Gonzales-Herrero and Pratt (1996, p. 90)

The key stages in this life-cycle are:

- o *Issues management* – The first stage of a life cycle is issues management, a form of environmental scanning to identify signals of emerging crises. This involves identifying and tracking stakeholders, including special interest groups, and determining priority issues.
- o *Planning prevention* – This second stage is where the issue is developing. Depending on the crisis, this can range from days to years. Typically, at this stage, it is clear that a crisis that may be problematic is emerging
- o *Crisis!* – A crisis emerging means that the organization has either failed to stop a problem, to recognize stakeholder concerns, or to change stakeholder attitudes to them. Activities of

this stage are largely reactive, as issues are either being ignored or denied within the organization or attitudes are already formed internally and externally, and polarized.

o *Post-crisis* – The crisis is over, and the long-term damage to the organization or the product is still unknown.

Table 5.3 Issues in contingency planning in the crisis life-cycle

	Issues management	Planning prevention	Crisis	Post-crisis
Objectives	Stem development of emerging issues	Prevent a crisis developing	Focus on crisis management objectives, prioritizing stakeholders	Rebuild trust
Communication strategies	Focus on addressing issues caused by lack of understanding	Identify key media to be used, and proactively seek opportunities to inform/present case	Use external evidence to support position and change attitudes	Apologize
			Pre-empt negative interactions from non-aligned stakeholders	Make good all criticisms
			Proactively seek opportunities to present cases to stakeholders	
Stakeholder action	Customize messages based on distinctive characteristics and interests of active stakeholders Cultivate relationships with passive stakeholders	Define target stakeholder audiences and messages	Seek information, supporting evidence and third party referrals	Seek to rebuild stakeholder relationships, including internal relationships if required
Internal actions	Identify and take action on controllable issues	Select and brief crisis management teams, including the key spokesperson Identify locations for crisis control, ensuring appropriate equipment	Develop: Spokesperson skills in managing the crisis	Withdraw or amend the product Offer damages or compensation payments to affected parties

		Brief internal stakeholders on issues and crisis procedures, to ensure buy-in and competence	Communication materials (e.g. advertising, video feeds, press releases, websites)	Start rebuilding brand values
				Undertake learning review
Monitoring	Evaluate strategy effectiveness by stakeholder group. Monitor issue intensity	Research stakeholder attitudes	Monitor media constantly	Monitor attitudes to the organization and the brand in key stakeholder groups
		Monitor media coverage of issue and organization	Monitor attitude change by stakeholder group	
Contingency plan focus	Develop plans in case issue cannot be influenced or blocked	Develop plans on issues threatening crisis	Develop plans to limit damage plans	Identifying and avoiding crisis

This life-cycle approach is consistent with other models for managing crises. For example, Pearson *et al.* (1997, pp. 55–57) identify that there are five phases of crisis management:

1. *Signal detection* – looking for warning signals – 'in the best prepared organizations, detecting signals is not left to chance'.
2. *Preparation* – when organizations do what they can to avoid crises, and manage those that occur.
3. *Damage containment* – Fortune 100 companies spend most crisis management resources to this phase, which attempts to limit the spread of the crisis damage. This should be prepared in advance as the costs of providing this service are high, and the processes are difficult.
4. *Recovery* – focuses on short- and long-term plans for the organization.
5. *Learning* – this is when the organization reviews what has happened to ensure better practice in the future. Often organizations want to forget the crisis, and so fail to learn.

Activity 5.8

Deep Vein Thrombosis is an issue that is threatening the transport sector. Assume you are responsible for contingency planning for one organization. What actions should you be undertaking to stop the crisis developing?

Extending knowledge

The outbreak of Foot and Mouth disease in the UK was a major catastrophe for the UK. You may want to read the report on this, and see the extent to which a failure to prepare contingency plans exacerbated the problem.

Check out http://www.warmwell.com/nov20eufinal.html

Case study

Johnson & Johnson and Tylenol

Many consider Johnson & Johnson's (J&J) handling of contamination of Tylenol products as a model of best practice.

In 1978, Tylenol was a market leading painkiller, with 37 per cent of the analgesic market in the US. It accounted for 17 per cent of J&J's corporate income. In 1982, someone tampered with the packs, adding potassium cyanide to the capsules, and seven people died as a result of taking the contaminated tablets.

Initially, all parties were in shock. J&J quickly withdrew all products from the shelves, at a cost of $100 million. J&J sent warnings to doctors and distributors, and stopped production of the brand in capsule form. J&J created triple seal, tamper-proof packs to show customers that the packs were secure. It invested $1 million in advertising over four days, followed in December 1982 by further TV advertising to increase consumers' trust in the brand. By February 2003, Tylenol had recovered 65 per cent of its sales and had about 30 per cent market share.

No one was ever identified as the poisoner, but J&J was not held responsible. Bordwin (1999) says that J&J's rules are simple and relevant to all companies:

'The lesson: be loud, be early, be forthright and err on the side of doing more than less. Show your customers and the public that they are your prime concern and that you are taking active measures to protect them. Convince them that you've corrected the situation and they don't have to stop doing business with you to protect themselves – you're protecting them.'

Source: Bordwin, M. (1999) 'Plan B...Or is it Plan C for Crisis?', *Management Review*, July–August, pp. 53–55.

Extending knowledge

Many consultants offer plan frameworks for crisis management. For example, Barry McLoughlin Associates Inc. (http://www.communicatewithpower.com) and Bernstein Communications (http://www.bernsteincrisismanagement.com/docs/10steps.html) shows how to prepare crisis contingency plans.

Case study

Coca-Cola

Coca-Cola is the world's greatest brand, and many more products bear the Coca-Cola logo. Former CEO, Douglas Daft said:

> *Fundamentally, The Coca-Cola Organization is built on a deep and abiding relationship of trust between it and all its constituents: bottlers ... customers ... consumers ... shareowners ... employees ... suppliers ... and the very communities of which successful companies are an integral part. That trust must be nurtured and maintained on a daily basis ... To be candid, every organization from time to time makes mistakes – including The Coca-Cola Organization. When we do, we face them and fix them ...*

A FMCG product must take action about claims before the crisis life-cycle can develop. It failed to do this in Belgium.

In 1999, Belgium – like many European countries – faced several food scares. On 9 June, customers complained of a strange taste and smell from Coca-Cola products. More than 100 Belgians, including school children, were taken ill after drinking these, many suffering nausea and headaches. Some people were hospitalized from their symptoms.

Five days later, the Belgian Health Ministry decided that Coca-Cola products should be withdrawn from sale in Belgium, and advised people against consuming previously purchased Coca-Cola products.

Coca-Cola's Atlanta headquarters responded one week after the initial allegations, on 16 June, when Coca-Cola's Chairman and CEO, Doug Ivester expressed regret for 'any problems encountered by our European consumers in the past few days'. He identified that 'off-quality' carbon dioxide could affect the taste and smell of bottled drinks, and that this smell intensified in vending machines.

The Belgian Health Ministry lifted its ban on Coca-Cola brands on 22 June, with conditions. Ivester immediately issued a statement expressing 'respect for the Ministry's obligation' to the Belgians, and issued Coca-Cola's first apology, saying:

> *We let down the people of Belgium and we're sorry for that, but now we're committed ... to earn their complete trust in us.*

It was suggested that the Belgian government had asked Coca-Cola to keep the issue out of the media initially. This explained Coca-Cola's silence, but it said it would be 'open and informative' in future. Coca-Cola bought advertising space in press and broadcast media to apologise to the Belgian government and people, and continued this promotional investment for some time. By August, research showed brand preference and purchase intention levels were at pre-crisis levels.

This crisis cost Coca-Cola more than $200 million in direct costs and lost profits. It caused some damage to its brand, not just in Belgium, but in neighbouring countries.

The illness was later deemed to be psychosomatic, and based on an over-reaction to the bad smell, coupled with fears left by the previous food scares.

Sources: Coca-Cola Worldwide Press Statements, http://www.coca-cola.com.

Daft, D., 'Re-building trust begins with us', Morehouse Coca-Cola lecture series, at http://www2.cocacola.com/presscenter/viewpoints_rebuilding_trust.html.

Johnson, V. and Peppas, S.C. (2003) 'Crisis management in Belgium: the case of Coca-Cola', *Corporate Communications: An International Journal*, Vol. 8, No. 1, pp. 18–22.

Managing moments of truth

Organizations increasingly recognize that 'moments of truth' make or break an organization's relationship with its customers. This section addresses element 3.6 of the *Managing Marketing Performance* syllabus:

> *Identify 'moments of truth' in delivering a service and activities that may add further value, and assess their likely impact on customers and intermediaries.*

Moments of truth and customer satisfaction

Managing reputations is especially important for service organizations. Services sell intangibles, through expectations and promises of what is to come. A critical moment which forms or destroys the relationship with customers is a 'moment of truth'. For service organizations, this is the point where the customer and the organization come together.

Jan Carlzon, former president and CEO of SAS (the Scandinavian airline) is credited with popularizing this term for business. Jan Carlzon built SAS into a profitable airline in the 1980s, through a total commitment to the customer, empowering front-line employees, and a flatter, leaner organization. These approaches enabled staff to meet customer needs when they came in contact with customers, as he believed that:

> *Last year [1986], each of our 10 million customers came in contact with approximately five SAS employees, and this contact lasted an average of 15 seconds each time. Thus, SAS is 'created' 50 million times a year, 15 seconds at a time. These 50 million 'moments of truth' are the moments that ultimately determine whether SAS will succeed or fail as a organization. They are the moments when we must prove to our customers that SAS is their best alternative.* (Carlzon, 1987)

These impressions – whether positive, neutral or negative - determine repeat business and referrals. Yet, the diversity of airline passengers, such as business people, young couples, students, families, disabled, etc. meant that travellers had different levels of experience of travel, and expectations of service. As a result, they have different needs, wants, expectations and tolerances. Training manuals and operating protocols cannot identify every possibility.

Until this time, more attention was given to other areas of marketing, such as advertising or product development, which were typically by managers and distant from consumers. Carlzon saw that these factors were less critical in driving satisfaction or referral. Companies' advertising effectiveness could be reduced in seconds by one contact with an employee who did not satisfy a customer. Even loyal customers could be so infuriated by one act of rudeness or inefficiency that they would be lost forever, and tell others of this experience.

The reverse was also true. Carlzon identified that that the organization could make an impact on customers, but often failed to exploit the opportunity. Simple situations like passengers walking past a help-desk could be turned into something that would build customer satisfaction and the organization's reputation.

While Carlzon's focus was on services, this applies to all organizations with customers, whether intermediaries or end consumers. His views brought about a step-change in how traditional airline businesses thought about their customers.

Activity 5.9

Think about a plane, train or bus journey you have made. Identify any moments of truth that have added to or reduced your enjoyment of the journey.

Based on your perceptions:

- ○ Evaluate whether the provider organization shares the views expressed by Carlzon on the importance of managing moments of truth.
- ○ What steps would you take to improve this?

The academic perspective

Academic literature focuses on understanding service quality and its impact on customer satisfaction. Managing service quality focuses on delivering services effectively through the ServQual dimensions identified in Table 5.4.

Table 5.4 ServQual dimensions

ServQual dimension	Description
Reliability	Ability to perform the promised service dependably and accurately
Responsiveness	Willingness to help customers and provide prompt service
Assurance	Employees' knowledge and courtesy and their ability to inspire trust and confidence
Empathy	Caring, individualised attention given to customers
Tangibles	Appearance of physical facilities, equipment, personnel and written materials

Source: Zeithaml, V.A. and Bitner, M.J. (2003)

Managers manage these internally, through definition and delivery of services, but customers also review these. Their satisfaction varies even with consistent service delivery and outcomes, because of other factors:

- ○ *Personal factors* – such as culture or demographic factors
- ○ *Situational factors* – such as the urgency of the need or the importance of the service
- ○ *Price*
- ○ *Service and product quality.*

These aspects are integrated in the model shown in Figure 5.8.

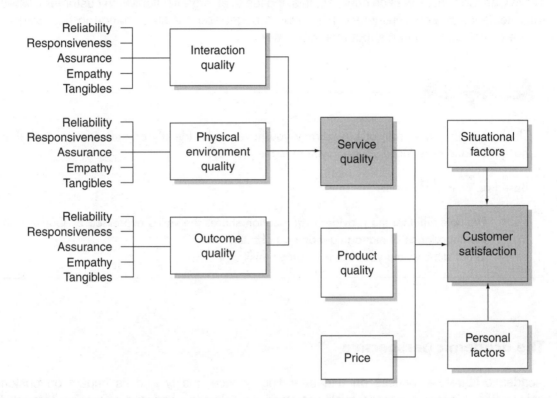

Figure 5.8 Customer perceptions of quality and customer satisfaction
Source: Zeithaml, V.A. and Bitner, M.J. (2003) *Services Marketing: Integrating Customer Focus Throughout the Firm*, McGraw-Hill, p. 85

 Activity 5.10

Does your perception of service change with price?

Do you expect more service from a restaurant that is more expensive or when you pay for a business class ticket?

What are the implications of your views on service delivery and on the physical environment?

Service interactions

'Moments of truth' are referred to as service interactions and service encounters in the management literature. These service encounters take place whenever customers, whether end consumers or intermediaries, come in contact (or *interact*) with the organization or its representatives (employees or intermediaries).

Shostack (1985) identified three distinct types of service encounters:

1. *Remote encounters* – customer contact with the organization is through impersonal means. Nowadays, this is usually through some form of computer interaction, such as people banking through ATMs and websites.
2. *Phone encounters* – whether for enquiries, orders, service delivery and customer service.
3. *Face-to-face encounters* – direct personal contacts between the customers and employees for any purpose, e.g. part of the sales process or the service delivery process.

These three categories are not discrete, as technology has developed since Shostack's work. For example, it is now possible to talk or 'chat' (computer-based contact) to someone through a link on a website, or place orders by phone without talking to a real person. Some situations offer variations on this, such as a service announcement from a pilot or driver on a plane, train or bus.

Technology is often used in interactions with customers for efficiency reasons, as mentioned in Unit 7. This does not always bring improvements from the consumer perspective. Negative experiences of using an ATM include:

o The machine unable to authorize payments, due to the bank's network failure.
o The machine not offering receipts or printed statements, because of lack of paper or ink.
o The area round the machine being dirty, through food or abandoned receipts.
o The machine being tampered with and the consumer losing money through fraud.

Human interaction could address these situations, or at least empathize with customers. Clearly, this places a higher priority on regular service for automated processes than for human ones.

Typically, service experiences have many component 'moments of truth'. A Disney theme park visitor has around 74 service encounters. These encounters are not equally important. The hotel organization Marriott found that most factors with the largest effect on customer loyalty occur during the first 10 minutes of a guest's stay, and so they place attention on the check-in process. Cram's (2003) findings differ, stating that a strong final impression is critical, which is usually ignored by providers. Hotel guests' last impression of a hotel can be the queue at checkout, and the last encounter for an airline is at the baggage reclaim at the terminal. Neither is a value-adding experience.

Clearly, customers combine perceptions of different encounters in a service experience to form an overall opinion. Cram recommends plotting these on a 'moodogram' to show how customer opinions develop throughout the service experience.

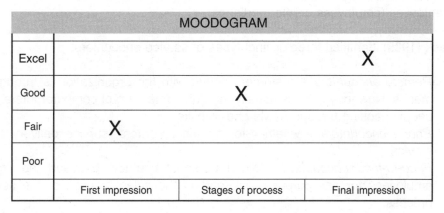

MOODOGRAM			
Excel			X
Good		X	
Fair	X		
Poor			
	First impression	Stages of process	Final impression

Figure 5.9 Service encounter Moodogram
Source: Cram, T. (2003) 'Seven of the Best', *The Ashridge Journal*, Summer

The idea of a service blueprint (Shostack, 1984) is associated with this. A service blueprint is a way of mapping the customer contact points and the necessary processes. The physical evidence associated with the service can be mapped. Mapping this process ensures that management attention is given to the support services for front-line workers at the time of contact. This concept is addressed in Unit 7.

Managing service encounters links to concepts such as the 'upside down' organization, which inverts the traditional organization chart that has the MD or CEO at the top in favour of placing those in front-line jobs at the top of the pyramid. Front-line staff impact directly on service customer satisfaction. They need support from the rest of the organization, including the senior management.

 Activity 5.11

Many service businesses are now using remote encounters:

- o Airlines are using e-ticketing systems
- o Telephone companies have Internet-based fault reporting
- o Retailers have online ordering.

What are the implications of these changes on customer expectations of the quality of the service encounter?

Case study

Emirates

Emirates was formed in 1985, with two leased aircraft. Now, it is recognised for delivering services of consistently high quality, retaining customers' enthusiasm and loyalty, which is evident in the awards they have won in recent years. These include:

- Airport Lounge of the Year – Skytrax The World's Best Airline Lounges Awards 2003
- Airline with the Best Cabin Crew – Business Traveller Middle East 2003
- Best Economy Class – Skytrax Research 2004
- Airline of the Year 2001 and 2002 – Skytrax Research – UK, runner up in 2003 and 2004.

Emirates' achievements are exceptional, given that they compete in a competitive market and against more established airlines.

Emirates' investment in its people is key to ensuring good service.

- It attracts high-quality staff, with attractive benefits.
- It invests heavily in training to enable them to perform to the best of their ability, and empowers them to solve customer problems.
- It encourages employee involvement in Emirates' service improvements through its Bright Ideas scheme.
- It has a Mabrouk (Arabic for congratulations) scheme, which rewards exceptional service and extra effort.

Emirates seeks the 'right' people by specifying the types of people required at the time of recruitment:

Emirates will be looking for confident, cheerful, flexible, mature and understanding candidates, with excellent social skills, and at ease with customers from every country and culture.

The latter point is critical. Emirates has a diverse customer base, and it reflects this in its diversity of employees' nationalities – more than 110 nationalities work alongside each other. This allows Emirates to offer multicultural crews which better understand and meet the needs of passengers from different ethnic groups.

Sources: http://www.emirates.com, http://www.emiratesgroupcareers.com/.

Adding value through service encounters

Jones and Sasser (1995) show that even satisfied customers may not remain loyal if they have no preference or commitment to the service provider. Service delivery must on moving customers from indifference or contentment to delight. Enabling an emotional response drives customer loyalty. Organizations now seek add value to create loyalty. In other words, they are trying to move from delivering acceptable service (moment of mediocrity) to delight (moment of magic). Service encounters offer the opportunity to:

- build trust in the relationship
- build brand differentiation
- increase loyalty.

Service encounters adding more functional added-value components, build the service surround. For example, guests at Disney resorts can take 'character breakfasts' where Disney characters mingle with the diners. Eating alongside their favourite character will remain in children's memories for some time. Other hotels may offer cheaper accommodation or meals, but only Disney hotels offer this added-value encounter.

Service encounters can be developed through the brand ethos. For example, Hard Rock Café, essentially a burger restaurant, whose service ethos are encapsulated in statements such as 'Love all ... Serve all' and 'Take Time to be Kind' enhances these through their brand M&Ms:

- Music
- Memorabilia
- Merchandize
- Menu
- Memories.

These dimensions add to the Hard Rock experience. Even if not receiving personal service, the M&Ms create a service experience. These also form a bond between staff and customers. This combination enables Hard Rock Café to deliver superior service encounters.

Adding values in routine aspects of interaction can differentiate services. Singapore Airlines comment that 'Anyone can pour a cup of coffee, but not everyone can pour coffee in a way that shows they care.' Apparently simple aspects, such as prompt attention, actively listening to customers, calling them by name, showing courtesy and respect all add value and distinguish Singapore Airlines service brand from other airlines and build their service brand. A strong organization service culture supports the service actions.

Case study

The Highland Wildlife Park

The Highland Wildlife Park is in the Cairngorms National Park. It is a paid-for tourist-attraction, and it currently charges £8 for an adult's entry to the Park.

The Park offers other packages with different levels of engagement in the park activities and involvement with the unique collection of animals. For example, one package, which costs £100 for the day, allows people to spend a day being a park warden. These visitors can choose which areas they want to be wardens for (and so get close to the animals they like), and get a complementary Park sweatshirt, staff discount on any purchases in the Park shop, and lunch.

Source: The Scottish Wildlifepark, http://highlandwildlifepark.org.

Researching service encounters

The key approach for identifying service delivery problems and identifying where value can be added to service encounters is Critical Incident Technique (CIT).

According to Johnston *et al.* (1997):

> CIT attempts to identify critical incidents in order to be able to understand customer-perceived quality ... and to help managers develop approaches to its improvement.

CIT is a qualitative approach that focuses on customers' descriptions of incidents that influenced their delight or dissatisfaction, developed by Flanagan (1954). Zeithaml and Bitner (2003, p. 104) suggest the following approach when undertaking CIT research:

- ○ Think of a time when, as a customer, you had a particularly satisfying (or dissatisfying) interaction with _____
- ○ When did the incident happen?
- ○ What specific instances led up to this situation?
- ○ Exactly what did the employee (or firm) do or say?
- ○ What resulted that made you feel that the interaction was satisfying (or dissatisfying)?
- ○ What could or should have been done differently?

A variation on CIT is the Five Whys approach, which was developed by Senge *et al.* (1994). This approach also attempts to understand what led to service satisfaction or dissatisfaction. This is an organizational (internal) review of what happened, and examines internal problems that underpinned complaints. This approach seeks to find the root of the problem, by simply asking 'why?' five times. This means that the focus is not on the symptoms of a system failure, but its cause.

Case study

The NHS and The Five Whys

The UK's NHS is placing ever increasing attention on the application of management techniques to improve service to its patients and community. Amongst these techniques is the Five Whys.

The NHS Improvement network cites the following example to illustrate how the Five Whys work in practice.

'A patient received the wrong medicine

Why?

The prescription was incorrect

Why?

A wrong decision was made by the doctor

Why?

The patient's chart did not contain all the information the doctor needed

Why?

The doctor's assistant had not entered the patient's latest lab test result

Why?

The lab technician had phoned the results through to the receptionist, who forgot to tell the assistant'

This questioning aims to allow management to take appropriate action in this area. In this instance, it is not the doctor's fault that the wrong medication was prescribed, or the fault of the doctor's assistant in not updating the chart. Rather, the absence of a formal system for recording lab test results was to blame.

Source: The NHS Improvement Network, accessed at http://www.tin.nhs.uk/sys_upl/templates/ StdLeft/StdLeft_disp.asp?pgid=1134&tid=144.

 ## Activity 5.12

Think of a problem that you have experienced in your work. It does not have to be a service problem.

Apply the Five Whys Approach. Does this help identify the root problem?

Using research findings

Keaveney (1995) used CIT to investigate why people switched service suppliers. The greatest number of failures reported (44 per cent of those reported) were due to core service failures, such as mistakes in delivering the services (e.g. 'botched' travel arrangements). Some failures were called 'catastrophes' as not only did they not provide the service, but they resulted in damage.

Failures at the 'moment of truth' (mentioned by 35 per cent or respondents) were the second most cited cause of customers switching suppliers. These were grouped mainly under the following categories, uncaring, impolite, unresponsive or acknowledgeable. Some (30 per cent) of respondents cited price problems. Others reported employees' poor responses to service failure, which ranged from no response to a reluctant response, or even responses where the customer was blamed for the problem.

Creating memorable service encounters

Research on service encounters helps identify priorities in service encounters. It also helps identify how to recover from service problems. Zeithaml and Bitner (2003) present four key themes in this:

1. *Service recovery* – is when organizations make good after a failure. Research shows that swift and effective service recovery can create a lasting and positive impression that enhances customer loyalty (Berry and Parasuraman, 1991). Generic advice for contact staff includes acknowledging the customer's problem, explaining causes, apologizing, taking responsibility, offering compensation or upgrades or presenting other options for resolution.
    Service recovery requires understanding causes of problems from both the customer perspective (using CIT) and the organization's perspectives (using the Five Whys). Front-line staff must know about the importance of service recovery and how to implement it effectively.
2. *Adaptability* – is essential to overcome the problems that customers believe stem from the organization's systems. While customers understand a general need for systems, they may need something at short notice, such as an emergency dental appointment or priority cheque clearing. Employees need to be able to recognize and acknowledge customers' needs, and explain why the systems are required.

Managers must determine why these problems arise, and seek to eliminate or reduce these in future. This may highlight aspects, e.g. staff workloads, staff empowerment and internal or bureaucratic barriers, for review. Strategies for managing unrealistic customer expectations might be required.

3. *Spontaneity* – adds to the service experience. Routine processes and instructions lead to service expectation. Often these merely satisfy and not delight. Unexpected staff actions and behaviours are what turn 'moments of truth' into 'moments of magic'. These are often simple acts, such as personalization, offering helpful advice, taking the initiative to resolve a customer problem, or generally having empathy with customers.

   Spontaneity comes from personal skills and attitudes, identified in the recruitment process and developed through training. Listening skills and a willingness to help are essential. Often organizations fail to allow for customers to listen, by setting targets for transaction times. The latter is common in call centre interactions, and is a barrier to satisfaction in service encounters.

4. *Coping strategies* – need to be developed, as often customers cause problems. The focus on customer satisfaction often puts employees under pressure to resolve problems, but within time and cost, and under attack from customers when they fail to meet their needs. Employees need to be able to make decisions and deal with conflict to avoid the situation escalating.

Case study

Thackray Museum

The Thackray Museum in Leeds, England, is a non-profit organization. The museum, originally called a medical museum, looks at how healthcare has developed over time.

The museum has a range of exhibits that are of high specialist interest, but the museum has identified a key role with younger people. It has formed close partnerships with school teachers, and works with them to prepare pupils for their trips. The museum encourages pupils' involvement in the exhibits through playing roles and interacting with different displays. The atmosphere, including sounds and smells, adds to the experience. Interactive displays have sought to build engagement.

School parties are important to the Thackray Museum, but to maintain service quality, it has a booking system to ensure that the service experience of the pupils, and other paying visitors, is not destroyed by crowds.

Source: Thackray Museum, http://www.thackraymuseum.org/.

Managing and monitoring service quality

The previous discussion examined the importance of the service encounter. This is part of managing quality in services. This section examines a range of service quality dimensions to address element 3.8 of the *Managing Marketing Performance* syllabus:

> *Establish and apply techniques for managing and monitoring service quality, including the use of specific measures.*

The challenge of service quality

The academic literature on services marketing developed in the 1980s, and mainly focused on the differences between services and products – the concepts of intangibility, variability, perishability and simultaneity. It shifted focus to managing service quality.

 Activity 5.13

Choose a physical product, e.g. a car, a computer or an item of clothing. What aspects are important in the quality of this product? How can companies ensure this?

Now, choose a service product, e.g. a hairdresser, a management consultant or an airline flight. What aspects are important in the quality of this service? How can companies ensure this?

For each of the key factors that distinguish services from products, identify how these influence or impact on service quality.

- ○ Intangibility (services cannot be touched)
- ○ Variability (Heterogeneity)
- ○ Simultaneity (inseparability; production and consumption are at the same time)
- ○ Perishability (cannot be stored).

Interest in service quality resulted from quality attracting increasing attention in management literature at this time (see Unit 7), and a growing awareness of the problems in defining and delivering quality for services.

Physical products can build quality in the product's manufacturing and design, based on achieving tangible outcomes. This can be managed in the organization's premises. The factors that influence service quality are varied and less controllable. Customers often report satisfaction or dissatisfaction, but the causes of these are complex.

Service delivery and customer satisfaction depend on employee actions; employee–customer interactions, customer–customer interactions or environmental factors. Most factors are outside the control of service providers.

The extended services marketing mix of people, process and physical evidence are not easily controllable in practice due to these other external influences. These are influenced by the ServQual factors, of reliability, responsiveness, assurance, empathy and tangibles, presented earlier in Table 5.3.

Although service quality can be difficult to manage, customers constantly evaluate services. Services which fail to satisfy will lose customers. Retaining customers requires understanding of dimensions that influence the quality of services. Once they understand these, they can monitor and improve the service quality.

This discussion has mentioned service quality, but there is no agreed definition of service quality. Bitner and Hubbert (1994, p. 77) defined service quality as 'the consumer's overall impression of the relative inferiority/superiority of the organization and its services'. Alternative views focus the match of the service delivery (i.e. the perceived service) and the customer's expectations.

Academics question whether quality and satisfaction are the same thing. Quality judgements in other fields are based on excellence, while customer satisfaction in services can result from mediocre service. Judgements on quality are usually cognitive (or reasoned), but customer impressions of satisfaction are usually affective (or subjective and emotional) (Oliver, 1997). Customer satisfaction is often based on an event or issue, such as a service encounter, rather than the more constant elements of a service.

The best service organizations manage service quality not just on the short-term 'moments of truth', but by building quality in their business. Once this is in place, adding quality in 'moments of truth' will help retain customers.

Case study

Vision Express

Vision Express, a retail supplier of spectacles and fashion eyewear, pioneered genuine one-hour dispensing service in the UK. The organization has grown to over 200 stores in the UK, Ireland and the Channel Islands, and has formed an alliance with Grand Optical Photoservice SA (GPS) to become the largest optical retailing group in Europe.

Vision Express wants to be viewed as the leading provider of professional eye care. This is supported by new store concepts – vision express | optical lab – which combines stylish and clinical dimensions, with state-of-the-art technology that have lens manufacturing laboratories that are central to the organization' score positioning.

Vision Express expresses a customer commitment. 'Total customer satisfaction is the foundation stone of our business. We work to a simple philosophy. Listen to the needs of each customer and help them to choose eyewear that meets their needs, guaranteeing total satisfaction. The shared vision of every one of our employees is our biggest asset.'

Their commitment is demonstrated in a 7 point guarantee of customer satisfaction.

1. *Your glasses in one hour, or free delivery*
2. *Perfectly satisfied with the comfort and appearance of your glasses*
3. *Totally satisfied with your prescription*
4. *Access to any frame in the world*
5. *Complimentary minor repairs and servicing*
6. *Glasses (frames) made to measure*
7. *Competitive price guaranteed.*

Source: http://www.visionexpress.com.

Models of service quality

Gronroos (1984) developed an early model of customer perceptions of service quality, focusing on how customers defined quality in terms of how the perceived service rated against their expectations of the service. The factors that influenced perceptions of service quality were:

- the outcome of the service delivery (i.e. its technical quality)
- how the service was delivered (i.e. its functional quality).

Parasuraman *et al.* (1985) developed this framework to produce a more comprehensive model of service quality. This model recognizes that satisfaction from service quality comes from a match between expectations of service quality and customer perceptions of the service. Where service perceptions were higher than expectations, service quality was deemed to be good. Where the reverse occurred, service quality was poor.

This model identified where and why service quality problems occurred. They referred to the gap between expectations and perceptions as the customer gap. The four reasons for a customer gap were termed provider gaps. These are considered in more detail later. Parasuraman *et al.* also noted that consumers use certain criteria to evaluate services. These criteria are the foundation of the ServQual criteria.

These two dimensions, managing the evaluation features (the ServQual factors) and managing the service gaps model are the key management tools for managing services.

Activity 5.14

Think of a recent good service experience. Were your perceptions of this service greater than your expectations of it?

Now think of a recent poor service experience. Were your perceptions of this service below your expectations?

The service gaps model

The gaps model of service quality identifies five problem areas:

1. *Customer Gap* – the difference between expectations and perceptions
2. *Provider Gap 1* – management not knowing what customers expect
3. *Provider Gap 2* – the organization not having the right service designs and standards
4. *Provider Gap 3* – the organization and its people not delivering to service standards
5. *Provider Gap 4* – the failure to match service performance to service promises.

These gaps are illustrated in Figure 5.10.

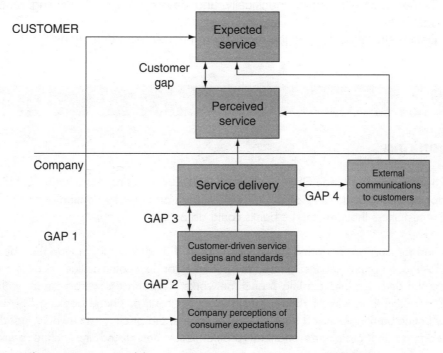

Figure 5.10 The service gaps model
Source: Zeithaml, V.A. and Bitner, M.J. (2003) *Services Marketing*, 3rd edition, McGraw-Hill

The customer gap – between perceived service and expected service – is the central gap. This gap is a function of the four provider gaps. Each provider gap has different causes and closing each gap has distinct solutions.

Provider Gap 1: management not knowing what customers expect

Knowing what customers expect is the first and possibly most critical step in delivering quality. Zeithaml, *et al.*, 1990

The main reasons for a gap emerging at this stage are:

o Poor or insufficient marketing research to help managers understand customer requirements
o Poor use of marketing and customer information
o Poor communication in the organization, especially between contact employees and managers
o Insufficient understanding of segments and/or lack of relationship orientation
o Inadequate service recovery.

To close this gap, managers must:

o Develop and implement market research programmes, including ongoing research with consumer panels and satisfaction tracking studies and qualitative research to determine unmet needs and customer priorities.
o Learn to turn customer insights into actions, such as use of customer complaints as signposts for service improvements.

   o   Develop programmes to help managers understand the problems of front-line workers, such as executive listening sessions, 'buddying' managers with front-line workers, undertaking front-line work, implementing internal satisfaction surveys and suggestion schemes.
   o   Target segments more specifically and develop ways of building relationships with customers.
   o   Define strategies for service recovery to ensure 'zero defections'.

Case study

Online banking

Novemetrie Institute and European Financial Management & Marketing Association (EFMA) in association with Capgemini, HP and Microsoft undertook research on European online banking. The findings were simple – customers thought that the banks could do better.

The core reason for the poor performance was that banks did not want to change their business model substantially. Although online services offered the potential for new value-added services, banks did not want to cause the demise of the existing branch networks. Respondents were happier with web-based banking (57 per cent) than with physical branches (35 per cent) or phone banking (29 per cent). The popularity of online banking resulted from its ease of access, the pricing frameworks, good advice and their knowledge of the customer's financial profile. Customers rated the online banks as being trustworthy.

Researchers commented that 'Users are frustrated … which leaves them confused when you think of the huge sums invested, among others, in CRM software. Banks haven't used the internet to transform their economic model; they've only seen it as a way to cut costs.'

Source: Dumout, E. (2004) 'European "online banks could do better"', July 02, accessed at http://www.silicon.com.

Provider Gap 2: the organization not having the right service designs and standards

Gap 2 arises because of having the wrong service quality standards and service designs. This is often caused by resistence to change existing patterns of service. Often this requires changes to staff, facilities, system, etc.

The major causes of Gap 2 are:

   o   Poor service design and new service development
   o   Lack of customer-driven standards
   o   Inappropriate physical evidence and servicescape.

To close this gap, managers must:

   o   Get managers to think 'outside the box' in terms of new business models rather than trying to improve things within the existing models; improving the innovation culture in the organization and generating new ideas for service.
   o   Set goals based on customer requirements of service to understand customer value and guide the service delivery and resourcing.
   o   Make sure the physical evidence and the servicescape (environment) matches customer needs and the service positioning.

Case study

The Easy Group

Stelios Haji-Ioannou is the founder and CEO of the Easy Group, which owns and operates a range of service businesses. He has been expanding his empire, but focusing on service activities, as he said 'We're not really makers of things'.

The Easy Group's business model is based on price-elasticity. It identifies what people will do more often if the price is cheap. Haji-Ioannou designs a service that can be delivered cheaply, while still meeting customer needs.

For example, most customers (95 per cent of them) make easyCar bookings online. Once they arrive at the location, they check in using mobile van units and laptop computers. This reduces the staff and office costs, and makes for a quicker customer experience.

The Easy Group companies cut out non-essential services, and offer customers a choice of what to pay for. For example, a large aspect of the cost for other car rental companies is cleaning the cars between hires. Most customers clean their cars before their return, rather than pay the £10 charge for car cleaning.

Haji-Ioannou uses the same approach in his airline group easyJet, and the credit card organization, easyMoney, allows customers the chance to select which benefits and services they want to pay for.

This model translates into other services, such as hotels (the Easy Group have announced they will launch a clean-it-yourself easyHotel). easyCinema has automated ticket-buying and ticket-taking.

Easy Group's success is in the willingness to change the existing way of doing things, and to design services that consider what customers value, and not just repeating what others do.

Source: Hanna, J. (2002), 'Profitable Business Model: It's Easy', HBS Conference Coverage, 2 December, accessed at http://hbswk.hbs.edu/pubitem.jhtml?id=3201&t=special_reports_eubc2002.

Provider Gap 3: the organization and its people not delivering to service standards

Often managers have a good understanding of customer requirements, and have designed good services, but services are not delivered effectively. Zeithaml *et al.* (1990) identified seven factors that led to this gap.

1. *Service role ambiguity* – people are not clear what they should be doing, or why.
2. *Service workers' role conflict* – workers cannot prioritize work roles or are placed in situations where work and customer requirements are in conflict.
3. *Poor employee* – job fit – people are in jobs they are poorly suited to. This is especially common in poorly paid service jobs.
4. *Poor technology* – job fit – the technology is unreliable or a barrier to effective service.
5. *Inappropriate supervisory controls* – focus on productivity rather than quality targets.
6. *Lack of employees' perceived control* – employees have little opportunity to resolve situations or feel helpless or powerless in resolving problems.
7. *Lack of teamwork* – employees feel little commitment to colleagues or to the organization.

To close this gap, managers must:

- o Define job roles and provide employees with information about their roles and feedback on how well they are undertaking these; ensure that employees have the training, on technical aspects of their role and of interpersonal skills, and knowledge of customers to give them competence and confidence.
- o Clarify instructions to the staff about priorities, and do not expose them to situations where they are being asked to do too many or inconsistent roles. Set appropriate measures, such as prioritizing customer satisfaction helps reinforce these roles.
- o Develop management understanding of required job skills and requirements, and developing sound recruitment policies to achieve these reduces problems in employee – job fit. Retaining good employees and paying fair salaries is critical.
- o Select technology on the basis of ease of use, error protection and overall reliability.
- o Include control components that recognize and reward good customer service, and take account of the importance of customer service.
- o Empower employees to make decisions that will affect their ability to solve customer problems.
- o Organize events and activities that build teamwork, monitoring and controlling based on team, rather than individual performance.

Case study

Ritz-Carlton Hotels

Ritz-Carlton has won many awards for service, and many of which result from its investment in its staff. It follows a rigorous selection process to identify team-players, with empathy for colleagues and customers. Ritz-Carlton's data shows that these become its top performing staff. This selection process has unusual approaches. For example, an applicant might be asked 'Do you wash your hands more or less often than others.' But this process helps Ritz-Carlton identify the right people, and communicates that Ritz-Carlton is only available to the best employees.

Ritz-Carlton spends about $5000 on training each new employee. All staff take part in a two-day programme that introduces organization values ('it's all about the service'), followed by a 21-day course on the specifics of their job responsibilities and the three steps of service. Employees are helped to understand how to use empowerment – all employees are authorized to spend up to $2000 to resolve problems, whether caused by the hotel or the guest. Solving these problems is a priority laid down in the organization code, which says '... when a guest has a problem ... break away from your regular duties to address and resolve the issue.'

For example, an administrator overheard a guest saying that he had not packed his work shoes and would be inappropriately dressed for a meeting the next day. She delivered a new pair in the right size and color to his room early the next morning.

Empowerment allows the staff to show they care, and their efforts are valued by customers. This in turn gives employees job satisfaction, which helps Ritz-Carton retain staff. While other luxury hotels have average staff turnover rates of 44 per cent, Ritz-Carlton's is only 25 per cent.

Ritz-Carlton says that 'We are ladies and gentlemen serving ladies and gentlemen'. It shows attention to employees by celebrating employee birthdays and employment anniversaries. Another cornerstone of its philosophy is that '. . . all employees have the right to be involved in the planning of the work that affects them.' This reduces the stress and allows processes to be improved.

Source: McDonald, D. (2004) 'Roll out the blue carpet – How Ritz-Carlton can teach you to serve your customers better', *Business* 2.0, May 6.

Provider Gap 4: the failure to match service performance to service promises

This gap is caused by the organization's communication, such as advertising, personal selling and sales promotions creating unrealistic expectations. The key contributing factors to this problem are:

- Lack of integrated marketing communications
- Poor horizontal communication between operations and advertising, salespeople, marketing and HR
- Ineffectively managing customer experiences
- Over-promising service levels.

To close this gap, managers must:

- Utilize integrated marketing communications for maximum consistency.
- Opening communication between the departments, involving employees in communications, either featuring in the advertising or seeing advertising before it is used externally; marketing should keep employees informed about and involved in new service developments, to ensure their commitment when these are launched; establishing liaison roles between HR and marketing helps overcome these problems.
- Develop common rules and system to ensure conformity to standards, but with the opportunity to add additional service where required. Only the core should be advertised or promoted to avoid over-promising.
- Educate customers in what is expected of them to reduce stress on staff and customer disappointment.
- Focus marketing communications on the customers' most valued service quality attributes, reflecting what is really delivered at the 'moment of truth', and helping customers to understand their role in the process.

Addressing these areas will help manage both customer expectations and customer perceptions, thus closing the customer gap.

Case study

IKEA

IKEA is now the world's leading home furnishings retailer. It requires customers to work – in self-assembling the products and in making the purchases. In order to avoid disappointment with this, IKEA give advice to customers on how to shop there.

For example, in advance, customers are advised to:

'Take measurements of spaces you want to fill with furniture. And be sure there's room in your car.'

They are advised that:

'Everything you need to shop is available at the entrance: pencils, paper, tape measures, store guides, catalogues, shopping trolleys, shopping bags.'

'Find smaller items in the market place.... Then collect your products from the warehouse in flat packages that are easy to take home.'

'IKEA stores are self-serve, but there's always someone around to answer your questions. You can bring your bulkier purchases to the Home Delivery desk to arrange delivery, for a fee.'

In addition to helping set expectations, this approach takes pressure off the staff who are asked to do things that are not in their job roles.

Source: http://www.ikea.com.

Methods of monitoring service quality

Organizations need performance measures or metrics to manage quality. The difficulties of defining service quality mean that general quality measures is difficult to apply. Two key issues to remember are:

1. Customers perceive service as an entirety, so measures should not just focus on individual activities, but on how these fit with the total service offering.
2. Metrics drive behaviour, so inappropriate performance measures can drive focus on activities that do not add value. (Managers often comment that what you measure is what you get.)

Sadly, both of these are poorly understood in practice. The latter is especially common in public sector organizations, which monitor 'service quality' to meet other stakeholder requirements. Clearly, service quality measurement will focus on meeting these requirements, rather than on improving service delivery for customer satisfaction.

Approaches to service quality measurement range from:

- o Simplistic mechanisms
- o Market research approaches
- o Service performance indexes
- o Integrated approaches, such as balanced scorecard.

Simplistic mechanisms

Typically, these approaches tend to be reactive rather than diagnostic, and appear as token attempts to understand or placate customers if used in isolation. These are common in public sector environments. Typically data analysis is limited too. These approaches include:

- o Comments cards, complaints procedures and suggestions boxes
- o Public meetings or user forums
- o Surgeries for dealing with complaints.

Market research approaches

Market research approaches check customer perceptions and customer satisfaction levels, and competitive service positioning dimensions.

Services marketing uses all the usual market research techniques, including internal analysis of sales records and customer behaviour; regular forms of tracking research, such as omnibus studies and consumer panels; external ad hoc research such as focus groups (for consultative approaches that give insight, rather than hard measures) and surveys (that give the quantitative support on customer perceptions of service quality measures).

Two key forms of market research for measuring service satisfaction are exit surveys and mystery shopping.

Exit surveys come in two forms. The first approach is an interview with customers leaving a service facility. The second form of exit surveys are with customers who are ceasing to buy from an organization, such as those closing down a bank account. Typically, these customers give very honest and forthright opinions about service quality.

Mystery shopping attempts to emulate the customer experience, monitoring a 'real time' customer experience. This reduces the problems with recall and individual issues that bias other forms of research. Airlines, hotels, shops, etc. use this to check both their own services and competitors' services.

Case study

McDonald's

McDonald's undertook 'mystery shops' in US restaurants and found that speed-of-service standards were met 'only 46 per cent of the time ... and that 3 of every 10 customers are waiting more than 4 minutes to complete their order', according to McDonald's Vice President Marty Ranft. Calls to the organization's freephone complaint line 'confirmed that rude service, slow service, unprofessional employees and inaccurate service are the source of the vast majority of customer complaints.'

Those customers that complain learn about the outcome of their complaint, and in many cases, vouchers for free food.

In the Middle East, McDonald's has had more success. Research agency Synovate rated McDonald's as the region's favourite fast food restaurant following a study of the region's informal eating out (IEO) market. The survey of over 2000 people from the GCC countries, researched the number of visits to quick service restaurants (QSR), and overall satisfaction with their most recent visit. All McDonald's restaurants in the region are owned by franchisees, but these restaurants were collectively rated the region's top restaurant, based on last visit satisfaction, market penetration, and market share.

Source: Gibson, R. (2002) 'McDonald's Sees Need To Speed Up US Service Improvements', *Dow Jones Newswires*, September 3.

Activity 5.15

You have been asked to set up mystery shopping programmes for:

HSBC

Hertz Car Rental

Public sector healthcare

What service standards should be assessed?

Extending knowledge

The ServQual methodology can be applied to an organization's services to determine where the gaps are in the service process. Full instructions of how to do this, including the questionnaires, are printed in Zeithaml *et al.* (1999).

Service performance indexes

Service performance indexes (SPIs) are 'comprehensive composites of the most critical performance standards' (Zeithaml and Bitner, 2003, p. 276). These can be set by an organization based on its own customer requirements and service provision. Singapore Airlines sets SPIs for the time at check-in, the time for luggage to arrive in the baggage claim area, etc. Other service performance indexes are operated on industry basis, such as for the public sector, for retailers or for airlines. In addition to offering tracking of performance, these offer benchmarking of service quality.

Integrated approaches, such as balanced scorecard

The breadth of issues involved in managing services make it appropriate to use composite models, such as Kaplan and Norton's Balanced Scorecard approach, to measure service quality, which is discussed in Unit 9. The balanced scorecard approach has four core areas, all of which are critical to effective service businesses (Figure 5.11).

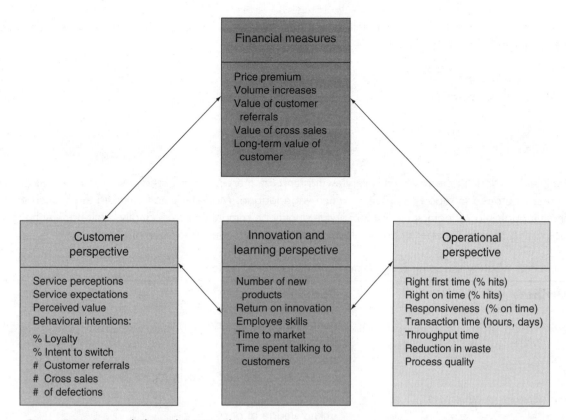

Figure 5.11 Service balanced scorecard
Source: Adapted by Zeithaml and Bitner (2003) from: Kaplan, R.S. and Norton, D.P. (1992) 'The Balanced Scorecard – Measures That Drive Performance', *Harvard Business Review*, January–February

Case study

Gulf Bank

Gulf Bank began a 'service excellence' programme in early 2003. A critical part of this process was a service quality system. Three key reporting requirements were set for this:

1. Focus on the drivers of customer satisfaction and retention
2. Drive action by channel and product managers
3. Simple in use and communications.

The drivers of customer satisfaction and retention were identified Kuwait's Institute of Banking Studies. This survey defined service excellence as 'that which the customer perceives as providing the services they require quickly, conveniently and without error, delivered courteously by knowledgeable staff at an acceptable cost.' The Bank measured its services against performance on these criteria, based on customer perceptions and on objective criteria. The latter assessed both technical effectiveness (accuracy, speed, etc.) and personal interaction (courtesy, knowledge, etc.) The former were addressed in a customer satisfaction questionnaire, including:

- ○ Excellent staff
- ○ Efficient operations
- ○ Convenience
- ○ Competitive costs
- ○ Excellent image.

Bank staff undertook the research, interviewing ten customers in each branch every month. Customers were encouraged to report complaints, which were logged. Marketing staff checked the branch environment against a 40 point checklist for service quality on a monthly basis. Finally, Gulf bank enhanced an existing mystery shopper approach focusing on the areas identified below in Table 5.5:

Table 5.5 Mystery shopping programme – areas for investigation

Attribute	Components
Appearance	conforms to dress code
	ID visible
	good posture
	not smoking, drinking, eating etc.
Interaction with customers	smile
	acknowledge at once
	greet appropriately
	use friendly tone of voice
	give uninterrupted attention
	be courteous
	use customer's name and title
	maintain eye contact
	excuse if leaving unattended
	ask if another service is required
	thank at end of service
Customer care	adopt professional manner
	maintain privacy
	serve one customer at a time
	do not redirect
Product knowledge	proactively provide appropriate product information
	execute the transaction 'right first time'
	provide transaction vouchers (receipts, etc.)
Phone service	comply with the telephone service guidelines
Exceptional effort	'going the extra mile'
Transaction and queuing time	
Service time, counter transactions	simple transaction
	complex transaction
Queuing time counter transactions	all counter transactions

Research on managers' information requirements identified the need for a 'one page' summary, with the opportunity to investigate further. Factors investigated, are detailed in the following table (Table 5.6):

Table 5.6 Service performance measures by channel

Channel/product	Metric
Branches	level of customer satisfaction number of customer complaints number of errors counter transactions – loan applications – credit card applications time queuing for counter service teller productivity counter transaction service time – simple transactions – complex transactions quality of the branch environment standard of employee behaviour
Automatic Teller Machines (ATMs)	level of customer satisfaction number of customer complaints system availability ATM machine downtime
Telephone banking (Call Centre)	level of customer satisfaction number of customer complaints service performance – average speed to answer – call response time – percentage of calls lost
Internet banking	level of customer satisfaction number of customer complaints system availability
Card products (ATM and credit cards)	level of customer satisfaction number of customer complaints time to issue card point of sale (merchant) system availability
Overall Gulf Bank	level of customer satisfaction number of customer complaints

The research findings were integrated into a scorecard to identify areas for attention. Issues currently under review are ATM availability, credit card delivery and loan processing time.

Source: Jones, C. (2004) 'Developing a scorecard for service quality', *Management Services*, April, pp. 8–13.

Summary

Managers are increasingly realizing the importance of managing brand equity. Brand equity refers to the value in a brand or the value from a brand. This topic has grown in importance due to the recognition of brands as a corporate asset, especially following major takeovers. There are several methods of determining brand equity, which include financial methods and methods that assess customer awareness. Brand equity measures can be used in valuing brands or companies for acquisitions, for identifying where, how and how much support is required for existing brands. The choice of brand equity method depends on the reason for measuring brand equity.

The value of an organization or brand's reputation is not fixed, but is susceptible to changes resulting from external or internal events and actions. Many organizations have faced major challenges in recent years, some of which have led to the organisation's or its loss of brand equity. The range of potential crises is increasing, as is the frequency of potentially damaging incidents. Organizations vary in how well they prepare for and respond to such issues. Some organizations are proactive (crisis-aware) and some are reactive (crisis-prone). Crisis-aware companies are those which prepare contingency plans and have crisis teams that can manage the crisis throughout the crisis life cycle. These crisis plans often include communications plans to limit the damage to the brand or corporate reputation.

Often customer views of organizations or brands can be damaged through careless interaction with a organization employee or distributor. These interactions are known as 'moments of truth', because they determine the extent of customer satisfaction. Management attention is increasingly focusing on these areas because of their impact on customer loyalty. These interactions can be face-to-face or remote interactions, and personal or impersonal. Research techniques to identify problem areas include CIT and the Five Whys. Identifying underlying problems allows managers to take action and help identify how to add value to the customer experience.

A closely associated concept is managing service quality. Service quality is harder to manage than tangible product quality due to the inherent characteristics of service products and the extended marketing mix. Assessing service quality spans the five ServQual factors, of reliability, responsiveness, assurance, empathy and tangibles. The service gaps model, which identifies the customer gap and the four contributory provider gaps, can be used to identify areas for attention. Other market research based measures, such as exit interviews, mystery shopping and service performance indices are helpful in managing service quality.

These areas are diverse, but interlinked. All are critical to effective implementation of business strategy.

Sample exam question

Feedback from customer focus groups suggests that an insurance organization is losing reputation as service quality declines. How can you determine the current level of service quality and how can it be measured and managed in the future. You are a consultant preparing a proposal for this client in order to gain the contract to undertake this work.

Discussion

The question is very clearly related to service quality in a service business. The context places you in the position of a consultant. What would a client like to see from a consultant bidding for their business, and what would the proposal document look like? Thinking this through as a basis for your answer will score many more marks than simply 'braindumping' about service quality models, benchmarking etc. Note that the question refers to determining, measuring and managing service quality it is not asking you to offer solutions to service problems at this stage.

Bibliography

Aaker, D.A. (1998) *Strategic Market Management*, Wiley.

Berry, L.L. and Parasuraman, A. (1991) *Marketing Services*, The Free Press.

Bitner, M.J. and Hubbert, A.R. (1994) 'Encounter satisfaction versus overall satisfaction versus quality: The customer's voice', in R.T. Rust and R.L. Oliver (eds), *Service Quality: New Directions in Theory and Practice*, Thousand Oaks, California: Sage, pp. 72–94.

Booth, S.A. (2000) 'How can organizations prepare for reputational crises?' *Journal of Contingencies and Crisis Management*, **8**(4), December, pp. 197–207.

Bordwin, M. (1999) 'Plan B...Or is it Plan C for Crisis?' *Management Review*, July–August, pp. 53–55.

Brand Finance (1999) *Brand Valuation in the Food Industry*, <http://www.brandfinance.com>.

Brand Finance (2000) *Current Practice in Brand Valuation*, Brand Finance, (www.brandfinance.com).

Brand Finance (2002) Measuring and Valuing Brand Equity, Brand Finance in collaboration with the Institute of Communications and Advertising, Canada.

Carlzon, J. (1987) *Moments of Truth*, New York: Harper & Row, pp. 2–3.

Cram, T. (2003) 'Seven of the best', *The Ashridge Journal*, Summer.

Flanagan, J.C. (1954) 'The critical incident technique', *Psychological Bulletin*, July, pp. 327–357.

Gonzales-Herrero and Pratt (1996) 'An integrated symmetrical model for crisis-communications management', *Journal of Public Relations Research*, **8**(2), pp. 79–105.

Gronroos, C. (1984) 'A service quality model and its marketing implications', *European Journal of Marketing*, **18**(4), pp. 36–44.

Hobby, J. (1999) 'Looking after the one who matters', *Accountancy Age*, 28 October, pp. 28–30.

Kapferer, J.-N. (1997) *Strategic Brand Management*, 2nd edition, Kogan Page.

Keaveney, S.M. (1995) 'Customer switching behavior in service industries: An exploratory study', *Journal of Marketing*, **59**(2), April, pp. 71–82.

Keller, K.L. and Lehmann, D.R. (2003) 'How do brands create value?', *Marketing Management*, **12**(3), May/June, pp. 26–31.

Mitroff, I. and Alspaslan, M.C. (2003) 'Preparing for evil', *Harvard Business Review*, April, pp. 109–115.

O'Connor, R. (1978) Planning under uncertainty, Conference Board.

Oliver, R.L. (1997) *Satisfaction: A Behavioral Perspective on the Consumer*, New York: McGraw-Hill.

Parasuraman, A., Zeithaml, V.A. and Berry, L.L. (1985) 'A conceptual model of service quality and its implications for future research', *Journal of Marketing*, **49**, Fall, pp. 41–50.

Pearson, C.M., Clair, J.A., Kovoor-Miara, S. and Mitroff, I. (1997) 'Managing the unthinkable', *Organizational Dynamics*, **26**(2), Autumn, pp. 51–64.

Senge, P., Kleiner, A., Roberts, C., Ross, R.B. and Smith, B.J. (1994) *The Fifth Discipline Fieldbook: Strategies and Tools for Building a Learning Organization*, Doubleday.

Shostack, G.L. (1984) 'Designing services that deliver', *Harvard Business Review*, January–February, pp. 133–139.

Shostack, G.L. (1985) 'Planning the service encounter', in *The Service Encounter*, J.A. Czepiel, M.R. Solomon and C.F. Superenant (eds), Lexington Books, pp. 243–254.

Siomokis, G. (1992) 'Conceptual and methodological propositions for assessing responses to industrial crises', *Review of Business*, **13**(4).

Zeithaml, V.A. and Bitner, M.J. (2003) *Services Marketing*, 3rd edition, McGraw-Hill.

Zeithaml, V.A., Parasuraman, A. and Berry, L.L. (1990) *Delivering Quality Service*, The Free Press, Unit 5.

unit 6
implementing business strategy through marketing activities 2

Objectives

Syllabus links

Learning outcomes

1. 'Demonstrate an ability to manage marketing activities as part of strategy implementation.'

2. 'Assess an organization's needs for marketing skills and resources and develop strategies for acquiring, developing and retaining them.'

Please see Appendix 4 for full details of the learning outcomes, related statements of practice and knowledge and skills requirements.

Information on the syllabus element (and its weighting) that is supported by this chapter can be found in Figure P.1, in the preface to this book.

Learning objectives

This is the final unit addressing element 3 of the Managing Marketing Performance syllabus, on implementing business strategy through marketing activities. The topics of this unit inter-relate with those in the previous units. At the end of the content on each topic, you should reflect on how this fits with the other topics in element 3 of the syllabus. This unit focuses on elements 3.7, 3.9 and 3.10 of the syllabus, on customer care, integrated marketing communications and managing customer relationships respectively, which are current priorities in effective business strategy delivery.

After completion of this section, you will be able to:

o   Propose and implement appropriate improvements to customer service by developing or enhancing customer care programmes

o   Develop and manage integrated marketing and communications programmes to establish and build relationships appropriate to the needs of customers, clients or intermediaries

o   Develop support for relationships with customers, clients and intermediaries using appropriate information systems and databases adhering to relevant privacy and data protection legislation.

Key definitions

Customer service – Customer service is a supplementary service to any organization's core offering (Parasuraman, 1998).

The activities that support orders, including application, advice, configuration, order processing, handling, post-sale communication and special services. The primary objective of customer service is to increase customer satisfaction, operational efficiency and customer loyalty.

www.fivetwelvegroup.com/question.html.

Integrated marketing communications (IMC) programmes – An integrated marketing communication program requires that: (1) multiple types of communication options are employed and (2) communication options are designed in a way to reflect the existence and content of other communication options in the program (Keller, 2001, p. 822).

Customer relationship management (CRM) – A comprehensive strategy and process of acquiring, retaining, and partnering with selective customers to create superior value for the company and the customer. It involves the integration of marketing, sales, customer service, and the supply-chain functions of the organization to achieve greater efficiencies and effectiveness in delivering customer value (Parvatiyar and Sheth, 2001).

A technology – enabled implementation of the marketing concept.

Study Guide

This unit will take about 4–5 hours to work through.

We suggest that you take a further 3–4 hours to do selected activities and reading in this unit.

Introduction

Retaining and engaging customers is a challenge in implementing relationship marketing. Business magazines comment on the importance of customer retention, excellence in sales and service support and the application of customer relationship management. Yet market data shows increasingly less customer loyalty, and little customer interest in contact from supplier organizations. Any actions may end up costing money, and not delivering marketing performance.

This unit addresses how to use customer service to enhance the customer experience, with the hope of retaining customers and growing their business, and how to maintain contact with these customers in an appropriate way, that builds impact and loyalty, through integrated marketing communications and new technologies.

Case study

Improving customer relationships?

In 2002, NOP surveyed people's attitudes towards call (or contact) centres, which are the major form of organization-customer dialogue for many organizations. The findings reported that customers think that call (or contact) centres waste their time. People are increasingly irritated by automated response systems (with instructions to 'Press 1 for...'). Call centre labour turnover varies, but estimates of between 15 per cent to 25 per cent annual staff turnover are common.

Although many organizations believe that an Internet presence adds to their customer communications, this only seems to be appealing to AB social grade customers. Many believe that the standard of follow up on online customer service enquiries is slow.

Source: Key Note reports on Call Centres (2002, 2004).

Customer service

This section addresses element 3.7 of the Managing Marketing Performance syllabus:

> *Propose and implement appropriate improvements to customer service by developing or enhancing customer care programmes.*

It is often said that if you ask marketing managers about how they demonstrate customer focus, they will tell you about their customer service levels. These concepts are linked, but they are different in many ways.

Activity 6.1

Think about the two terms identified in the CIM syllabus element – customer service and customer care.

Do you see any distinctions between these?

How does your organization approach and define these?

Definitions of customer service

There are few academic definitions of customer service, but many commercial or practical ones. The following definitions set the context for this section:

> *The area of the company that provides product information, help and/or technical support to new customers and sells them the products or services they need or want.*

> (www.biztroubleshooter.com/Glossary/glossary_a-n.htm)

> *The activities that support orders, including application, advice, configuration, order processing, handling, post-sale communication and special services. The primary objective of customer service is to increase customer satisfaction, operational efficiency and customer loyalty.*

> (www.fivetwelvegroup.com/question.html)

> *A function of an organization that interacts with customers, e.g. responds to inquiries or complaints. Can also describe the positive attitude of an organization towards its client base, and taking active steps (as opposed to always REacting) to improve product or service delivery.*

> (www.homebusinessmanual.com.au/glossary.html)

These definitions identify that customer service can be:

o   a business department or function
o   a series of activities or
o   an approach to improving customer satisfaction.

Customer service is a supplement to any organization's core offering (Parasuraman, 1998). Customer service can be added to a physical product, such as a washing machine or a car, or to a service, such as software or telecommunications. Customer service is not services marketing, but many services marketing principles apply to delivery of customer service.

The aim of good customer service is to benefit:

o   *The organization*, through customer retention, referrals and cross-selling
o   *The customer*, through attention in the delivery of added value
o   *The staff*, in creating a more rewarding role.

Several terms are commonly used synonymously with customer service, although some differences exist:

o   *Customer care* – encompasses an organization-wide commitment to customers to ensure that the organization meets and exceeds customer expectations – as indicated in the acronym of Customers Are Really Everything. It does not need to have defined processes and goals.
o   *Customer support* – is the service provided by suppliers and third-parties to help customers in their purchase, use or maintenance of products. This may be part of an overall customer service strategy.
o   *Technical support* – specifically focuses on solving technical problems, and is common in commercial and technical markets. This is commonly used in the installation and repair of products or in problem solving. This is also a part of an organization's customer services strategy.

These forms of service and support can be delivered in a range of different ways:

- *Face- to-face* – in the customers' premises, in a local store or commercial location or in the supplying organizations' premises
- *Phone* – either inbound or outbound and personal or computer automated response
- *Fax* – either inbound or outbound, can be computer automated
- *Online* – in a help facility, FAQ sheets, bulletin boards or using an e-mail, chat or 'call me' response.

In addition, customers also support other customers, such as the online bulletin boards which are common for software problems.

Marketing managers with the responsibility for customer service must focus and co-ordinate these forms of support and the various media to meet and exceed customer expectations.

Case study

Direct Line

Direct Line brought radical change to the UK insurance industry. Bypassing middlemen, with 'their fat commissions', it sold insurance directly to consumers by telephone. It trained operators to talk about insurance without jargon, and brought customer service that equalled or exceeded many traditional brokers. It was faster, easier and simpler than ever before to buy insurance.

However, its success was not just in selling the policies, but also in how it dealt with claims. Much of this was handled by phone, avoiding the long delays associated with insurance claims.

Now Direct Line is innovating in online customer service, allowing customers people to:

- Amend car or home policies
- Renew policies
- Register a car claim
- Register a home claim
- Track the progress of car repairs
- View policy details
- Retrieve and accept quotes
- Get quotes for products.

Source: http://www.directline.com.

 ## Activity 6.2

Review the discussion on customer service and the Direct Line case. How does Direct Line view the role of customer service?

How does that influence its forms of customer service?

The importance of customer service

The economic and competitive arguments for customer retention and the need for differentiation are major factors behind improving customer service. For example, a Mintel (2001) report on UK Grocery retailing comments:

> *The value in using service to differentiate an offer is that it can be harder to negate by a competitor. Unlike price-matching, which negates a competitor's price advantage, service provision reflects a company's 'personality' and enhances a retailer's brand value.*

Customer service is a controllable aspect of the organization's marketing activity. While not included in common definitions of the marketing mix, Christopher, Payne and Ballantyne (2002) view it as being one of three foundations of relationship marketing, as shown in Figure 6.1, and part of the expanded marketing mix, as shown in Figure 6.2.

Figure 6.1 The relationship marketing orientation
Source: Christopher, Payne and Ballantyne (2002, p. 9)

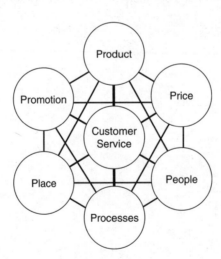

Figure 6.2 The expanded marketing mix
Source: Christopher, Payne and Ballantyne (2002, p. 11)

Banks and financial services institutions often sell their core services based on the additional levels of customer support they offer customers (Gray, 2004). These approaches are based on need to deliver and delight customers. The underlying principle is that such customers will return, buy more, refer others, and be cheaper to serve.

However widely understood this principle is, there is a reality gap. Achieving total customer satisfaction has to be reconciled with costs. As a result, complaints about customer service are widely reported. However, marketing managers, often the first to complain about poor service, should question why service levels are so bad and determine the impact of poor customer service on their business performance (Table 6.1).

Table 6.1 Selected research findings on customer service

Portland Research Group found:

On average, consumers call a company 2.3 times before their issues are resolved. Their future purchase intentions drop from 76% to 55% with the second contact. On average, callers are transferred 1.5 times before speaking to the 'right person'. Customer satisfaction or loyalty is not affected by the first call transfer, but being passed on a second time reduces future purchase intentions from 64% to 48%.

Source: destinationCRM.com, 12 April 2004

BearingPoint, Inc. identified that only 22% of financial services executives believed that customers would actively refer family and friends to their company, despite the expenditure on CRM. A significant opportunity to enhance customer loyalty by improving the quality of their customers' experience was reported by 92% of executives.

Source: Call Center Management Review, 1 April 2004

Mintel (2001) found that 49% of adult respondents have left a store without buying anything because of poor service. The research also shows that 21% of adult respondents will never use that retailer's stores again because of poor service. The negative reactions are greatest in the affluent, upmarket customers.

Source: Mintel (2001)

As customers, marketers understand that customer service matters, but as managers, customer service is rarely central to their marketing strategy and resourced accordingly.

These findings are borne out by recent research from a consultancy Strativity Group Inc who in a year-long study of attitudes of customer service and marketing executives found that:

o 32 per cent said their compensation was tied to quality of service.
o 37 per cent agreed that they were equipped to service and resolve customer problems.
o 36 per cent of European respondents thought their company deserved loyalty from customers.

Source: (Strativity Group Inc. http://www.strativitygroup.com/ 2004)

These data indicate that marketers are not prioritizing and supporting customer satisfaction, so not delivering customer retention and customer referrals. The management challenge is to make customer service happen in a cost-effective way.

The commercial argument must consider the costs and benefits from improved customer service. In addition to calculating specific costs of any improvement, the generic issue of how improving customer service will affect revenues and profitability must be considered. This can be weighed against the failure to improve customer service, in terms of customer defections, adverse word of mouth and the cost of new customer acquisition.

Extending knowledge

Use the Internet to identify a consultancy that specialises in advising on customer service, such as the Strativity Group website, http://www.strativity.com. Identify the case for customer service, and the key issues to be considered.

Roles of customer service

Understanding the role of customer service is essential for its effective delivery.

Levitt (1980) showed the ability of adding benefits to a core product or service as a means of differentiation. The augmented product adds various forms of service to the product core, delivering additional value to customers. This is commonly presented as a diagram with a series of concentric circles, with the basic product at the core. Many aspects of the augmented product are forms of customer service. Thus customer service may be seen as a key part of the total product concept.

A second role of customer service is evident in early approaches. Different forms of customer service were based on the timing of service (Christopher, 1992) as indicated in Table 6.2. Customer service helps customers gain information, buy or use products. These time dimensions have developed and form the core of customer relationship management, which is addressed later.

Table 6.2 Customer service components at different stages in product purchase and use

Pre-transaction	Pre-contact	Advertising Technical information Written policies System flexibility
Transaction	Personal contact	Sales call Presentation/demonstration Order placement
	Pre-delivery	Document processing Inventory policy Order assembly Transportation
Post-transaction	Delivery	Receiving Installation
	Post-delivery	Product performance Product support Implementation Training

Source: Christopher, M. (1992) *The Customer Service Planner*, Butterworth-Heinemann, p. 8

An alternative role is evident in Lovelock and Wirtz's (2004) 'flower of service' framework that shows the total offering to a customer as a flower, based round the core of the product (Figure 6.3). The petals represent the key elements of service to the customer (e.g. information, billing, etc.).

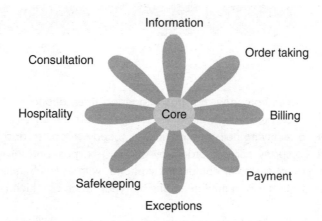

Figure 6.3 Flower of service
Source: Lovelock, C. and Wirtz, J. (2004) *Services Marketing*, 5th edition

This approach identifies various forms of opportunities for customer service:

o **Facilitating services**

  – *Information*: about how or where to buy or use a product, or reminders, documents and manuals
  – *Order-taking*: recording orders and giving information or availability and delivery
  – *Billing*: customers want bills that are accurate and easy to understand and contact if there are any areas of confusion
  – *Payment*: offering payment options, such as annual, monthly or weekly payments and cash, credit card or direct bank payments may reduce the 'pain' of paying for something.

o **Enhancing services**

  – *Consultation*: adding advice and customization round customer needs can add value
  – *Hospitality*: welcoming customers who are making time to contact a business is essential to their repeat business
  – *Safekeeping*: reducing the risks and concerns, such as after-sales service, also adds value
  – *Exceptions*: allowing for flexibility, when things go wrong or in exceptional circumstances, is valued by customers.

These activities are not always within the domain of marketing staff. For example, exceptions are often dealt with by technical engineers; billing is normally a financial function; and information may be provided by an independent agent, such as a distributor. Managing customer service must be an organization-wide activity, often spanning those in the organization's microenvironment, such as suppliers, alliance partners and intermediaries. Within the organization, it commonly involves co-operation of marketing, operations, technology and human resources departments.

Case study

Lands' End

Lands' End is a US direct sales company that has expanded internationally. It is widely cited as an example of a customer focused business. Its customer service covers the entire customer buying process 'from initiating the order, to receiving help and advice, to speedy shipping, and further follow-up when necessary'. Although the company accepts orders by phone, fax, post and through the Internet (email and live chat), the main form of customer contact is by phone, with over 15 million calls a year. Emails are increasing, with over a quarter of a million emails per year, each of which is answered personally.

The company website states that Lands' End people 'go the extra mile' by:

- A simple guarantee – Guaranteed Period. ® – allows customers to return items for any reason, whenever they like.
- Freephone (toll-free) phone lines are open 24 hour a day, for ordering and customer service.
- Offering free electronic greeting cards and gift certificates to help customers celebrate holidays and events.
- Giving newly hired representatives 70–80 hours of training in products, customer service and computer, and 24 hours of training in each subsequent year.
- Having speciality shoppers to answer sizing questions, make gift suggestions and advise on wardrobe coordination.
- Allowing customers to 'shop with a friend' and add items to a shared shopping basket.
- Creating a virtual model of the customer, to allow them to see what they would look like wearing items.
- Offering gift-wrapping, monogramming and hemming of items.
- Offering free fabrics swatches, buttons, luggage repairs.
- Fast delivery.

Source: www.landsend.com, www.landsend.co.uk.

Guaranteeing service

A central way of communicating, facilitating and enhancing aspects of the customer service is through service guarantees. Guarantees address aspects of customer service, such as the speed with which calls are taken, the speed of delivery, the accuracy of billing, etc.

Organisations may levy additional charges for customer service guarantees. For example, Dell offers various forms and lengths of guarantees, with different prices for different response solutions. The extent to which these customer services become part of the core product, rather than the augmented surround is subject to debate. Parasuraman (1998) states that when the services are provided for a fee, then they no longer become part of customer service, but part of the product core.

In B2B markets, guarantees are often formalized into service level agreements (SLAs). SLAs are details of agreed levels of service provision, priorities and responsibilities. It is debatable whether these fall within Parasuram's definition of being independent support, or part of the core.

Service level agreements are a way of managing customer expectations, to avoid or resolve conflicts between service providers and customers, and to monitor service delivery. Typically, SLAs address:

- ○ *Service delivery issues* include the eligibility for service, the standards for service (e.g. response times and outcomes), the roles and responsibilities of customers and suppliers, the means of managing disputes.
- ○ *Management issues* detail how service performance will be measured, reported, and how problems will be addressed; when and how revisions to the SLA will take place.
- ○ *Conditions* for payment, compensation or penalties.

Activity 6.3

Check out the website for a computer manufacturer, bookstore or online supermarket. What levels of service commitments are these offering? Are these addressing facilitating and enhancing services?

Compare these with the service commitments offered by your organization and its competitors. Are your organization and your industry customer service standard setters or followers?

Improving customer service

Service enhancements are required when an organization fails to meet service standards or where key performance indicators are falling below acceptable levels. Scheuring (1989) suggests using customer service audits – 'periodic, comprehensive, systematic and independent reviews of a customer service functions environmental influences and operations' – to determine areas for improvement.

This process is similar to the generic marketing audit, focusing analysing, planning, implementing, controlling and organizing for customer service, and examining the tasks, policies and procedures, people, and resources for customer service. Scheuring comments that 'the purpose of this candid, objective review is rather to pinpoint opportunities for improvement and stimulate discussion about potential strategic and tactical changes'.

Extending knowledge

Look at the checklist for undertaking a customer service audit in Scheuring's article to identify the range of issues involved in customer service auditing. A shorter version of a customer service audit is included in the Appendix of Christopher's book.

Parasuraman (1998) proposes an alternative model for identifying problems (and thus areas for improvement) in customer service in B2B markets. This identifies four key categories of problems, similar to the Service Gaps model discussed in Unit 6. At a generic level, this applies to all sectors seeking customer service improvement, including B2C and non-profit customer service. This is shown in Figure 6.4.

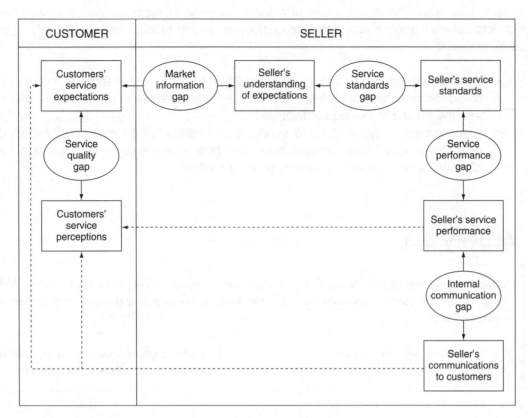

Figure 6.4 Parasuraman's model of service shortfalls in seller–customer interactions
Source: Parasuraman, A. (1998, p. 315)

Parasuraman's four seller organization gaps are:

1. *Market information gap* – where the seller has incomplete or inaccurate knowledge of the customers' service expectations.

    – **The solution** is more customer information, gathered through qualitative and quantitative approaches.

2. *Service standards gap* – where the seller fails to interpret customers' service expectations and transform these into specifications or guidelines for company personnel.

    – **The solution** is to redefine the customer service activities, and pilot these before rolling these out.

3. *Service performance gap* – where internal support systems (e.g. recruitment, training, technology, rewards) to support the employees' delivery of service standards are inadequate.

    – **The solution** is to map the customer service process and identify where problems occur, and to design training or other HR responses, and acquire or implement new systems and processes.

4. *Internal communication gap* – where there are inconsistencies between customer communication about the service and the actual service delivery, caused from poor internal communication about the service.

    – **The solutions** are better flow of information internally through new inter-departmental process and more effective review of such requirements.

These gaps show that customer research cannot identify all improvements and enhancements to customer service. Management need to refine roles, and communicate these better. Organization and support systems are key success factors in successful customer service (Jones, 2000).

Therefore, organizations must also undertake continuous evaluation and improvements to the process. This will involve the use of techniques such as quality management, process management and benchmarking (see Unit 7 for further information).

Case study

That won't do nicely

A well known financial services provider, famed for its ability to solve customers' problems wherever they are in the world, has customer service advisors on call 24 hours a day, seven days a week.

However, despite this, there is no fax machine in the customer service area. Customers needing assistance and support have to wait 2 days for the fax to be delivered through a slow internal mail system before a customer service advisor can action this.

Activity 6.4

Refer the case study.

What customer service gap causes this problem?

How can it be resolved?

Customer services planning

Christopher (1992, p. 23) states that:

> If customer service is to play a significant role in the organization's marketing mix programme, then it must be planned and managed just as any other marketing element such as price or promotion.

He advocates that customer service planning should follow the generic planning framework of:

- ○ *Mission* – in this instance, customer service is the mission for the organization. It should be set in the context of the importance of customer service and effective communication with customers, and examining the culture and values of service within the organization, including training, staff empowerment and teamwork. This sets the foundations for service, such as in the level of product expertise, the quality standards for service and the importance of customer satisfaction.

183

     ○ *Objectives* – the defined service objectives for the organization, linked to the marketing mix. This addresses the importance of customer service relative to other activities, such as promotional activity, or product development, and defines objectives for pre-transaction, transaction and post-transaction stages.

     ○ *Strategy* – the generic approach to achieving these objectives is the customer service strategy. Customer service strategy may have tiers of response, for example, distinguishing between key accounts, business customers and individual consumers or gold, silver and 'lead' customers, based on their spend or level of commitment to the organization. This enables the organization to develop the service package to meet the needs of these customers in a way that reflects their value to the organization.

     ○ *Implementation* – addresses the activities involved in making the plan work. This addresses the training required to develop skills, such as listening, empathy, trust, self-organization and knowledge, about the technology and product; the protocols or procedures for diffusing conflict and handling complaints; the codes of conduct for behaviour, including acceptable and unacceptable behaviour and actions by employees and customers; the means by which service satisfaction will be measured and developed (e.g. surveys, mystery customers, suggestion schemes, employee attitude surveys).

This planning process and the plan must be resourced appropriately. The level of resourcing should reflect the importance of customer service in the organization's strategy, linked to the benefits and costs of delivery. This includes many contentious decisions, such as the use of computerized systems to handle calls, which can substantially reduce the costs of handling customer calls.

Case study

Yorkshire Water

Yorkshire Water is the water supplier in Yorkshire, UK. It was formed during the privatization of UK water services in the late 20th century and its vision is to be 'the best water company in the UK' and the customer service leader in the water industry.

Its Customer Service strategy is agreed at Board level. Known as Exceeding Expectations, this communicates the importance of setting ever higher standards of performance throughout the business. This strategy is supported by research – for example, in-depth research with the top 15 housebuilders in its region led to a Developer Charter for housebuilders and it is piloting account management with the largest housebuilders in response to the research findings.

The Exceeding Expectations strategy is agreed at Board level, championed by the Head of Customer Service. This strategy is delivered across the organization, as all departments, and all contacted service partners, have responsibilities for delivering against this, for both internal and external customer contact. The strategy is aligned with the marketing strategy, and supports the corporate brand values. Initiatives are targeted at specific improvements in service – for example, staff handling water supply investigations now work flexible hours to give customers a choice of appointment times, that includes evenings and weekends.

A CRM system is central to the Exceeding Expectations strategy, and its use of this resulted in Yorkshire Water's success in the 'best use of technology in customer services' at the National Customer Service Awards and Gartner European CRM Awards. This helps Yorkshire Water monitor its performance on several operational dimensions. In addition, Yorkshire Water also monitor the satisfaction levels overall.

Source: http://www.yorkshirewater.com/yorkshirewater/cservices.html, http://www.keldagroup.com/kel/investors/reports/presentations/pres2004/analystvisit/analystvisit.pdf.

Managing integrated marketing communications

Customer service offerings are strongly linked to personal interaction. Marketers' focus on communication with customers is typically through marketing communications programmes. This section focuses on managing marketing communications within a relationship marketing approach, addressing element 3.9 of the *Managing Marketing Performance* syllabus:

> *Develop and manage integrated marketing communications programmes to establish and build relationships appropriate to the needs of customers, clients or intermediaries.*

Marketing communications is covered extensively in the CIM syllabus. The goal of this section is to highlight key issues about delivering valued and consistent communications to customers.

Background principles

Historically many promotional approaches, such as personal selling, advertising and publicity have been managed within separate parts of the organization. This has often led to barriers between different functional areas (Cespedes, 1994) and organizations have failed to gain leverage from integration of promotional activities.

Keller (2001, p. 822) identifies that Integrated Marketing Communications (IMC) programmes have:

> *(1) multiple types of communication options…and (2) communication options are designed in a way to reflect the existence and content of other communication options in the program.*

 ## Activity 6.5

What marketing communications activities does your organization undertake?

Who is responsible for their delivery?

How are these integrated?

Integration of marketing and communications programmes applies at different levels.

- ○ *Integration of the overall marketing programmes with the promotional activity* – This means that marketing communications activity should be consistent with the marketing objectives and strategy. This is often managed well in advertising, but poorly when transferred to and implemented by the sales force, who are more focused on activity and results.
- ○ *Integration of the various aspects of marketing and promotional activity* – Consistent presentation of the company or its brands, such as the colours, the visual layout, the messages, the logos, etc. leads to integrated marketing communications. In some instances, this extends to staff uniforms matching the corporate colours or even independent dealerships or franchises having a consistent look and feel.
- ○ *Media choice to produce integrated campaigns* – Integration of above-the-line promotional activity (such as traditional press or TV advertising) and below-the-line activities (such as sales promotions or direct marketing) into through-the-line campaigns, results

in the optimum blend such approaches, e.g. using advertising to create awareness and other techniques to involve, persuade or retain customers.

○ *Integration of brand strategies and promotional delivery in different markets* – The growing importance of the Internet and telecoms technologies is encouraging organizations to make brand identities work internationally, as Mars did by harmonising Snickers (formerly Marathon in the UK) and Twix (formerly Raiders in some countries).

○ *Integrated marketing communications programmes for trade and consumer channels* – Intermediaries usually prefer products that are 'easy to sell'. Because of this, trade salespeople (those selling to intermediaries) leverage the value of appropriate consumer campaigns in their contacts with trade customers. In some settings, such as in grocery retailing where the intermediaries are dominant, key account managers work with key accounts to develop and customize co-operative consumer advertising campaigns. Matching the requirements of trade customers and the internal requirements for consistency is essential.

Case study

Volvo's S40 integrated campaigns

By 2004, Volvo had lost share in the car market, as the brand positioning of the 1980s was no longer compelling or desirable, especially for younger and more aspirational customers.

The target for the Volvo S40 campaign was 'heavy' and 'mature' internet users, who like the latest technology. These are experienced digital consumers, and heavy users of news, travel, business info, cinema listings, directories and sports sites. They use e-mail and buy online.

Volvo wanted to challenge brand perceptions through an integrated campaign that was reminiscent of the *Blair Witch Project*. Trailers of 'The Mystery of Dalarö' ran in cinemas, on TV and online as a teaser campaign to drive people to the website, where they could watch the full 5 minutes documentary that showed the car in great detail, with owners explaining their reasons for choosing the brand. The campaign was supported by a spoof site from the supposed director of the campaign, as a viral marketing activity, which was 'apparently' independent of Volvo. The toolkit asked Volvo personnel and dealers not to acknowledge this as being from Volvo to maximise the buzz from the campaign.

Prior to the campaign, Volvo circulated a toolkit of information on its marketing communications to Volvo marketing people in the UK, France, Italy, Spain and Germany. The purpose of this document was to 'ensure a robust and innovative campaign in all channels'. The toolkit contained recommendations and guidance on media opportunities; scripts, print executions and strategic recommendations across all media. This was circulated in advance of the final creative work, offering advance information to help the local markets (and local dealers) prepare for the forthcoming launches. The toolkit reminded local Volvo managers that all communications should refer to the S40 as 'The All New S40' to communicate the novel positioning and the campaign feel.

The document included discussion of the creative tools, overall communications strategy, the above-the-line campaign information, outline media schedules and on-line creative concepts. Print work guidelines detailed how to format activities, such as double page spreads, single page ads, advertorial an inserts, outdoor advertising and posters, point of sale displays and direct marketing, and suggested uses of these options.

Although the core materials were standardized, the campaign had local market adaptations. For example, in Spain, digital TV viewers could view the documentary on a digital mystery TV channel and a CD-Rom of the documentary was included in Sunday newspaper supplements. An advertorial was placed opposite the TV listings on the first day of the campaign. Ambient media, including postcards in trendy restaurants in Madrid and Barcelona, was also used. In the UK, the dealers also ran local Mystery campaigns and Volvo sponsored a series of showings of 'Cult' films, which were preceded by a showing of the video. (Details of the results of this feature in Unit 7.)

Source: Volvo and Mindshare.

Activity 6.6

Refer to the Volvo case.

1. What advantages exist in Volvo giving the responsibility for control of the local implementation of this campaign to its agency?
2. What factors need to be considered to gain local market buy-in to such a toolkit?
3. What evidence is there that these factors were considered in this campaign?

Establishing relationships

Increasingly organizations are moving from a monologue approach in customer contact (typical of a transactional way of doing business), to a relationship approach that integrated communications over the customer lifecycle.

Integrated marketing plans take account of communication in all the relationship marketing domains, and within the overall marketing (and marketing communications) strategy and programmes. Direct marketing is increasingly important as the dialogue in develop understanding of customers, and of promotional effectiveness. This in turn drives increased profitability from relationship marketing.

Further, changing the customer contact process from casual interaction to customer dialogue helps build value from customers, increasing the intensity of the customer relationship and moving customers up the ladder of loyalty (Figure 6.5).

Partner – someone who has the relationship of a partner with you
Advocate – someone who actively recommends you to others
Supporter – someone who likes your organization, but supports you only passively
Client – someone who has done business with you on a repeat basis but may be negative, or at best neutral, towards your organization
Customer – someone who has done business just once with your organization
Prospect – someone whom you believe may do business with you.

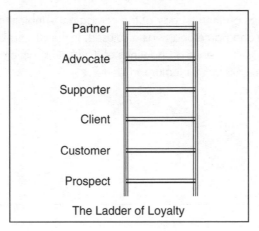

Figure 6.5 The ladder of loyalty
Source: Peck, H., Payne, A., Christopher, M. and Clark, M. (1999) *Relationship Marketing – Strategy and Implementation*, Butterworth-Heinemann

 Activity 6.7

Marketers talk about forming relationships with customers.

What organizations do you want to have a relationship with, if any?

Do some organizations, which you are not interested in, try to form relationships with you?

What are the implications of this for marketing communications practice?

Case study

Franz Ferdinand

Franz Ferdinand has achieved worldwide recognition for its music. The band members are digitally aware (singer/guitarist Alex Kapranos used to teach IT), so it is no surprise that it is also recognised as having excellent digital marketing activity. Its website has details of its forthcoming album, tour dates, events, and band members regularly upload information (blogs) to the site.

The band is especially popular with students, who are highly IT literate. An independent site for the band already exists, where fans post articles and photos. The band now plans further development of the official site and the 30 000 fans who are registered on the site will be asked to confirm existing details, asked for mobile phone details, which may be used for future mobile SMS and MMS communications and opt in to a newsletter.

Agency DS.Emotion, said: 'Digital is the way forward in building interactive relationships with young net-savvy music fans.'

Source: Whitehead, J. (2005), 'Franz Ferdinand boosts web activity before new album', *Brand Republic*, 15 February, accessed at http://www.brandrepublic.com/news/newsArticle.cfm?articleID=235394.

Customer relationships are intended to grow lifetime value. McCorkell (1999) shows how direct marketing measurability grows through building a stronger relationship with customers. He contrasts the number of and revenue from charity donors, who pay in cash (i.e. essentially transactional customers) with those who pay by direct debit (relationship customers). Table 6.3 shows the effects of customer defections from 100 donors in a year for each form of payment. Table 6.4 converts this to show the cumulative income from each group.

Table 6.3 Comparison of cash vs. direct debit customers – defection rates

	Cash payer	Direct debit
Year 1	100	100
Year 2	55 (–45%)	85 (–15%)
Year 3	36 (–35%)	77 (–10%)
Year 4	25 (–30%)	70 (–7.5%)

Source: McCorkell, G. (1999)

Table 6.4 Comparison of cash vs. direct debit customers – impact on revenue

	Cash payer (number of customers by annual payment)	Direct debit (number of customers by annual payment)
Year 1	100×60^1 £6000	100×55^1 £5500
Year 2	55×60^2 £3300	85×60^2 £5100
Year 3	36×60^2 £2160	77×60^2 £4620
Year 4	25×60^2 £1500	70×60^2 £4200
Cumulative income	£12 900	£19 420

Source: McCorkell, G. (1999)

[1]An annual payment of £60 is equal to a monthly payment of £5. Commonly, an initial discount would be offered to encourage a customer to commit to paying by direct debit.
[2]The number of customers declines according to the customer defection rate identified earlier.

Managing marketing performance in marketing communications means building relationships to improve revenue and profit. Success should be measured through customer satisfaction and retention, not through sales alone.

The following award winning case study from the non-profit sector shows the benefits of integrated marketing communications to acquire and retain customers.

Case study

Concern

Concern, an Irish charity, is known mainly for its work in emergency relief. Its scope is wider than this, both in its markets, having expanded to undertake fundraising activities in the UK and US, and in its work in long-term development activities in 28 countries, and generally looking after the interests of the world's poor.

Concern had rapid growth during the early 1990s, although most of its income was generated following emergency appeals for the large-scale disasters, such as those in Rwanda and Somalia. Concern's income fluctuated substantially between campaigns, often leaving the charity with insufficient resources.

This problem was exacerbated by Concern's move to new markets. Marketing activities were a local responsibility, which brought few donations except when timed alongside emergency appeals. Concern's income, which peaked at £16 million in 1992, had reached a low of £7 million in 1995.

Concern set a marketing objective of doubling net fundraising contribution to £14 million by 2003. This was to be achieved through more regular sources of income, especially through growing regular monthly donations by standing orders or direct debits. (The target was to increase this from £1 million in 1999 to £4 million by 2004.)

Concern created a new central marketing team with direct marketing knowledge and expertise, and commissioned two new agencies, one for creative work and integration, and the second for media buying. Core material was developed, which could be adapted for different markets. The positioning was on Concern's superior ability to make aid available quickly and cost-effectively in the areas of greatest need.

The centralized marketing function combined the four existing databases from the different offices into one new marketing database. This formed part of a new information system, which would be used to predict Donor Lifetime Value (the cumulative income from a donor). Concern sought regular monthly donations, rather than one-off contributions, so processes for handling donations and processing standing orders were developed, ensuring that these could expand in periods of crisis.

Direct response ads were placed in media in the UK and Ireland. The media were tested to identify their ability to achieve a target return on investment, against increasing targets over the donor lifecycle. All media used for donor acquisition had to cover their costs in the donations received.

Creative work focused on hard-hitting messages about cash being required to help people. Generic campaigns were developed for use across all media, and supplemented with specific direct mail packs for emergency appeals, customized for high and normal value donors. The high value donor packs included information about the crisis situation in a letter; an update on the aid programme; photographs of individual families; a donation slip and a reply paid envelope.

The non-donor or normal donor pack was printed on cheaper materials, had fewer inserts, but had a stronger tone and more dramatic plea, and asked for a direct debit. The simplicity stressed that Concern used funds for the needy.

Concern developed two generic advertisements for direct response TV (DRTV) advertising to be used when disasters occurred. One such use was for the plight of Afghanistan's people soon after 11 September 2001, supported by press advertising. Concern had customised direct mail packs produced quickly for key market segments. This appeal raised £4 million.

Concern explored e-mail as a promotional medium. This could be sent within two hours of a disaster and created a viral approach for referrals (asking people to pass the message to friends). News updates could be sent to the e-mail list, usually accompanied by with requests for further donations. In addition, donation response websites were developed for each specific campaign.

The database integration and the various promotional activities helped Concern's income from fundraising grow from £14.8 million to £26 million, with a contribution of £18 million. This exceeded the target of £14 million. This resulted mainly from the increase in regular donors, from 8000 to 95 000, with the resulting impact on regular donor income achieving £10 million in 2002.

Concern's marketing success also had further benefits. In Ireland, it increased brand awareness by six percentage points, achieving 55 per cent spontaneous and 96 per cent prompted awareness. It doubled its market share in England, Wales and Scotland. Over a 5-year period, it achieved a 7 to 1 return on its investment. DRTV was the most successful medium. Online income rose from £5000 in 1999 to £250 000 by 2001.

Concern's activities in both acquiring customers and building relationships was build round building customer relationships and measuring communications performance.

Source: Institute of Direct Marketing, 2002 IDM Business Performance Award – Gold Award Winner, Concern – Integrated Direct Marketing To Build Donor Loyalty.

The integrated approach

Keller (2001) states that: 'the overriding goal (of Integrated Marketing Communications) is to create the most effective and efficient communication program possible'.

He identifies six criteria that impact on this:

1. *Coverage* – the proportion of target customers reached by each marketing communications option.
2. *Contribution* – the ability of a form of marketing communication to create the desired response in isolation of any other form of communication.
3. *Commonality* – the common associations that exist and are reinforced in communication options, i.e. the extent to which meaning is shared in different marketing communications.
4. *Complementarity* – the extent to which communications options can show, emphasize or develop different associations.
5. *Robustness* – the extent to which forms of marketing communication are effective for different consumers, bearing in mind the different levels of prior experience and exposure.
6. *Cost* – these criteria should be considered in the context of cost to determine their value in an Integrated Marketing Communications programme.

Keller advocates that a choice of communications options takes account of the objectives, priorities and tradeoffs, not only of the attributes and satiability of different approaches, but also in their ability to work together, as indicated in Tables 6.5 and 6.6.

Table 6.5 Micro-evaluation of promotional approaches

Ability to ...	TV	Print	Sales promotions	Sponsorship	Interactive
Attract attention or be intrusive	++	++	++	+	+
Convey product info	+	+++	+++	+	+++
Create emotional response	+++	++	+	++	+
Link to brand	+	++	++	+++	+++
Encourage or facilitate purchase	+	++	+++	+	+++

Source: Keller, K.L. (2001) 'Mastering the Marketing Communications Mix: Micro and Macro Perspectives on Integrated Marketing Communication Programs', *Journal of Marketing Management*, Sept. Vol. 17, Issue 7/8, p. 836

Table 6.6 Macro-evaluation of promotional options

Ability to ...	TV	Print	Sales promotions	Sponsorship	Interactive
Coverage					
Breadth	+++	+	++	+++	+
Depth	+	++	++	++	+++
Contribution	+++	+++	+++	+++	+++
Commonality	+++	++	++	+	+++
Complementarity	+++	+++	+++	+++	+++
Robustness	+	++	+	+	+++
Cost	+++	+++	+++	+++	+++

Source: Keller, K.L. (2001) 'Mastering the Marketing Communications Mix: Micro and Macro Perspectives on Integrated Marketing Communication Programs', *Journal of Marketing Management,* Sept. Vol. 17, Issue 7/8, p. 836

Evaluating these approaches considers the fit of elements in an integrated communications mix, and their fit to the purpose (i.e. customer acquisition, or forming or building relationships). While the examples in this section have focused on direct marketing as a core component because of its measurability, Keller (2001, p. 841) comments:

> *Undoubtedly, a myriad of different sets of communications options can create nearly equivalent effects, suggesting there is not necessarily a singularly best communication program.*

Keller's work and the case studies in this section show the need for synergy within the mix, 'so that the effects of any one communication option are enhanced by the presence of another'. (Keller, 2001, p. 841). Synergy brings benefits in communication of brand attributes or benefits, increasing exposure to marketing communications messages, increasing the propensity to purchase or even read messages, irrespective of the customer's level of experience with the brand.

 Activity 6.8

For an organization of your choice, identify the factors considered when developing or evaluating marketing communications.

What gaps exist in the choice criteria?

Using information systems and databases

This final section of this unit addresses element 3.10 of the *Managing Marketing Performance* syllabus:

> *Develop support for relationships with customers, clients and intermediaries using appropriate information systems and databases and adhering to relevant privacy and data protection legislation.*

This builds on Units 4 and 5, and earlier sections of this unit.

The early developments

In little over 30 years, technology has radically changed the process of understanding and managing customer relationships.

In the 1980s and early 1990s, information on customers, clients and intermediaries was stored in a customer database (sometimes paper based), which recorded basic customer information, which typically addressed three core areas of attention:

1. *Who* – are the customers?
2. *What* – are they buying?
3. *Where* – are they located?

This demographic information and transaction history gave sufficient information to profile customers and gain some insight into their purchase behaviour. This was often supplemented by data from a customer contact history.

However, later the focus moved to:

o *When* – how often do they spend and when did they last spend?
o *How much* – are they buying?
o *Why* – what prompts them to buy?

This data gives the potential to analyse the customer database using criteria that are at the heart of much current marketing practice. These include the FRAC factors:

o **F**requency of purchase
o **R**ecency of purchase
o **A**mount spent per transaction and overall
o **C**ategory or type of goods purchased.

Early databases were rarely integrated with other organizational data or external databases. Nevertheless, these guided marketing decisions, such as targeting and promotional testing. They were also used for direct sales and cross selling. These databases initiated computerized customer account management, and through this, of computerized data-based marketing.

Although there is growing interest in CRM systems, many organizations still fail to record or analyse basic information to understand their customers, improve their customer contact and grow their business.

Activity 6.9

Identify a range of potential uses of information from the basic databases (using the six questions), and identify the limitations – what is not possible – from such databases.

Consider the databases that your organization has. Do they use them fully? Or are they used for administrative activities rather than management activities?

Integrated databases

A step change came about when organizations were able to merge databases, which offered the potential for richer data and deeper analysis. Key internal databases included sales, accounts, production and dealer support systems. Organizations also accessed, used or acquired external databases, such as those from list brokers and segmentation consultancies, to add depth to their understanding of existing customers and to identify new targets.

Recognition grew that databases, analysis tools and applications could run alongside each other. This was the start of integrated contact management. The customer contact history could be stored, and accessed by, for example, telemarketing, to drive or respond to customer contact. This became known as database marketing.

> *Database marketing is the ability to use the vast potential of today's computer and telecommunication technology in driving customer oriented programmes in a personalised, articulated and cost-effective manner.* (Stan Rapp)

Rapp's comment identifies that the power of data-based database marketing results from delivering customized, personalized communications to meet customer needs, building on IT capabilities.

Case study

Manchester United

Manchester United is probably the best known and most popular football club in the world, with an estimated fan base of 53 million people worldwide. The challenge for Manchester United is to convert this commitment and loyalty into revenue and profits. Manchester United's supporters' club has more than 100 000 members, most of which are in the UK. A new membership scheme – One United – seeks to broaden the existing membership base.

The first step in this initiative involved integrating the existing databases – transactional files holding data on ticket sales, credit card holders, mail order buyers and members of the old United membership scheme. Fans were identified and targeted for membership of the new One United membership scheme, based on recency, frequency and value.

Manchester United had previously failed to exploit the value of Manchester United fanbase. Manchester United's head of membership, Helen Busby said, 'Football clubs are in a unique position in that they can boast cradle-to-grave loyalty,' she says. 'Unlike other brands, our aim is not to convert people to our brand, but rather to identify fans and develop a mutually beneficial, transacting relationship... We'd used a lot of Old Trafford media to promote the membership scheme, but that only reached those already attending matches'.

One United is focused on moving existing fans up the ladder of loyalty. Activities that do this, such as sponsored questions in lifestyle surveys, and use of road shows and of direct response advertising, have been developed. Registered members of the official website, www.manutd.com, can join online, and a competition 'Who wants to be a United Millionaire?' tests others to qualify as fans. In return, the members are offered exclusive items, such as a yearbook that reviews the previous season, DVDs and store discounts. As the club cannot offer match tickets for all fans, these benefits offer relevant ways of building the Manchester United brand. It also offers value to international fans.

One United acquired 50 000 new members in its first year, resulting in a record 163 000 members, at an overall cost of £2.70 per response. The future focus is on building One United's strength abroad. Country-specific programmes can be developed for fans, working with overseas supporters clubs.

Source: McElhatton, N. (2004) 'Data Clinic: Case Study – Manchester United FC', *Direct Response*, 30 April.

Customer relationship management

McCorkell (1999) identifies that direct and database marketing is built on four dimensions, which he refers to as the TICC system:

1. *Targeting* – who are the targets for the offer?
2. *Interaction* – how can we communicate and what should we communicate?
3. *Control* – what is the return on the investment?
4. *Continuity* – how can we build the relationship?

The targeting, continuity and control are aspects that build the interaction, as illustrated in Figure 6.6.

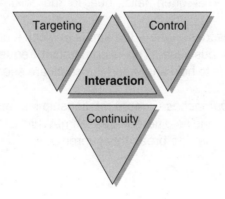

Figure 6.6
Source: McCorkell, G. (1999)

These principles, coupled with the company-wide access to databases for use in applications are at the heart of CRM systems.

Hobby (1999, p. 28) defines CRM as:

> *a management approach that enables organizations to identify, attract and increase retention of profitable customers by managing relationships with them*

This view of CRM does not mention the IT component of CRM, as this is not the most important dimension. The hardware and software dimensions of CRM often dominate discussions of this topic. Effective CRM is grounded in an understanding of *value* – both providing value and delivering value to customers. Delivery of value to customers is weighed against the value of customers to the organization, which drives the level and mechanics of the required support. It builds on understanding who customers are, what their current and likely future spend will be.

In part, this value comes from personalization and customization. CRM is frequently cited as being about 'one-to-one marketing' (Peppers *et al.*, 1999), responding to an individual customer based on what you know about that customer.

Extending knowledge

Don Peppers and Martha Rogers have been exponents of one-to-one marketing for many years. Check out their website http://www.1to1.com and also read one of their many books or articles on the individualized marketing activities.

Many reports show that CRM is not delivering in practice. Fundamentally, delivery of value and customization for customers are not at the heart of most CRM implementation, as CRM implementation is not always being grounded in a marketing-oriented organization. Day (2002) identified four approaches to CRM:

1. *Customer-driven approaches* – where CRM is at the heart of a strategy to deliver customer value through an augmented solution, comprising superior customer service and customization. In these organizations, CRM technologies support business process to save customers' time and effort.
2. *Inner-directed approaches* – gain understanding of customers through CRM technology, to cut service costs, reduce the time in closing deals and have more targeted marketing efforts. Much of this work is undertaken by IT on standard software with little strategic focus. This often fails, due to the failure to deliver improved value to customers.
3. *Defensive approaches* – where the aim is to block a competitor from obtaining a share of the customers' business. (This is common in frequent flyer miles, for example.) The purpose of CRM is to hold share and the costs are seen as an inevitable part of being in the market.
4. *Market-driven approaches* – where relationship leaders have an advantage that others find 'hard to copy' and so differentiates them. While competitors find it hard to compete, challengers find it hard to break this supremacy.

Activity 6.10

Many organizations, from government departments to financial services organizations, claim to be operating CRM systems to improve customer value.

Identify a few of these organizations that you have contact with, either personally or at work.

Which of Day's approaches do these organizations appear to have?

Now think about your organization, if it has implemented CRM. Which of Day's approaches does it have?

Day also identified that relationship leaders had higher levels of customer retention, better sales growth, and higher profitability than others in the sector. Further, he identified two kinds of advantage:

1. *Relational advantages* – such as the customer service and responsiveness to unique requirements, and
2. *Product advantages* – such as quality, performance, and value for money.

Day's research shows that an organization's ability to deliver relational advantages explained their levels of customer retention and growth. This demonstrates that the value to customers is delivered through the 'soft' aspects of relationship management, and not through technology.

Relationship management and information technology have to be married carefully. The relentless drive to sell is more commonly associated with CRM systems than the soft people aspects of service and responsiveness. CRM systems should not be about technology, but about customer focus and its delivery throughout the organization. It is a technology-enabled implementation of marketing.

This integrated relationship marketing perspective is evident in Parvatiyar and Sheth's (2001, p. 5) definition of CRM:

> *a comprehensive strategy and process of acquiring, retaining, and partnering with selective customers to create superior value for the company and the customer. It involves the integration of marketing, sales, customer service, and the supply-chain functions of the organization to achieve greater efficiencies and effectiveness in delivering customer value.*

Various models detail how to develop these selective customer relationships, such as Peppers and Rogers' approach of:

o *Identify* – each customer should be identified individually
o *Differentiate* – customers by value and need
o *Interact* – and remember previous interactions
o *Customize* – the product or service on the future interactions.

However, these do not work in isolation. CRM must be used as part of an integrated relationship marketing strategy to be effective.

Case study

Tesco and Tops

Tesco has achieved an amazing turnaround within the last decade. In the early 1990s, it was struggling in the UK's competitive retailing environment, and now it is one of the world's leading retailers.

Initial attempts to turn the business round focused on cutting prices, which brought poor returns and lost customers. The company commissioned research to understand the market. This showed that the customer profile of its competitors differed, while Tesco had no single customer profile. It decided that its strategy should span and deliver value across the UK population. This seemingly impractical remit has been at the heart of its success.

Tesco's research indicated that customers wanted improvements in customer service, such as faster checkout service, shorter checkout queues and importantly, discounts for loyal customers. Tesco set about improving customer service, and then addressed the need for loyalty rewards in 1995, when Tesco launched its Clubcard initiative. Clubcard was a major investment for the company, with set up costs of £10 million and customer discounts at 1 per cent of income.

Although the scheme was initially launched as a way of rewarding customers, Clubcard data provided regularly updated information on customer preferences and purchases. This enabled Tesco to communicate directly with customers, offering relevant, focused offers to chosen groups of customers, in a cost-effective and value-adding way.

The two-way dialogue offered Tesco a chance to listen to customers too, and Tesco responded to customers' requests for partner organizations by forming alliances with other organizations offering improved opportunities to earn points. A Clubcard magazine was tailored for five different lifestyle segments identified in its Club card data.

The company began to share information with suppliers to gain closer links to improve the quality of forecasting and inventory management. Tesco charged suppliers for access to this information.

Tesco is hoping to develop its share in Thailand. However, a competitor, Tops Supermarket, launched a loyalty programme – 'Spot rewards card' – offering benefits such as discounts and personal shopping lists, in what it claims is the first of these loyalty programmes in Asia. Like Tesco's UK Clubcard, this also helps Tops build an understanding of shopping patterns of its customers. Tops hopes to issue more than 1.2 million cards in 2004, and aims to move customers up the ladder of loyalty, increasing their spending by 20 per cent on average. It aims for a 6 per cent increase in sales.

Sources: The Grocer Insight (2004) 'Media spend's a vital growth aid', *The Grocer*, 7th April, p. 17.

Peck, H. (2002) 'Tesco Clubcard Forever?', Cranfield School of Management Case Study.

Prasad, G. (2004) 'One-To-One Marketing: Tops goes electronic with CRM', *Media Asia* 4th June.

Using CRM

Relationship marketing seeks profit from satisfied customers. The challenge is how to make customers more profitable. The delivery of this in day-to-day transactions and exchanges is critical to the execution of the strategy. This relationship is shown in Figure 6.7.

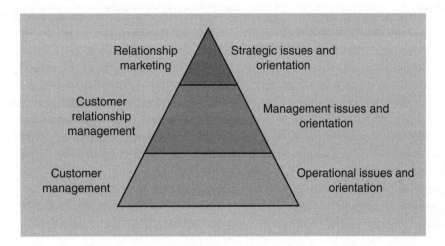

Figure 6.7 Relationship management at strategic, tactical and operational levels
Source: Payne, A. (2004) 'The Role of Stakeholders in Relationship Marketing' ESRC Seminar Series on Relationship Marketing, Nottingham University Business School

This diagram links the content of Units 4, 5 and 6. This final section in Unit 6 focuses on managing implementation within this framework. This involves all points of contact with customers over their life cycle, from before purchase, during the purchase and after the purchase, and with contact throughout the organization.

Contacts should build on, use and replenish the core customer databases, of customer information, customer response and purchasing behaviour to deliver value through customer contact. An integrative framework for this is shown in Figure 6.8.

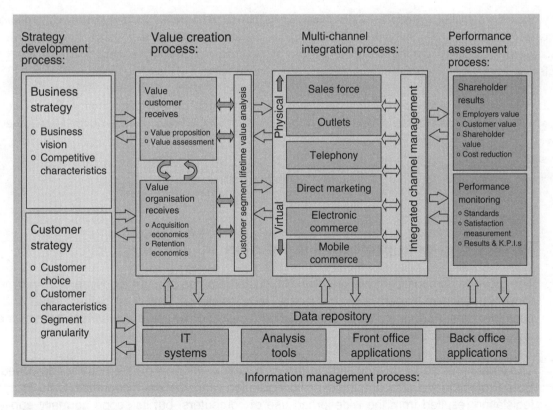

Figure 6.8 The CRM strategy framework
Source: Payne, A. (2004)

Case study

Sky

Sky supplies the UK's satellite broadcasting. It is an extensive advertiser, and uses on-air trails and consumer and trade sales promotions to recruit new customers. Often its promotions offer free or subsidized installation of satellite dishes or free or subsidized set-top boxes. Many of these promotions are timed around key viewing times, such as Christmas or major sporting events.

Sky's calculations show that subscriptions for 6–12 months will recover the cost of this activity and further subscriptions will result in profit for Sky. Clearly, this means that Sky must ensure that the direct cost of acquisition is addressed and that customer retention is managed.

Sky's churn rate is reported at 9.4 per cent, meaning that almost 1 in 10 customers does not renew the subscription. This is substantially lower than the two other major commercial multichannel companies, cable operators NTL and Telewest, in the UK. They have respectively 14.4 per cent and 15.2 per cent churn rates (Ofcom 2004).

Sky develops its customer relationship through many different approaches, aimed at enhancing or upselling. These include:

o Monthly magazines, showing the key programmes in its broadcast schedules
o Frequent direct mail activities to remind customers about events, to inform about new subscription packages or to promote special deals
o Channel 999,which has an interactive 'back chat' component.

Sky is sales-driven, but it responds to customers. It has introduced parental locks to protect children from accessing inappropriate channels, and it innovates in enhanced services, such as personal video recorders, interactive shopping, computer gaming and interactive gambling facilities. These cross-selling activities benefit customers through immediacy of fulfilment of their wishes.

Customer contact is at the heart of new developments and at the heart of implementation. Sky's success has built a considerable loyalty in its customers, and profit for Sky, in a market that did not exist 20 years ago.

Source: http://www.sky.com and http://www.ofcom.org.uk.

Privacy and data protection legislation

The move to personalized relationships with customers has brought the issue of privacy to the fore. Marketing managers are now legally responsible for how they gather, store and use customer data. Further, some issues about data collection or use may be legal, but still require critical ethical review.

The legal rights about privacy and storage of customer information are usually addressed in a Data Protection Act, although the specific legislation varies between countries. Data Protection legislation resulted from the widespread use of computers, but its scope normally applies to both electronic and hard copy of data.

Data Protection in Europe operates under eight principles, presented in Table 6.7.

Table 6.7 Principles of Data Protection in Europe

1. Data should be processed fairly and lawfully.
2. Data should be processed for limited purposes and not in any way that is incompatible with these purposes.
3. Data is adequate, relevant and not excessive.
4. Data is accurate.
5. Data is kept only as long as necessary.
6. Data is processed in line with individual's rights.
7. Data is kept secure.
8. Data is not transferred to other countries that cannot provide adequate data protection.

Source: *Business Link,* www.businesslink.gov.uk (2004)

A key concern is managing personal data, which is defined under the legislation as being any information that identifies a person. This includes their name, address, e-mail address, telephone number, etc. Further, it also 'includes any expression of opinion about the individual' which is stored in records (DPA, 1998, s1).

Data protection legislation gives the customers rights about this information and its use, such as:

- o The right of access, such as to see information held on them.
- o The right to prevent processing of data that can cause distress, such as revealing financial information to a third party without consent.
- o The right to prevent processing for direct marketing, such as preventing organizations from using data for direct-marketing purposes.
- o The right to compensation for damage or distress resulting from inappropriate use of personal data, where the Data Controller cannot show reasonable care in complying with the Act.
- o The right to have data rectified, blocked, erased or destroyed.
- o The right to prevent an organization from selling or passing on information without permission.
- o The right to have personal data kept secure from unauthorized access.
- o The right not to have data that is important deleted from an organization's records.

Restrictions are placed on organizations holding such records. Data Protection legislation requires that the people (called data controllers) 'who (either alone or jointly or in common with other persons) determine the purposes for which and the manner in which any personal data are, or are to be, processed' (DPA, 1998, s1) register with the Office of the Information Commissioner and pay an annual registration fee. It is a criminal offence for organizations to process personal data without this registration.

Extending knowledge

For information on the Data Protection Act in the UK, look at: http://www.informationcommissioner.gov.uk/ For information on the Data Protection Act in the EU, look at http://europa.eu.int/comm/internal_market/privacy/index_en.htm.

Students from other countries should use a good search engine to identify the relevant authorities and legislation in their country.

In some cases, the application of the Data Protection Act leads to a deterioration in customer service. For example, some insurers have passed the obligations for some support

201

services – such as managing windscreen repairs – to third parties outside working hours. However, third parties cannot access some customer records, and so therefore customers may not get the required service when they need it. Organizations also may not pass customer information outside the country (or region for regulations that apply across countries) without explicit permission.

Other laws address privacy matters and the use of information. These include legislation that addresses the use of different media for contact. In Europe, The Privacy and Electronic Communications (EC Directive) Regulations 2003 restricts the use of telephone networks for direct marketing purposes and prohibits unsolicited direct marketing activity by telephone, by fax, by electronic mail (this means text/video/picture messaging and e-mail) and by automated calling systems. This act also addresses the use of caller ID systems in direct marketing activities, and the use of directories of subscribers.

A range of other legislation also addresses the sale of goods and services generally or through specific media (e.g. Direct Mail). Further restrictions apply in different sectors, such as financial services, alcoholic beverages and children's products.

 ## Activity 6.11

What customer information is held in your organization?

Who is the 'data controller'?

Who is ensuring compliance with legal developments on customer information and contact?

Customers are gaining more rights over their personal privacy. As a result, increasingly, organizations have to ask customers to opt-in, rather than wait for them to say that they opt out of these activities. This is being referred to as permission marketing.

Permission marketing is strongly advocated for e-mail marketing. Spam is a topic of much concern in government and in the marketing community. Some countries and locations have implemented legislation to make this illegal, but few have managed successful prosecutions against people who spam. Indeed, many marketers in many large organizations are unaware of the legal requirements, as indicated by Crush (2004):

> *Despite laws banning unsolicited emails to people who have not opted in to receive them, only 52 per cent of the top 50 companies by turnover in the banking, insurance, publishing, retail and telecoms sectors are playing by the rules. And retail is the least compliant, with just 42 per cent playing ball . . . .*

Voluntary codes also limit the direct marketing contact they receive by mail (through the Mailing Preference Service) and by fax (through the Fax Preference Service). Customers can report to the regulators any approach that has not checked the register.

The biggest challenge facing marketing is to self-regulate and conform to the existing require-ments. As Crush states:

> *More legislation is likely in the near future with penalties.*

Arguably the biggest penalty is the damage to the customer relationship.

Extending knowledge

The following weblinks apply in the UK.

The Telephone Preference Service – http://www.tpsonline.org.uk/tps/.

The Mailing Preference Service – http://www.tpsonline.org.uk/mpsr/.

The Fax Preference Service – http://www.mpsonline.org.uk/fps/.

Case study

PowerGen

In 2000, PowerGen's reputation suffered through poor online data protection. PowerGen had to release a statement to customers asking them to change their credit card numbers after it left the information available on its website.

PowerGen offered each of its 7000 online customers compensation for inconvenience caused by this security lapse. This was, however, not a legal obligation. Phil Jones, assistant commissioner at the Data Protection Registrar, said although customer details were published online, they were not eligible for any compensation unless the data had been used fraudulently.

PowerGen offered the cash as a goodwill payment to compensate customers for its lapse, the inconvenience caused by PowerGen's lapse and to protect the PowerGen brand.

Summary

Implementing business strategy is essential to deliver marketing performance. Key ways of implementing business strategy are through customer service, integrated marketing communications and building customer relationships based on IT systems.

With rising customer expectations, organizations increasingly add service and support activities to enhance the customer experience and show their commitment to customers. Customer service takes place pre-purchase, during the purchase process or post-purchase, and service facilitates the sale or enhances the product or service offering. Service guarantees add to the customer benefit and show a priority to delivering customer care and satisfaction. Customer service audits identify means of improving customer service. However, once again, a gaps model can help identify underlying causes of problems.

The concept of the integrated marketing mix has been long established in marketing. A core component of this is the promotional mix. However, while academic textbooks identify the need for an integrated and balanced promotional mix, this is often not followed in practice, as the responsibility for different areas lies in different parts of the organization, with limited co-operation or co-ordination of activity. Such integrated marketing communications programmes differ based on whether the task is to acquire new customers or to retain and grow existing customers and can involve intermediaries in their delivery. Effective integrated marketing communications plans show that synergy results from such co-ordination.

Information and communications technology (ICT) fuels integration of customer service and integrated marketing communications. This is often referred to as customer relationship management. Managing customer interactions up the ladder of loyalty to recognize the customer (based on their contact and purchase histories) and personalize interactions builds effective and profitable customer relationships. Understanding the legal requirements of record-keeping, such as permission to store or use the information and controlling access to personal information, is essential for legal compliance.

These areas are diverse, but interlinked. All are critical to effective implementation of the business strategy.

Sample exam question

You have taken over as marketing manager for a medium sized business that has offices in three different regions of your country. Marketing communications budgets are allocated, proportionate to sales in each of these offices. Each manager has a different view of the appeal, visual layout, market targets and media, and each believes that his/her view is best. Examine how you could evaluate this and how you could bring about a more integrated approach to managing marketing communications budgets.

Discussion

The question is very clearly related to managing integrated marketing communications. You have the role of managing a disparate group of campaigns. It is clear that each manager is satisfied with the local approach, so you will have to ensure that you have measures of results that will show the effectiveness of your proposals. Clearly, direct/database marketing is a means of achieving this. Case studies of best practice will guide thinking on this, and give ideas about issues to address. Note that the question refers asks about evaluation and implementation of a more integrated approach, not for a communications plan.

Bibliography

Cespedes, F. (1994) 'Industrial Marketing: Managing New Requirements', *Sloan Management Review*, **365**(3), Spring, pp. 45–60.

Christopher, M. (1992) *The Customer Service Planner*, Butterworth-Heinemann.

Christopher, M., Payne, A. and Ballantyne, D. (2002) *Relationship Marketing, Creating Stakeholder Value*, Butterworth-Heinemann.

Crush, P. (2004) 'Email marketing: Uninvited and illegal', *Marketing*, 7 July. Data Protection Act (1998) HMSO.

Gray, R. (2004) 'Service brands: Customer service is not a strategy', *Marketing*, 21 July.

Hobby, J. (1999) 'Looking after the one who matters', *Accountancy Age*, 28 October, pp. 28–30.

Jones, C.A. (2000) 'Extraordinary customer service management: The critical success factors', *Business Perspectives*, Summer, **2**(4), pp. 26–31.